CATALOGUING OF NON BOOK MATERIALS

CATALOGUING OF NON BOOK MATERIALS

By

Dr. Anil Kumar Dhiman

Information Scientist
Gurukul Kangri University
Hardwar- 249 404 (U.A.)

Ess Ess Publications

4837/24, Ansari Road, Darya Ganj,
New Delhi-110002
✆ : 23260807
Fax : 23274173
E-mail: essess@del3.vsnl.net.in
url:http://www.essessbook.com

First Published 2004

ISBN : 81-7000 - 374 - 1

Price : Rs. 1150/-

Published by :

Ess Ess Publications

4837/24, Ansari Road, Darya Ganj,

New Delhi - 110 002

Phone : 23260807

Fax : 23274173

E-mail : essess@del3.vsnl.net.in

url:http://www.essessbooks.com

Printed at :

Print Line

To

My Son

Aman

CONTENTS

PREFACE

The catalogue aims to provide complete information about the holdings of library at a particular time so that the users may get the desired documents in a short span of time. In earlier times, the libraries were having only books and some other printed materials in their collection but today a variety of publications in different forms are coming in the book world or rather in the world of knowledge. Nowadays, libraries have become the center of not only of providing the information but also the producer of generating the information and its dissemination, so the libraries are to rely upon the different information sources hence they have to acquire the published sources in all forms. As a result, the libraries are acquiring non-book materials also.

This book is written basically to provide a concise amount of information on the cataloguing of non -book materials. In this book, emphasis has been made on both the aspects of cataloguing i.e., the manual cataloguing and computerized cataloguing. As majority of libraries in India, still prevailing the manual cataloguing hence, a complete chapter has been retained on manual cataloguing of various forms of non-book materials. The book starts with Introduction on cataloguing. Its second chapter is devoted to AACR, which seems to be the only cataloguing standard for cataloguing on non-book materials. Its third chapter gives a brief account of history of non-book materials' cataloguing. The fourth chapter of the book is the main thrust of the book, in which manual cataloguing of different types of the non-book materials is discussed with the help of examples. In implementing today's online catalogues, librarian accustomed to the traditional cataloguing may find it difficult to change from old ones to new trends. So the next chapter has been retained to discuss the latest aspects of cataloguing viz., Database online cataloguing, MARC format for cataloguing besides, the tags as suggested by INFLIBNET, Ahmedabad for cataloguing. The last chapter of the book is for the latest trends in the field of cataloguing, where online cataloguing, recent standards for cataloguing etc are discussed.

The author does not claim to be an authority on the subject but an attempt has been made to make the work simple and understandable. In writing this book, the author have drawn the information from number of sources, especially the matter of MLISc courses of Annamalai University, Annamalai Nagar (TN) and BLISc course of IGNOU, New Delhi is frequently consulted; which is thankfully acknowledged. The help received from Mr. S.C. Sinha, Ex Library Officer, Central Building Research Institute, Roorkee and Mr. Sushil Kumar Sharma, Central Library, IIT, Roorkee is also acknowledged. The Author is also thankful to Mr. Sumit Sethi and Mrs. Sheel Sethi, the owners of Ess Ess Publications, New Delhi for publishing this book in a nice form in time.

In writing of this book, my sister Alka Rani, *M.A., M.Lib Sc.*, working as Library Incharge at Vyapar Mandal P.G. College, Manglour (U.A.) and my wife, Mrs. Yashoda Rani, *M.A., B.Lib. Sc.*, have assisted me; their assistance is highly acknowledged. The author is highly indebted to his parents Mr. Ramlal Dhiman and Mrs. Kamla Devi, who encouraged him like his earlier works as usual during the preparation of this book.

This is hoped the work will be welcome by the librarians' world and Teaching Community as well.

Dr. Anil Kumar Dhiman
Information Scientist
Central Library
Gurukul Kangri University
Hardwar -249 404 (U.A.)

Dated : April 2003

Other Books of the Author

i. Citation Analysis of the Research Field and Information Technology Development. Ess Ess Publications, New Delhi. (2001).

ii. Prolegomena to Universe of Knowledge. Ess Ess Publications, New Delhi. (2002).

iii. Research Methodology. 2 Vols. Ess Ess Publications, New Delhi. (2002).

iv. Special Libraries: Technical and Research Libraries. Ess Ess Publications, New Delhi (2002).

v. Academic Libraries. Ess Ess Publications, New Delhi. (2002).

vi. Basics of Information Technology for Librarians and Information Scientists. Ess Ess Publications, New Delhi. (2003).

vii. Medicinal Plants and Raw Drugs of India. Bishen Singh Mahendra Pal Singh, Dehradun. (2000).

viii. Medicinal Plants of Uttaranchal State. Chowkhamba Sanskrit Series Office, Varanasi (2003).

ix. Wild Medicinal Plants of India. Bishen Singh Mahendra Pal Singh, Dehradun (2003). (In Press).

x Sacred Plants and their Medicinal Uses. Daya Publishing House, New Delhi (2003).

1
INTRODUCTION

The word "catalogue" has been derived from a Greek phrase kata logos. "Kata" means "by" or "according to" and "logos" has various meanings like "word" or "order" or "reason". Thus "catalogue" may be regarded as a "work in which contents are arranged in a reasonable way, according to a set plan or merely word by word".

It is difficult to reach at an agreed definition of catalogue in the wake of its various kinds used within and without libraries. However CCC attempts to define catalogue as a "list of reading materials available in the hodings of a library or group of libraries". In order to provide access to the holding of library an index or list of the material is always prepared and maintained for the readers. This tool is basically called a catalogue. A more plausible definition thus comes in an expression: "a calalogue is a list arranged by alphabet, by number, or by subject of books, maps, coins, stamps, sound recordings, or materials in any other medium that constitute a collection". Its prime purpose is to record, describe, and index the holdings of a specific collection. Cataloguing is the process of preparing a catalogue, or of preparing bidliographic records that will become entries in a catalogue.

The *Library Catalogue* is a list of books and other reading material in the holdings of a library or a group of libraries. The list contains entries of books, arranged according to some definite plan. As distinguished from a *bibliography*, it is a list which records, describes and indexes the resources of a collection of a library or libraries in a locality or country.

In the early modern period, the library catalogue contained entries of books on paper, either hand written/type written. Subsequently, it was printed in book form; and lastly it was on cards of standard size 7.3x 5.3 cm, and filed in trays, which were kept in cabinets, placed on a stand at a convenient height, usually 3 ft. 6 inches, in order that persons of average height could reach the topmost trays and refer them. Perhaps the British Museum catalogue, consisting of handwritten slips of paper pasted on the appropriate page guard books of an unusual size, (and not available to the public, only the staff of the British Museum, on request by a reader for a book or information would refer, and locate the given author/book) had to be converted into machine readable catalogue.

Since 1980, all these manual methods adopted for the physical forms of library catalogues have given way to automated systems: specially the MARC system, and computer storage of information and its retrieval, and on-line interactive catalogues are found in their places.

Cataloguing denotes the various processes adopted in preparing the entries of the reading material in a catalogue and its maintenance. *Cataloguing and classification* are the twin processes adopted in modern *library administration* to help readers in locating the desired books and other reading material quickly and conveniently. They are intended "to relate and display together the editions which a library has of a given work and the works which it has of a given author." In view of the importance of the catalogue in providing access to the resources of a library, large sums of money are spent and competent persons are employed as cataloguers.

"The library catalogue does not-or should not-exist as an end itself. It is one part of the total bibliographic system and must be responsive to changes that take place in other parts of the system". *Studies of catalogues and cataloguing* carried out indicate the gradual changes in the form, style and techniques of catalogues. The reader's approach to books and reading, the physical features of the book, and the advances made in the field of classification have all had their impact on the library catalogue. "The modification. however, have been unnecessarily slow, and sometimes inadequate, because of incomplete understanding of the nature and *functions of the catalogue* and its place; in the system as a whole." *Cataloguing practice* from the beginning is determined by the set of rules followed by a library, *e.g., the British Museum* has its "Rules for compiling the catalogues of Printed Books Maps and Music in the British Museum" revised edition, 1936; and the *Library of Congress* has its own Rules, "Despite the fact that cataloguing has been referred to as an art, these rules as *Seymour Lubetzky points out have shaped our catalogues and detemtined their usefulness*.

A *Sumerian clay tablet* (2000 B.C.)? inscribed with 62 titles is one of the earliest artifacts, that can be considered a catalogue. The earliest known form of library catalogue indicates that it was compiled to serve as a simple inventory or list of the library resources. The lists 'piivakes' which Callimachus drew up at Alexandria probably contained the names of those authors, only which he found in the library with which he was connected there and they may, therefore, be regarded as class-catalogues for that particular subject. It is that analytical and critical mind of Callimachus, as a classifier and cataloguer, which is evidenced in his 'piivakes' that is of far-reaching importance to the modern cataloguer. Callimachus gave the name of the *author,* place of birth, name of his father, his teachers and education, his nickname or pseudonym, a short biography, the title of his work or works; if the work lacked a title he provided one, a comment on its authenticity, and finally a stichiometric note giving the first words of the work (often the ancient title) and the exact number of lines of the manuscript (of each work and of all the author's writings). The last was an important bibliographical detail, used to control the size of the manuscript and determine the compensation to the scribe as well as for general reference.

"There is no doubt that our whole concept of author entry first came with the Greeks; it never once appeared in any work which has survived from the earlier civilizations of the East. Even today in the "Orient; the traditional entry for a book is its title. Most of the oriental writings of well known authors have been better known under their titles than under their names, e.g. Raghuvamsa of Kalidasa; Kadambari of Bana; Leelavati of Bhaskaracharya; perhaps the approach of the readers was towards the title or subject covered; by it rather than the person who wrote it. It signifies the impersonal and objective bent of mind of oriental readers which seems to be better than the subjective approach. Will not people read and appreciate the dramas of Shakespeare, had they been written by some person other than Shakespeare as superbly as was done by him? It cannot be said that the title approach to the work of an author signifies unnaturalness or an undemocratic attitude.—

Callimachus seems to have adopted the following main divisions of knowldge for classifying the manuscripts:

I. Epic and other Non-Dramatic Poetry

II. The Drama

III. Laws

IV. Philosophy

V. History

VI. Oratory

VIII. Mathematical Science

IX. Natural Science

X. Miscellanea

The authors were arranged in the alphabetical order of their names, under the appropriate class of knowledge to which their works related. The 'pinakes' (the tablets) were kept with the wall book cases.

Thus the *Pinakes* was the first great library catalogues of western civilization, just as the *Bible of Gutenberg* was the first great printed book. Thus, as in all intellectual efforts, the Greeks fixed the canons *of cataloguing, which have been incorporated, more or less, in our Library of Congress*, European and other system. However, the Pinakes was more than a catalogue. It was the work of the foremost man of letters of his age.... That the original Pinakes (120) is lost is a major disaster to learning. We repeat we would rather have the priceless 120 volumes of Callimachus even than 'Livy whole'.

The catalogue of the library at the *Convent of St. Francis of Assisi*, dated 1 January 1381 indicates that the library was in two divisions: (1) for the use of the brethren; (2) for loans to outsiders. This catalogue has a brief preface stating that it includes "all the books belonging to the library of the Holy *Convent of St. Francis* at Assisi whether they be chained, or whether they be not chained."

The compiler of the catalogue goes through the library case by case, noting the position of the case, the subjects of the books contained in it, and their titles. This is succeeded; by an enumeration of the number of volumes, so as to show in a couple of pages, how many the whole library contained.

The foregoing examples of *catalogues* of the early and medieval libraries tend to indicate that the catalogue was more a record for the keeper or custodian of the books than one for the public.

It also discloses that the number of books 'or manuscripts' in those' libraries was small and did not create problems which great national university, and public libraries of today with millions of volumes have to face. The use of the library was also restricted to certain classes of people.

Many *medieval libraries* had such small collections that lists of any kind were found unnecessary. In several cases it was only a rough inventory. Books were valuable property and so had to be protected and enumerated among, the treasures of a house. The emphasis on the material values of books continued in many library records until the sixteenth century. Secular corporations followed the example set by the church and lent their manuscripts, but only on security. A remarkable example of a loan transaction of a work on medicine at the *Ecole de Medecine, Paris,* astonishingly illustrates the property value attached to library books and manuscripts. When Lous XI, the King of France, wanted a work on medicine from this library, he was asked to deposit a security of 12 marks' worth of plate and 100 gold crowns before he could borrow it. The king deposited the security, borrowed the work, and after use returned it on 24 January 1472, when the money was returned to him.

There were some monastic libraries which listed books not to catalogue them but to commemorate the donations received. Some other medieval libraries maintained lists of works as a check against loss or theft. Still, again, there were *'catalogues'* written in metrical form which suggests that the young monks were required to commit the lists to memory. Only in the larger monasteries do we find real, catalogues., i.e. guides to the content and location of books available, for use. Thus, the earlier *medieval catalogues* were primarily shelf lists. True author and subject records were a later development.

With the advent of the printing press and its product-printed books-the volume of literature has been growing steadily. Books became not only cheap to suit the means of ordinary people but also grew in variety. Booksellers established standards for the description of titles in their lists or catalogues by giving the size, number of pages, quality of binding, price and also a brief annotation of the books or its contents. Library catalogues soon adopted this practice more or less fully in describing the books in catalogue entries, in order to help the readers to identify the books from the catalogue. With the growth in the number of serial publications, specially in the field of science and technology, newer techniques and standards of description became necessary.

What scholars expect of cataloguing now can be gauged from the views ecpressed by William B. Hamilton, a Professor of History of Duke University, and Joseph S. Fruton, a Professor of Biochemistry of Yale University: A *library catalogue* is expected to satisfy every kind of bibliographic demand made on it, if possible without reference to other types of services in a library. But this is an untenable proposition, because a library catalogue is largely dependent on ordering, *acquisition, classification, stock control* verification, revision. discarding and other operations in a library.

A modern library catalogue of a satisfactory type, in general, displays the record of a library's resources with a view to making them easily, accessible for study and reference; serves as a dependable tool of communication of ideas and subjects dealt with in the books to the readers who use the library; provides basic bibliographic information to systematic study and research· functions as a select author and subject bibliography.

The above characteristics of a modern library catalogue distinguish from the early and medieval catalogues, which were little more than inventories of the collections in libraries. The shelf list and the accession records maintained in libraries today perform the functions of an inventory of the stock, thereby relieving the load on the catalogue of the library. It is but natural that as the reader became more important than the books, the objectives of the library catalogue changed from inventory to retrieval or location of particular items or groups of items in a library collection, which has become the most important function of the library catalogue. The catalague entry may provide a wide variety of information on or about the *author,* his *collaborators, subjects* and *titles,* forms and aspects, etc.

OBJECTIVES OF A LIBRARY CATALOGUE

The objectives of a library catalogue are as follows:—

(i) It should enable a person to find a book of which either (a) the author, or (b) the title, or (c) the subject is known;

(ii) It should depict what the library has (a) by a given author, (b) on a given subject (c) in a given kind of literature,

(iii) It should assist in the choice of book (a) as to its edition, and (b) its character.

Thus a library catalogue should be an effective tool to serve the following two purposes:

i) to locate a particular document by its author, collaborator (editor, translator, reviser, adapter, commentator etc), subject, title or any other specifications a user may look under; and

ii) to bring to notice of users all works written by an author, on a subject and all the editions etc. of a work.

DEVELOPMENT OF CATALOGUING CODES

The term cataloguing refers to the process of preparing entries for a catalogue. History of catalogues reveals that it was the religious institutions and later the universities which developed strong collections of books and therefore provided catalogues. Entries tended to be very brief because the main object of the catalogue was to serve as inventory control record. Subject and author cataloguesc began to appear in the thirteenth and fourteenth centuries. The use of alphabetical order in author catalogues was introduced in the sixteenth century.

Since the early catalogues were mainly inventories of book stock rather than a bibliographical tools, cataloguing codes were almost non-existent. The sixteenth century saw three notable codes such as: *Conrad Gerner's* Cataloguing Methods of 1548 suggesting a basic catalogue of book in the order in which they stood on the shelves with a alphabetical author index; the cataloguing methods of *Florianus Treflerus* (1560)- a monk who wrote perhaps the first manual on library economy; and the cataloguing methods of *Andrew Maunsell* a London Bookseller, outlined rules in catalogue of 1595.

The seventeenth century saw further developments in the making of catalogue codes with the beginnings of the *Bodleian Library* catalogues and the cataloguing method of *John Durie* and *Frederic de Rostgaard,* a Danish Scholar.

By the eighteenth century catalogues had become finding lists rather than mere inventory control records. Entry under surname, use of imprint and bound with, notes, references, and analytical entries was common. The card catalogue was introduced in France in 1743. France also produced the first national cataloguing code in 1791. This made a card catalogue arranged alphabetically by author. The first printed catalogue of the British Museum was produced in 1787 and notable catalogues from the United States were those of Harvard and Yale. The Harvard Catalogue of 1790 was the earliest example of an *alphabetico-classed catalogue*.

NEED FOR CODES

The need for codes of cataloguing rules was largely felt in the beginning of nineteenth century. By the middle of this century a long series of cataloguing codes was developed. Each new code sought to, improve on the preceding one. The earlier codes were mostly the efforts of individuals, but the later codes were developed as result of joint efforts and undertakings. The important cataloguing codes are now discussed briefly.

The British Museum Cataloguing Rules

The British Museum cataloguing Rules (BM) also konwn as Panizzi's "91 Rules", under the caption: 'Rules for the Compilation of the Catalogue' were developed in 1839 and published in 1841 as a guide for the compilation of the British

Museum catalogues. This was the first major catalogue code which influenced other subsequent codes. The rules are directly related to the particular functions of the British Museum catalogue, which are to (a) to provide an inventory of the stock of the library and (b) to allow the rapid location of any book. The bibliographical function is a secondary one, and the rules produce a finding-list catalogue.

Charles C. Jewett, the Librarian of the Smithsonian Institution, Washington D.C. produced an important pamphet titled "Smithsonian Report on the Construction of Catalog of Libraries," and their Publication by means of separate stereotyped titles, with Rules and Examples in 1853. This code contained 33 rules largely based on Panizzi's rules. Jewett suggested a system of subject headings which is earliest attempt at codifying subject heading practice. Jewett is also remembered for his proposal of centralized and cooperative cataloguing by means of a union catalogue which provides "stereotyped" cataloguing entries for all libraries.

Cutter's Rules for Dictionary Catalogue

The first edition appeared in 1876 with the title Rules for a Printed Dictionay Catalogue. The fourth edition with complete set of rules under the title Rules for a Dictionary Catalogue came out in 1904. Cutter's purpose was to "investigate what might be called the first principles of cataloguing", because of this his code left deep impact on the subsequent codes than any other work in the field of cataloguing. It contains the well-known statement of the objectives of the catalogue and the means to attain them.

This comprehensive code of 369 rules covers author, title, subject, and form entry, description, and filing and arrangement. One of its most valuable features is the frequent discussion of cataloguing problems-for example, pseudonymous work and corporate authorship-which makes the code almost a textbook on cataloguing as well as a code of rules.

Cutter advocates frequently main entry under "best-known" name. His concern for the convenience of the reader is further shown by his use of "double entry" on several occasions. Although the code is based on certain well-defined principles, it does contain a great deal of repetition for identical cases.

AA 1908

American Library Association Catalog Rules: Author and Title Entries was published in 1908. It was a joint venture of American and the British Librarians in developing a cataloguing code. However the two groups did not reach full agreement on all details and the code was published in two editions (English and American).

AA 1908 reflected the influence of the previous codes. It excluded Cutter's statements of objectives and means. The rules for subject headings were also ommited. The major aim of this code was to meet the "requirements of larger libraries of a scholarly character".

The rules in this code were extremely pedantic. The authors were to be entered under their surnames followed by full names, not the initials; pseudonymous authors were always to be antered under their real name although not known to the users. An excessive amount of detail was called for in the description including all places of publication and publishers if there were more than one and the division of illustrations into ten arbitrary groups etc. The worst example was the separation of rules 2 (joint authors) and 126 (collections), which caused considerable confusion over the years.

The Vatican Code

The Vatican Code had its origins in the 1920s when the Vatican Library was reorganized. Vatican Library Rules for the catalog of printed books was translated from the 2nd Italian edition and published by ALA in 1948.

The rules were developed for the purpose of compiling a general catalogue of printed books in the Vatican Library after its reorganization in the 1920s. The persons responsible were either Americans or American-trained Librarians. Therefore, this code of cosmopolitan nature is described as an international code with a definite American bias. Its significance lies in the fact that for many years, the Vatican code was as Wyllis E. Wright states in the foreword to the English translation. (2nd ed.) "the most complete statement of American cataloguing practice".

Probably the most comprehensive and best-structured code at the time, the Vatican code contains rules for Entry Word, Description, Subject Entry and Filing with sufficient number of examples. The treatment of periodicals is much complete than that of AA 1908.

Library of Congress Descriptive Cataloguing Rules 1949

The extensive use of Library of Congress printed cardes by the libraries in the United States caused considerable interest in the Library Cataloguing rules. The Library of Congress started revising its rules for descriptive cataloguing. It published in 1946 its Studies of Descriptive Cataloguing: A Report to the librarian of Congress by the Director of the Processing Department which advocated simplification of cataloguing details. The result of this effort was that the ALA had to omit its rules of ALA Draft (1941) for descriptive cataloguing which had not been received well in 1941.

The L.C. rules cover description only that phase of the process of cataloguing which concerns itself with the identification and description of books. These rules cover description for book and non-book materials.

American Library Association Rules 1949

ALA Cataloguing Rules for Author and Title Entries (2nd ed.) came out in 1949. It omitted description part of cataloguing rules. It attempted to codify experience aiming, according to the introduction to represent "the best or the most general current practice in cataloguing of the libraries of the United States". It contained a number of changes from AA 1908 adding, more rules. The basic rules were emphasized with amplifications clearly subordinated.

ALA 1949 and LC 1949 served as standards for descriptive cataloguing for American libraries until the appearance of the Anglo-American Cataloguing Rules in 1967 (AACR1).

ALA 1949 was subjected to criticism by Osborn and Lubetzky. It was taken as a pedantic approach likely to result in a bio-bibliographical tool rather than an efficient location tool etc.

Classified Catalogue Code

S.R. Ranganathan (1892-1972). *Classified Catalogue Code with Additional Rules for Dictionary Catalogue Code.* ED 5. Assisted by A Neelameghan.

The first edition of classificed catalogue code was appeared in 1934 and was continued through five editions, the last (i.e., the 5th edition) coming in 1964. Each later edition was an improvement on the earlier one, the revision, addition or improvement made on the basis of practical application and critical examination supported by teaching and reasoning. This empirical, analytical and critical approach shaped the code progressively.

The second edition (1945) demonstrated the symbiolic relationship between classification and cataloging and evolved chain procedure for subject cataloguing/indexing. Rules for style of writing and alphabetisation correlating the two through Gestalt theory of alphabetisation were other added features of this edition.

Ranganathan's comparative study of classified and dictionary catalogues and evaluation of Cutter's rules helped him publish his Dictionary Catalogue Cooe in 1945.

The third edition (1951) added rules for compiling union catalogue of periodical publications, abstracting periodical and incorpórating as well, a glossary of English Sanskrit terms to be helpful for developing cognate terminology in other Indian languages.

The fourth edition (1955) implemented the lay-out for a catalogue code in the light of Heading and Canons, added supplementary rules for national bibliography, rearranged the rules for determination of authorship, choice of heading and rendering the heading. It also incorporated further additional rules for style of writing effecting correponding changes in the rules for alphabetisation. This edition, as a result of his comparative study of five codes (Heading and Canons published in 1955) made necessary further corrections and alterations which eliminated the need for a separate dictionary catalogue code.

The fifth edition (1964) included new chapters on law of parsimony, physical form, centralised cataloguing, homonyms in class index entries and feature headings, and non-conventional documents. Typographical and other simple errors were corrected, a little rewording was done and better examples were added.

While thc codes for alphahelical, author and dictionary catalogues are quite large in number, thc codes oriented to classified catalogue are few in number. Ranganathan's Classified Catalogue code (CCC) is one prominent code of these few. After Cutter's rules and Vatican code, the (CCC) is thc only other code which is complete to cover all thc cataloguing procedures and to provide rules for entry, description, subject cataloguing/indexing and filing.

Before Ranganathan, there were no catalogue codes ever produced in India. Neither was there an established bibliographic/ cataloguing tradition. The Classified Catalogue Code is the first and the only code designed in India. It was mostly an intuitive effort but applying scientific method to ensure precision and correctness. This is however, does not go to say that the code was entirely a product of prestine mind. Ranganathan, educated in England had the benefit of exposure to western thought and practice, which definitely provided the needed background to work out independently. There are, therefore, many influences. Yet the code is distinctively Rangnathn's own. What is his own adds to the merit, and what is not to its weakness.

The code can be divided into three Units. The first 9 parts/ chapters (A to H and J) form the approach. Many basic issues, more importantly, canons and normative principles; parts and physical form of catalogue, centralised cataloguing; recording, style, language and script, arrangement of entries; conflict of authorship and resolution (determintion of authership); name of person, (i.e., structure, element, etc.) are dealt with. The next 11 chapters (K to N, P to V) constitute the substantial part, i.e., rules for rendering names persons, corporate bodies, geographical entities; preparation of class index entries; main and book index entries for different catagories of books and perodicals; additional rules for compilation of union catalogues of books and periodical publications; National bibliography; indexing periodical; abstracting periodical; and cataloguing of incunabula and non-book materials. The last part (W) constitutes end matter (glossary of terms, bibliographic references and index).

The rules are marked for the simplicity, clarity and brevity. It draws a distinction between a library catalogue and a bibliography. Elaborate description is a necessity in bibliography and not in a library catalogue. Therefore, CCC does not prescribe recording of imprint, collation, many details in notes, statment of responsibility in the title section, etc. The rules for determining authorship are based on a set of problems explained as conflicts of authorship. The rules relating to rendering of names/headings for persons, corporate bodies and geographic entities are based on language, nationality and cultural preferences which are postulated through principles.

The empirical approach and application of normative principles in drafting and arranging the rules have made CC a model code. The fact that it does not cover the entire range of various types of material makes it a less comprehensive code. No code can be perfect in all details and the CCC is no exception.

It needs revision and rethinking so as to caipture and respond to the changes that have come about after its publication in 1964.

Anglo- American Cataloguing Rules 1967 (AACR)

The strongest criticism of ALA rules 1949 by Lubetzky paved the way for a new code. He criticised that code for being unnecessarily long and confusing as it provided duplicate and overlapping rules to meet identical condtion.

An International Conference on Cataloguing Principles was held in Paris in 1961. As a result, a statment of Principles known as the "Paris Statement" or the "Paris Principles" was issued. It drew heavily to the choice of entry and the forms of headings only. It starts with a statment of the functions of the catalogue which represents a restatment of Lubetzky's Cutter's objectives.

Since the Paris Principles deal with the problems of entry and headings only and there were no internnationl guidelines for the development of the rules for description, LC 1949 code was used as the basis for descriptive information of monographs, serials, as well as for the rules for cataloguing non-book material.

Atthough the "Paris Principles" contributed toward international standardization, the demand for national cataloguing code remained strong.

Lubetzky had porvided a preliminary review of AACR in 1964. His successor C. Summer Spalding began a complete reappraisal based on the work of Lubetzky and on the Paris Principle. The American and British Committees, working for the revision of code, could not reach complete agreement on a number of points. This disagreement resulted in the publication of two separate texts of the Anglo-American Cataloguing Rules (AACR)- the North American text and the British text in 1967.

The New code (known as AACR 1) appeared in 1967 and was received by the profession with a mixed reaction. The rules in the code were organised in 2 parts, part 1 dealing with entry and heading consisting of four chapters, and part 2 covering description presented in 10 chapters.

The code applied reevalution of the existing practice. It was seen as a better code in terms of its more logical grouping of the rules with emphasis on conditions of authorship rather than on classes of authors (married women, princes of blood, etc.) and kinds of publication (anna, dictionaries encyclopaedias. etc). It corresponded, more than the earlier codes to the patterns of intelligent users instead of blindly ruling preparation of entries, which may be precise; consistent and technically correct. It gave preference to the form of name preferred or used by the author than his real/official name. Title page of the item catalogued was prescribed as the source of information for cataloguing against the old practice of deriving details from outside sources. Similarly, in the case of change of names of corporate bodies, entry was required under the changed/new name. The code, further emphasized the function of assembling bibliographic units by providing uniform title entry more widely. But some of the vestiges of old practices remained. For example, the authorial status to editors and compilers, entry under, place names for certain corporate bodies continued. On this and certain other points since the American and British Committees could not reach agreement, the code was published in two slightly differing texts like the 1908 code.

When work on AACR 1 began, books and periodicals were the basic and popular materials, Card catalogue was the norm. But when the code appeared in 1967 the situation changed vastly. As a result of technology, a variety of new media as non-book materials found their way into libraires Computer mainpulation of data made possible other forms of catalogue. The need to integrate the descriptive records (catalogue entries) of different forms of material (book and non-book items) necessitated studies to find analogies between their characteristics. IFLA brought out a document entitled International Standard Bibliographic Description (for single and multi-volume monographic publication) in 1971. This was later improved/ revised and published in 1974, as ISBD(M): International Standard Bibliographic Description for Monographic Publications, 1st standard edition. Along with it another standard for serials, viz., ISBD(S) International Standard Bibliographic Description for Serials was also published. The AACR I incorporated these documents and revised chapter 6 (separatly published monographs) in 1974 followed by chapter 12 (for audio-visual media and special instructional materials) in 1975 and chapter 14 (for sound recodings) in 1976. IFLA's International standards for other kinds of material including a general one followed in succession.

This piecemeal revision was found unsatisfactory. It needs development of overall principles and integration of descriptive rules for various media. The expanded cooperation between the cataloguing agencies in Great Britain, America and other countries as well as the increase in the use of UKMARC and LCMARC brought about agreement for a single unified text of code, the ambiguities and differences resolved.

AACR 2 (1978)

Anglo-American cataloging rules/ Prepared by the American Library Association, the British Library, the Canadian Committee on Cataloguing, the Library Association, the Library of Congress; edited by Michael Gorman and Paul W. Winkler, 2nd ed.- London: Library Association; Chicago: American Library Association, 1978.

This second edition proved superior revealing basic pirnciples that porvided the edifice of the code. It followed "the sequence of cataloguers' operation in most present-day libraries and bibliographic agencies," i.e., first examinaing the item and describing it and then determining the access points. The code therefore, presented the descriptive rules in part 1 followed by rules for determining and establishing headings/access points in part 2. Part 1 begins with a general chapter which can be applied to all materials in general chapter. In the description, the code permitted alternative rules and options to suit the needs of the libraries and cataloguing agencies. In the rules for access points, it worked out many terminological improvement to remove conceptual irritants, eg., statement of responsibility in place of statement of authorship, corporate entry, instead of corporate author, etc. It standardized punctuation to conform to the pattern established in ISBDs.

ACCR 2, 1988 revised

Anglo-American cataloging rules/ prepared under the direction of the Joint Steering Committee for Revision of AACR, a committee of the American Library Association, the Australian Committee on Cataloguing, the British Library, the Canadian Committe on Cataloguing the Library Association, the Library of Congress: edited by Michael Gorman and Paul W Winkler.- 2nd ed., 1988 revision.- Ottawa: Candian Library Association; London, Library Association Publishing Limited; Chicago: American Library Association 1988.

The implementation of AACR 2 (1978) code was begun by the Library of Congress in Jan 1981. Like the earlier edition (AACR1), the second edition too appeared at a time when there were rapid developments taking place. More important and of greater immediate relevance was the emergence of many new forms of material which were still in shaping.

Although the code (AACR2) resolved the problems of authorship more satisfactorily, the rules were found inadequate in dealing with new media. In course of implementation of the code, some rules presented themselves as confusing, insufficient and complicated. This gave rise to differences in interpretation.

Therefore, attempts were made to clarify, expand or alter rules in necessary cases. The Library of Congress notified the interpretations and modifications in its Cataloguing service bulletin.

Three sets of revisions of AACR2 comprising of Geographical corrections, Textual amendments, and altered and additional rules were issued in 1982, 1984 and 1986. These were followed also by a draft revision of chapter 9 for computer files. The code too came into wide use and found translation in many languages. In view of the changes and additions that were brought out and the growing popularity and use of the code, it was decided to revise it. The revised code, it was further decided, to be named as AACR 2, 1988 revision and not as 3rd edition. The revision sought to incoporate the additions and modifications already made as well as further revisions contemplated, viz., description of material for the blind, rethinking of the concept of separate bibliographical identities, tretment of titles, author heading, geographic names and corporate bodies, corrections, rewording and addition of new examples.

The revision, therefore, did not result either in the change of basic concepts, principles or structure. While the prominent changes applied to computer files, other changes related to the material for the blind, sound recordings, music, etc. In order to achieve greater conformity in establishing heading, a few rules were changed. These changes include redetermining of title proper, redesignation of GMD in a few instances, addition of distinction in the rules for choice of pseudonyms, deletion of option to qualify place names (by adding larger areas/jurisdictions), addition of geographical identifiers to identical corporate bodies, redefining the type 3 subordinate corporate body, recasting of uniform titles, entry additionally under corporate name other than publisher, distributor, etc. in the case of some cartographic material, etc.

The rules are presented in two parts; part one consists of description rules in 13 chapter. Chapter 1 has the general rules which provide the general frame within which descriptive rules for specific classes of material follow. Chapter 13 also contains general rules for analysis of specific types. These are as follow:—

Part 1 Description: Chapter 1, General rules of description, 2. Books, Pamphlets and monographs, 3. Cartographic Materials, 4.

Manuscripts (including manuscripts collection), 5. Music (Published music), 6. Sound Recordings, 7. Motion Pictures and Video-Recording, 8. Cartographic Materials, 9. Computer Files, 10. Three-dimensional Artifacts and Realia, 11. Microforms, 12. Serials, and 13. Analysis.

Part2. Heading, uniform titles and references: Chapter 21. Choice of Access Points, 22. Headings for Persons, 23. Geographic Names, 24. Heading for Coporate Bodies, 25. Uniform Title, and 26. References.

The third part contitutes the end matter. It consists of Appendices, A. Capitalization, B. Abbreviations, C. Numerals, and D. Glossary, and An Index.

Each part has one introductory chapter. The rules in the 12 chapters of part 1 (Description) have mnemonic numbering to facilitate to and for reference to rules applying to appropriate areas. The descriptive rules are presented first, obviously because cataloguing begins with description, then follow the tasks of determination and establishment of heading. So, rules for access points, choice of forms of heading are given in the second part. The gap between chapters 13 and 21 is left to incorporate descriptive rules for new classes of materials that may come (in which case Chapter 13 may be renumbered). In both parts, the rules follow the order of general to specific. The code has provision for optional rules and alternatvie rules to accommodate the varying requirments of libraries.

The preface that "cataloging rules cannot be static, they must be allowed to respond to changing needs". What is meant by this is that revision does not stop at any time; it goes on. Further revisions become necessary.

With technological developments, media for storage and publication of information appeared ranging from microforms (microfilms, microfiche, etc.) to magnetic (floppy discs, tapes, etc.) and optical media (CD-ROM families). Consequently, the catalogue code had to incorporate new rules to handle these new media.

One of the most significant developments has been emergence of the Online Public Access Catalogue (OPAC) which is basically the gateway to a library's collection. This is an interface through which users can search a library's catalogue, and can also perform a number of other operations, such as borrower record checking, reservation of items, online renewal, and so on. Although OPACs made their first appearance in the mid-1970s, it was only at the beginning of the next decade that libraries is significant numbers began to switch from card to automated catalogues. Library management software packages usually come with an OPAC Module which can be used. The library can identify and design specific menus for staff and users, dialogues on specific fields, such as author, title, subject, ISBN, etc. with right truncation facilities, and keyword searching with Boolean search facilities. With the recent advent of graphical user interface, it has become possible to include a range of information retrieval facilities menus or as options on buttons or check boxes.

The other developments include various online cataloguing networks and service, sometimes called bibliographic utilities, These networks, or bibliographic utilities, such as OCLC (Online Computer Library Center), RLIN (Research Library Information Network), etc., provide cataloguing facilities to their member librareis. These are basically central cataloguing facilities whereby member libraries can download the catalogue entries of specific materials. The largest of these is the OCLC. OCLC's world Cat (the OCLC Online Union Catalog) offer access to catalogue resources that no other single institutions possesses.

The most recent, and porbably the most prominent, developement of the era has been the internet which has drastically changed the various aspects of our lives. Internet, and one of its most porminent services, the World Web (WWW), has become the most widely used source of information for all concerned, and due to its exponential growth it has been extermely important to catalogue, and thereby exert some kind of bibliographic control on the infomation available on the Internet.

Cataloguing of Non-Book Materials

A modern library today is flooded with a variety of "non book", "non print", "audio visual" materials apart from monographs, serials and sophisticated machine-readable media of information.

Non-book materials generally understood to be any resource material which is not a printed book. Thus a range of non-book materials would include item such as sound recording, filmstrips, motion pictures and video-recording. Other items are print and these include maps, chart, posters, and other are non-print. The term non-book may extend to pamphlets, microforms and serials, or these items may be classified as book.

It is worth noting that audio-visual material is only one form of non-book material. Audio-visual resources are designed to transmit information either by sound or vision, and as such are library resources which do not depend on the printed word in order to make communication with users. Since, however, non-book material includes such printed items as pamphlets and newspapers, it becomes clear that although all audio-visual materials can be considered to be non-book materials, not all non-book materials are audio-visual materials.

Rapid technological developments have caused librarians to reassess their library stock provision in the light of the demands and needs of borrowers living and working in the moderen era. The need for the swift transmission of information in the fields of industry, within the home itself we surround ourselves with a range of media such as television, radio and sound-recorders, all of which communication in other ways than by printed word. At the same time changes in the world of education have prompted increased individualized learning and information seeking on the part of school children and students alike. These are three of the main factor which have resulted in librarians acquiring a varied collection of non-book materials to supplement their traditional book-stock.

Ccataloguing Standards for Non-Book Materials

Dr. Ranganathan in chapter VA has enumerated various kinds of non-book material:—

1. Incunabula;
2. Document in non-conventional script

   21 Braille;

   22 Stenograph;

23 Music in notation; and

24 Cipher.

3. Document similar to conventionl book in physical appearance but using drawings, pictures, maps and similar graphical media instead of phonetical symbols.

4. Manuscript in

41 Paper of Cloth in codex form;

42 Paper or cloth in roll form;

43 Leaves;

44 Parchment;

45 Wood;

46 Metal;

47 Stone; and

48 Clay tablets

5. Reprographs of other than normal or near-normal size such as

51 Microfilm

52 Microfiche; and

53 Micro-card

6. Reprographs such as

61 Sound record of conventional books;

62 Speaking book or pirnted book with a companion attachment of the sound record of the letter-press in it; and

63 Conventional phonograph records.

7. Cinema reels including

71 Silent ones; and

72 Talkies

8. Metadocuments or instrument-record of phenomena.

Ranganathan has not provided specific rules for cataloguing of the above non-conventional documents. He said "sufficient experience has not been gained in India with the kind of documents other than manuscripts. Even in regard to manuscripts, certain traditions have been evolved largely by scholars using the manuscripts without much confirmity to the current principles of cataloguing. However time has come to work out the modification necessary in the catalogue code in the case of manuscripts as well as other kinds of documents under consideration. It is our hope that future editions of this book CCC will be able to add progressively chapters to this part dealing with the respective kinds of documents. "But unfortunately no new edition of the *Classified Catalogue Code* came after 1964.

Before the publication of AACR 2 little standardization in the descriptive cataloguing rules for non-book materials was available. These materials were catalogued "just like books", but not considered the equal to books. This attitude has changed and the importance of other media established.

The publication of the revised second edition of the Anglo-American cataloguing rules (AACR2) confirmed that all format could be catalogued to the same standard. It simply stated that 'The rules cover the description of, and provision of access point for all library materials commonly collected at the present time. The integrated structure of the text makes the general rules usable as a basic for cataloguing uncommonly collected materials of all kinds and library materials yet unknown.

The revised edition notes that technological developments such as videodisc and microcomputer files have necessitated rule revision, particulary in chapter 9, computer files. Nevertheless, these new information carriers can be catalogued by the librarian and they do not differ in substance from other non-books. The pirnciples that underline AACR2 are a sound guide for the cataloguing of all NBM. Further the publication of ISBD (NBM) for non-book materials and ISBD (G)- a general framework for description by IFLA further helped resolve cataloguing problems and made the rules so flexible that they could be applied even to a medium unknown when the rules were developed. They become principles as much as rules.

Table : History of Cataloguing Standards Development

Year	People	Reports and Publications	Institutions	Organizations	Conferences	Codes and standards	Cataloguing and cataloguing services	Comments
1787							First British Museum Printed catalogues	
1841	Panizzi		British Museum			Rules for compling the catalogue of printed books, maps and music in the British Museum (Rev ed 1936)		The first of the modern codes. Great influence
1852	Jevett	On the construction of catalogs						First American rules for author entry, with suggested supplementary subject list. Also advocated centralized/ cooperative cataloguing
1856	Crestadoro	The art of making catalogues						Advocated detailed main entries beginning with author. Accession number arrangement with indexes of names and subjects. Applied to Manchester Public Librarycatalogue in 1864
1864			Manchester Public Lubrary				Catalogue constructed according to Crestadoro's principles (1856)- First KWIC index	

Year	People	Reports and Publications	Institutions	Organizations	Conferences	Codes and standards	Cataloguing and cataloguing services	Comments
1876	Cutter					Rules for a dictionary catalogue (4th ed 1904)		Tremendous influence. Basis of American Practice. Includes rules for author and subject entries and also filing rules
1881							First Library of Congress general card catalogue begun	
1897							Volume one of Bibliotheque National catalogue published	Only now nearing completion
1899						Prussian Instructions		Rules widely adopted in Germany and many other European countries. Unusual ideas on coporate authorship and anonymous works
1899-1901	Putnam		Library of Congress				Library of congress adopts dictionary catalog and begins distribution of catalogue cards	The Library of congress has since held a central position in US cataloguing
1908				Library Association American Library Association		AA code (the 'Joint' code)		Intended to bring uniformity to the cataloguing practice of English speaking countries
1911	Kaiser	Systematic indexing						Significant contribution to the theory of subject heading

Year	People	Reports and Publications	Institutions	Organizations	Conferences	Codes and standards	Cataloguing and cataloguing services	Comments
1914			Library of Congress			Subject heading used in the dictionary catalogs of the Library of Congress		US practice is still largely based upon these working tools which reflect Cutter's rules
1923	Sears					Sears' List of subject heading which was based on Library of Congress list		
1927		Kenyon Report (Public Libraries Committee Report on public libraries in England and Wales; Cmd 2868)						Plea for local cooperation
1931			Vatican Library			Vatican Code		Includes rules for alphabetical subject entries and filing rules. Has been described as 'the best statement of American catalogue practice'
1934	Cranchaw	Cutting cataloguing costs 50% (In *Library world* 39 1934 179-184)						Anitcipated Osborn and Lubetzky with his ideas on simplification
1934	Ranganathan					Classified Catalogue code (6th ed 1964)		The only code of rules specifically for the classified catalogue
1941	Osborn	The crisis in cataloguing (In *Library quarterly* 11 (4) 1941 393-411)						Voiced the dissatisfaction felt by many cataloguers with existing codes, especially the preliminary edition of ALA 1949

Year	People	Reports and Publications	Institutions	Organizations	Conferences	Codes and standards	Cataloguing and cataloguing services	Comments
1942			American Library Association			ALA rules for filing catalogue card, First edition (2nd ed 1968; rewritten 1980)		
1942-1946			Library of Congress				First Library of Congress Printed catalogues published (167 volumes)	
1945	Ranganathan					Dictionary catalogue code		
1949			Library of Congress	American Library Association		ALA rules and the Library of Congress rules for descriptive cataloguing		The ALA rules were heavily criticized for 'enumerating' case and for being too detailed
1950			British National Bibliography				The British national bibliography begins publications. A classified arrangement using chain procedure for subject indexing	
1951			Library of Congress				Introduced 'limited cataloguing' policy ceased 1964	
1951				British Standards Institution		BS 1749: Specification for alphabetical arrange-ment and the filings order of numberals and symbols (2nd ed 1969)		

Year	People	Reports and Publications	Institutions	Organizations	Conferences	Codes and standards	Cataloguing and cataloguing services	Comments
1953	Lubetzky	Cataloging rules and principles						Very important. Aruges for rules besed upon prino-iples- 'conditions' rather than 'cases'
1954				IFLA Working Group on the Coordination of Cataloguing principles				The International Federation of Library Association has played, and is playing, a vital role in international cataloguing. ICCP was to blossom from this working party
1955	Ranga-nathan	Heading and canons						Animportant comparative study of five codes of cataloguing rules
1956			British National Bibliography				First printed cards from BNB	
1956			Library of Congress				National Union catalog begins	
1956			Library of Congress			Filing rules for the dic-tionary cataloges of the Library of Congress (rewritten 1980)		Originally issued in loose-leaf form, as Filling manual, for LC staff only
1958-1959			Library of Congress				CIS (Cataloguing In Source) experiment	Now CIP (Cataloguing In Publication)

Year	People	Reports and Publications	Institutions	Organizations	Conferences	Codes and standards	Cataloguing and cataloguing services	Comments
1959-1966			British Museum				BM General catalogue published in photo litho edition (263 volumes)	
1960	Coates	Subject catalogues: headings and Structure						Analyses approach of Cutter and Kaiser and Develops his own theories, put into practice in British technology index
1960	Lubetzky	Code of cataloging rules... an unfinished draft						Incomplete but showed what could be achieved with a drastic reduction in the number of rules
1961							First automated production of catalogue cards	The Douglas Aircraft Co. introduces the first *cataloguing* application of computer had been used with post-coordinate indexing since 1950s
1961 upon					ICCP (International Conference on Cataloguing Principles)- Paris			A 'statement of principles' based Lubetzky's work was adopted at this Conference which has had an enormouseffecton cataloguing and cataloguing rules throught the world

Year	People	Reports and Publications	Institutions	Organizations	Conferences	Codes and standards	Cataloguing and cataloguing services	Comments
1963		King report on automation and the Library of Congress						Led to the MARC project
1965							The Library of Congress National Program for Acquisition and Cataloguing (NPAC) otherwise known as the 'Shared Cataloguing Program' begun	
1965							First computerization of catalogues in the UK (the public libraries of Camden and Barnet)	
1966				Brasenose conference on the automation of libraries				Put forward the argument that the computer can produce a 'reactive catalogue', that it can generate from a common bibliographic store a system of catalogues that are all mutually compatible
1966			Library of Congress				Project MARC begun	
1967			Library of Congress	Library Association/ American Library Association/ Canadian Library Association		Anglo-American Cataloguing Rules		Based upon 'conditions of author-ship' and not types of publication

Year	People	Reports and Publications	Institutions	Organizations	Conferences	Codes and standards	Cataloguing and cataloguing services	Comments
1967							Introduction of the SBN (Standard Book) Number- now ISBN)	
1967							Attention first focussed upon possibility of microform catalogues	At the Lockheed Missiles and Space Co
1967			British National Bibliography				UK MARC begun	
1967			Ohio College Library center				OCLC network set up	
1968			Library of Congress				National union catalog pre-1956 imprints began publication	
1969			BLCMP				First UK network	
1970							Introduction of ISSN (International Standard Serial Number)	
1970						Canadian rules of non-book materials		
1970				IFLA			Introduction of ISBD (International Standard Bibliographic Description)	
1971	Austin						PRECIS first used in BNB	

Year	People	Reports and Publications	Institutions	Organizations	Conferences	Codes and standards	Cataloguing and cataloguing services	Comments
1973				Library Association/ National Council for Educational Technology (now Council for Educational Technology for the UK)		LANCET rules for non-book materials		
1973							Books in English first published	An ultra-microfiche bibliography based upon MARC
1975			British Library formed					
1977			British Library				BLAISE goes live	
1978			Library of Congress/ British Library	Library Association American Library Association/ Canadian Library Association		AACR 2nd ed published		Emphasizes integrated approach to cataloguing different library materials
1980				American Library Association		ALA filing rules		New version of 1968 rules
1980			British Library			BLAISE filing rules		
1980			Library of Congress			Filing rules		New version of 1956 rules

Year	People	Reports and Publications	Institutions	Organizations	Conferences	Codes and standards	Cataloguing and cataloguing services	Comments
1981			British Library/ Library of Congress/ National Libraries of Canada and Australia					Adopted AACR 2
1981			Library of Congress					Policy of whereby new rules 'superimposition', are only used if they do not lead to conflict with existing headings, to be abandoned, Replaced by 'compatible heading'
1981	Gorman					Concise AACR 2		
1982								Compatible headings policy of LC ceases
1982								Microcomputer application in libraries for cataloguing and indexing becoming more widespread

Year	People	Reports and Publications	Institutions	Organizations	Conferences	Codes and standards	Cataloguing and cataloguing services	Comments
1988	Gorman					AACR-II revision		
1998	Gorman					AACR-II revision		
2000						XML		It enjoys the wide spread acceptance in Library field as a cataloguing standard
2001						MARC-21 format		

2

PRELIMINARIES OF AACR - II

The Anglo-American Cataloguing rules, second edition AACR-II published in the year 1978 was jointly prepared by the American Library Association, the Brithish library, the Canadian Committee on cataloguing, the library Association and the Library of Congress. It is edited by Michael Gorman and Paul W. Winkler and published by the American Library Association and Canadian Library Association.

Anglo-American Cataloguing Rules, edition 2, 1988 Revision consists of two parts. Part I covers rules for standard description of all kinds of material. Part II deals with the determination and establishment of heading or access points in the catalouge. The rules in these parts proceed from general of specific.

In part I, the basic rules for the description of all library materials are included in Chapter I. They are of general applicability. The rules for specific types of materials are given in Chapters :2-12 and chapter 13 deals with analytical entries.

The areas/items to be included in the description are :

- Title and statement of responsibility
- Edition
- Material or type of publication specific details
- Publication, distribution, etc.
- Physical description
- Series
- Note
- Standard number and terms of availability.

In part II, the rules for determination of choice of access points and form of heading are provided. These rules are applicable to all library materials irrespective of the medium. These are discussed in chapter 21-26. There are no chapter in between 13 and 21. The appendices A-C provide rules for capitalisation, abbreviations and numerals.

Appendix A contains instruction for capitalization

Appendix B contains lists of standard Abbreviations

Appendix C deals with numerals

Appendix D glossary

Glossary is the very important part providing most of the terminology used, beginners of cataloguing must use this part more frequently to understand the meaning, definition and the context of terms used in the AACR II.

An index is provided at the end of the code and it has been compiled by KGB Backwell.

LEVELS OF DESCRIPTION

The catalogue entries very from library to library on the basis of description of the items. The descriptions are catagorised into levels on the basis of amount of information to be included. The code has recommended that all descriptive elements may not be useful to all types of libraries. The inclusion of these descriptive elements is catagorised according to three levels. The library can choose any level of description for all the materials. The library also has a choice to use all the levels in on catalogue, depending on the type of materials described.

First level provides minimum information, which is necessary to identify a given document. This level is used in small libraries. The second level can be called a standard description. It provides all the data, which may be considered necessary for description of documents. This level is used for all the data, which may be considered necessary for description of documents. This level is used for medium to large-size libraries. This is normally used the majority of libraries, as it serves the requirements of most users. The third level description of the documents covering every possible elements of description included in the code. This level is used in large and special libraries.

First level of Description:— The first level of description, includes at least the elements set out in this shcematic illustration: Title proper/first statment of responsiblity, if different from main entry heading in form or number or if there is no main entry heading.- Edition statement.- Materials (or type of publication) specification details.- First publisher, etc., date of publication, etc.- Extent of item.- Note(s).- Standard number.

Small libraries such as school, children libraries, where the patron's needs are not sophisticated, and small collections without large growth potential or where staff make detailed cataloguing impractical are likely to adopt the first level of description.

Example :

2:55 q N 65		Ranganathan, S.R.
  1919	 Sarada 1965	Classified catalogue code/ S.R. Ranganathan. Ranganathan Endowment for Library Science, 884p. 1. Cataloguing I. Title

Second Level of Description: — For the second level of description, it includes at least the elements set out in the schematic illustration below:

Title proper (general material designation)= parallel title: other title information/first statement of responsibility relative to the edition.- Material (or type of publication) specific details-First place of publication, etc.: first publisher, etc., date of publication etc.-Extent of item: other physical details; dimensions.- (Title proper of series/ statement of responsibility relating to series, ISSN of series: numbering within the series. Title of subseries, ISSN of subseries; numbering with in subseries).-Note(s).- Standard number.

The good majority of information centers such as College Libraries, District Library adopt the second level of description.

Example :

2.55 qN65	Ranganathan, Shiyali Ramamrita.	
1919	Classified catalogue code: with additional rules for Dictionary catalogue code/ S.R. Ranganathan; assisted by A. Neelemeghan. -5th ed. - Bangalore:Sarada Ranganathan Endowment for Library Science, 1965. vii, 637, p.; 20 cm,- (Ranganathan Series in Library Science;2). Practical manual for classified catalogue intended for librarians. 1. cataloguing I. Neelameghan, A II. Title III. series	

Third Level of Description: All elements are required at this level. The third level of description is intended for national libraries, research libraries, and those with a need for detailed cataloguing information.

Example :

2.55 qN65	Ranganathan, Shiyali Ramamrita.	
1919	Classified catalogue code: with additional rules for Dictionary catalogue code/ S.R. Ranganathan; assisted by A. Neelemeghan. 5th ed. - Bangalore: Sarada Ranganathan Endowment for Library Science, 1965. vii, 637, p.; 20 cm,- (Ranganathan Series in Library Science; 2). Practical manual for classified catalogue code intended for librarians. ISER0191: Rs. 200/- 1. Cataloguing 2. Information Processing & retrieval I. Title A. II Series.	

Entry Format

In most of the libraries in India, the entries are written on a card form, and it is the most flexible one. It can be kept up to date and it suits to unit entry catalouing. The entry is made on standard size cards of 12.5 cm. x 7.5 cm (5"x3"). Certain vertical and horizontal lines are drawn on the card. The vertical lines are known as indentions. There are two vertical lines and one horizontal line in red.

The first vertical is known as the first indention and the second vertical line is known as the second indention. There is one more indention known as third indention, but this is an imaginary line on the card.

The horizontal line is used for writing the heading of the entry.

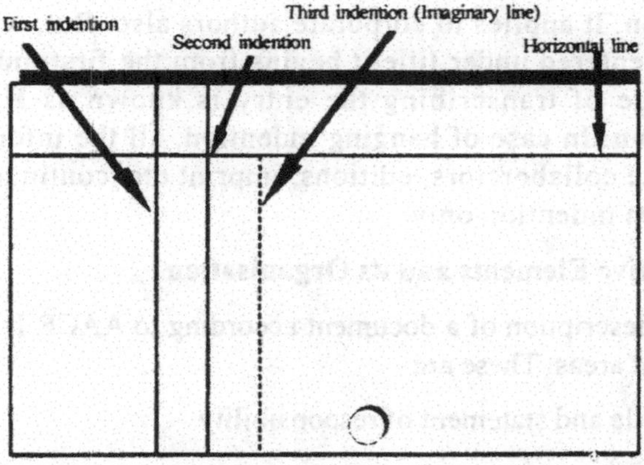

ITEMS IN THE CATALOGUE ENTRY

The total information that is to be included is to be taken from one or more sources of information. However, if the information is not supplied in the title page, the information may be taken from any other bibliographical sources. The information, taken from outside of the title page should be enclosed in square brackets.

The details of information to be written in a catalogue entry are:

* Heading
* Descriptive elements
* Punctuation marks

* Call number
* Tracing

Heading

It is the word groups under which the entry is made. This may be the name of a person, a coroprate body, pseudonym, or the title of the book. In the case of name of a person, the heading comprises of the surname (family name) followed by the forename (personal name) of the person. For example:

Dhiman, Anil Kumar

In case the name of author can not be accommodated on the first line then it continues form the third imaginary indention. It applies to corporate authors also. But, when the book is entered under title it begins from the first indention. This type of transcribing the entry is known as **Hanging Indention**. In case of hanging indention, all the information about the collaborators, editions, imprint etc. continues form the secon indention only.

Descriptive Elements and its Organisation

The description of a document according to AACR II divided into eight areas. These are

1. Title and statement of responsibility
2. Edition
3. Material (or type of publication) specific details
4. Publication, distribution, etc
5. Physical description
6. Series
7. Notes
8. Standard number and terms of availability

Each of these areas are futher extended into number of subsection using appropriate connection symbols.

Class No	Choice of access points (Author/ title)
Book No	Title/statement of responsibility; subsequent statement of responsibility. Edition- place of publication: name of the publisher, year of publication.
ACC No	preliminary pages, textual pages: illustrations; size+ accompaning materials. — (series).
	Note
	Standard Number
	Tracing

Rules for Description

I. Title and statement of responsibility area:

Rule 1.1.B. Title proper

Transcribe the title proper exactly as to wording, order, and spelling, but not necessarily as to punctuation and capitalization.

Example:

The merchant of venice

A midsummer night's dream

Text book of Econocmic

Alternative Title

An alternative title is the second part of a title proper that consists of two parts, each of which is a title: the parts are joined by the word or its equivalent in another language.

e.g. : The tempest, or, the enchanted island

Rule 1.1B2

If the title proper includes two statement of resonsibility or the name of a publisher, distributor, etc. and the statement or name is an integral part of the title proper, transcribe it as such

eg: Marlowe's plays

Rule 1.1B4 Long Title

A long title proper only if this can be done without loss of essential information. Never omit the first words of the title proper. Indicate ommissions by the mark of ommissions.

eg. Basics of Information Technology...

Rule 1.1D Parallel titles

The title proper in another language and/or script is parallel title. It should be recorded immediately after title proper in the order indicated by the sequence, or by the layout of the chief source of information. The parallel title should be preceded by a connecting symbol equal sign "=" The first letter is in capital.

eg: Tyres and Wheels= Penus it rows + Reifen and Radier

Rule 1. 1E Other title information

The other title information should be recorded after the title proper or parallel title if any, and will be preceded by the connecting symbol colon (:). The first letter of the other title information will be in ordinary hand (Roman lower case letter).

eg: Physical Chemistry: a study in his dramatic criticism.

Rule 1. 1F Statement of Responsiblity

Statement of responsibility is a statement, transcribed from the item being described, relating to persons responsibility for the intellectual or artistic content of the item, to corporate bodies from which the content emanates, or to persons or corporate bodies responsible for the performance of the content of the item.

This area should be preceded by the connecting symbol diagonal slash '/'.

Rules 1. 1F1

Record the statement of responsibility appearing porminently in the item in the form in which they appear there. If a statement of responsibility is taken from a source other that the chief source of information, enclose it in square brackets.

eg: Eastern religion and western thoughts/ S. Radhakrishnan Regional development planning in India/ [R.K. Misra]

Shared Responsibility (Two authors)

For two or three authors, in first and second mentioned author the connecting symbol is comma ','.

eg: Statistical Methods for biologists/ S. Palanichamy, M. Sehgal.

Note:

Cataloguer is also given more autonomy to supply a word group 'and' but it should be enclosed in square brackets.

eg: Dark room/James Brown (and) Seymour Lubertsky

Shared responsibility (Three authors)

eg: An introductory practical organic chemistry/V.K. Chadda, R.L. sehgal and P.K. Garg

Rule 1.1F5 Shared responsibility (four or more authors)

When a single statement of responsibility names more than three persons or corporate bodies performoing the same function or with the same degree of responsibility, omit all but the first of each group of such persons or bodies. Indicate the omission by the mark of omission (...) and add et al. in square brackets.

eg: Energy for a sustainable world/Jose Golde Smith... [et al.]

Rule 1. 1F6 Subsequent Statement of responsibility

This sub-section subseqent statement of responsibility, should be preceded by a connecting symbol semicolon.

If there is more than one statement of responsibility, record them in the order indicated by their sequnce on, by the layout of, the chief source of information of the sequence and if layout are ambiguous or insufficent to determine the order, record the statements in the order that makes the most sense.

eg: Glimpses of indian ethno botany/ P.S.Misra; edited by S.K. Jain

II. Edition Area

This area should be preceded with the connecting symbol full stop space dash space.

Rule 1.2B1 Edition Statement

Record the edition statement as formed on the item. Use standard abbreviation.

eg:. 2nd ed.

._ 4th rev. ed._

._ 12th enlarged ed._

Rule 1.2B3

In case of doubt whether a statement is an edition statement, take the presence of such words as edition, issue, version as evidence that such a statement is an edition statement, and record it as such.

eg: ._ Somerset ed.

._ New English ed.

._ New vararium ed.

Rule 1.2B4 Optional Addition

If an item lacks an edition statement but is known to contain significant change from previous editions, supply a suitable brief statement in the language and script of the title proper and enclose it in square brackets.

eg.:_ (2nd ed., Partly rev.)

Rule 1.2C Statement of Responsibility Relating to Edition

Record a Statement of responsibility relating to one or more editions, but not to all editions, of a given work following the edition statement if there is one.

eg: The nether world: a novel/ George Kissing._ (New ed., repr.)/edited, with an introduction, by Johan Susgrave

Rule 1. 2D Subsequent edition statement

If an item is designed as a reissue containing changes from a particular edition, give that statement following the edition statement and its statement of responsibility.

eg: The natural history of Selborne in the country of Southampton/by Gilbert White.- world's classic ed., New ed., rev., reset, and illustrated.

III. Material (or Type of Publication) Specific Details Area

This area is absent in the case of monographs. It should be used for cartographic materials and serial publication.

IV. Publication, Distribution Etc Area

This area is preceeded by a full stop, space dash space (._).

Rule 1.4.C Place of Publication, Distribution etc.

Record the place of publication, etc., in the form and the grammatical case in which it appears.

eg: New York

New Delhi

Rules 1.4C3

Add the name of the country, state, province, etc., to the name of the place if it is considered necessary for identification, or if it is considered necessary to distinguish the place from other of the same name.

eg: Oxford (English) Santiago (Chile)

Rule 1.4C5

If a publisher, distributor, etc., has offices in more than one place and these are named in the item, always give the first named place, and the first of any subsequently named places that is in the home country of the cataloguing agency or is given prominence by the layout of the source of information. Omit all other places.

eg: London; New York

(For a cataloguing agency in United States)

Paris; New Delhi

(For a cataloguing agency in India)

Rule 1.4C6

If the place of publication, distribution, etc., is uncertain, give the probable place in the language of the chief source of information, with a question mark.

eg: (New Delhi ?)

If no probable place can be given, give the name of the country, state, province, etc. If, in such a case, the country, state, province, etc., is not certain, give it with a question mark.

eg:

[India ?]

[Chain ?]

If no place or probable place can be given, give the abbreviations s.l. (sine loco), or its equivalent in non roman scripts.

Rule 1.4D Name of publisher, distributor, etc.

This is the second subsection in the publication, distribution, etc. area, and it should be preceded by a connecting symbol colon (:)

Rule 1.4D1

Give the name of the publisher, distributor, etc., following the place(s) to which it relates

eg: Harmondsworth : Penguin

New Delhi : S. Chand

Madras : AITBS

Rule 1.4D2

Give the name of a publisher, distributor, etc., in the short form in which it can be understood and identified internationally.

eg: Penguin

Not : Penguin Books

: W.H. Allen

Not: Allen

Rule 1.4D3

Do not omit from the phrase naming a publisher, distributor, etc:

(a) Words or phrases indicating the function (other than solely publishing) performed by the person or body

: Distributed by Higginbothoms Pvt. Ltd.

but : Allen & Unwin

Not : Published by Allen & Unwin

(b) Parts of the name required to differentiate between publishers, distributors, etc.

: Longmans, Green

: Longmans, Educational

Not : Longmans

Rule 1.4D6

If the name of the publisher, distributor, etc., is unkown, give the abbreviations s.n (sine nomine) or its equivalent in nonroman scripts.

eg: Delhi : (s.n.)

India : (s.n.)

Rule 1.4F Date of publication, distribution etc.

That is the third sub-section in the publication, distribution etc. area and it should be preceded by a connecting symbol comma i.e. ','.

Rule 1.4F1

Give the date of publication, distribution, etc., of the edition named in the edition area. If there is no edition statement, give the date of the first edition. Give dates in western- style arabic numerals. If the date found in the item is not of Gregorian or Julian Calendar, give the date as found and follow it with the year(s) of the Gregorian or Julian Calendar

eg:,

,1978

Rule 1.4F2

Give the date as found in the item even if it is known to be incorrect. If a date is known to be incorrect add the correct date

eg:, 1893 (i.e. 1993)

Rule 1.4F4

If the publication date differs from the date of distribution, add the date of distribution if it is considered to be significant by the cataloguing agency. If the publisher and distributor are different, give the date(s) after the name(s) to which they apply

eg: London : Macmilan, 1991 (distributed 1993)

Rule 1.4F6

If the date of publication, distribution, etc., copyright date, or date of manufacture can be assigned to an item, give an approximate date of publication.

eg: ,[1979?] Probable date

,[1992?] Probable date

, [ca 1979?] Approximate date

,[199-] Decade certain

,[197-?] Probable decade

,[19-] Century certain

,[20-?] Probable century

V. Physical Discription Area

There are five important sub-section in Physical Description area and their relevant connecting symbols are given below

1. Preliminary pages (comma)
2. Texual pages (Abbreviated from for pages (p.))
3. Illustrative matters (colon)
4. Size (semicolon)
5. Accompanying material (plus sign)

Physical description area should be rendered in a new paragraph starting from second indent and if there is any continuation will start from the first indent.

Rule 1.5B2... Directs to Refer Rule 2.5B2

Record the number of pages, leaves, or coloumns in terres of the numberd of lettered sequences in the volume. Record the last number page leaf, or column in each sequence and follow it with the appropriate term or abbreviations

eg:

859p.

xxii, 629p

15 leaves

10 broadside

Rule 1.5B3

Specify, in addition, the number of components as detailed in the following chapters

eg: 5v (1848p.)

Rule 1.5C1

Give physical date (Other than extent or dimensions) about an item as instructed in the following chapter

eg: 517p. : ill. (some col.)

Rule 1.5D Dimensions (2.5D1)

Give the height of the volume (s) in centimeters, to the next whole centimeter up (eg. if a volume measures 14.2 centemetres, record it as 15 cm). Measure the height of the binding if the volume is bound. Otherwise, measure the height of the item itself. If the volume measures less than 10 centimetres, give the height in millimeters.

eg:. 417. :ill.; 23cm.

87p. : ill, : 18cm

Rule 2.5D2

If the width of the volume is either less than half the height or greater than the height, give the width following the height preceded by a multipilication sign.

eg: ;22 x 8cm

; 20 x 35cm

Rule 2.5D3

If the volume in a multivolume set differ in height and the difference is two centimetres or less, give the largest size. If the difference is more than two centimetres, give the small size and the largest size, seprated by a hypen.

Rule 2.5E Accompanying Material (1.5E1)

There are four ways of recording information about accompanying material.

1. record the details of the accompanying material in a seprate entry or
2 record the details of the accompanying material in a multilevel description or
3 record the details of the accompanying material in a note or
4 record the name of accompanying material at the end of the physical description

eg: 721p.: col.ill.; 28cm.+ 2 maps

iv, 771p. :ill., : 22cm. + 5 atlas (30X20cm.)

VI. Series Area

This area should be rendered using a circular brackets and preceded by a connecting symbol, full stop, space, dash, space.

Series should be recorded exactly to the wording, spelling, order available in the document

eg._ (Ranganathan Series in Library Science)

._ (Clive Bingly publications in Science and Technology).

Rule 1.6E Statements of Responsibility Relating to Series

Give statement of responsiblity appearing in conjuction with the series title if they are considered to be necessary for identification of the series.

eg:_. (Research monographs/Institute of Economic Affairs)

Rule 1.6G1 Numbering within series

Record the numbering of the item within the series in the terms given in the item. Use standard abbreviations and substitute arabic numerals for other numerals or spelled out numbers.

eg: Environment Science Research ; v.7

VII. Note Area

Note area should be rendered in sperate paragraphs.

If there is any information left out in the appropriate areas 1-6, this should be given in note.

Rule 1.7B Notes

Give notes in the order in which they are listed below.

Rule 1.7B1 Nature, Scope, or artistic form of the item

eg:

Commedy in two acts

Documentary

Rule 1.7B2 Language of the item and/or translation or adaption

eg: Commentary in Hindi

Text in French.

Rule 1.7B3 Source of Title proper

eg: Title from the container

Rule 1.7B4 Variations in title

eg: Original title : L' education sentimental

Rule 1.7B13 Dissertations

eg: Thesis (M.Phill.)- University of Delhi.

Rule 1.7B17 Summary

Summary: Pictures the highlight of the play 'Julias Caesar' using photographs of an actual porduction.

Rule 1.7 B 18 Contents

Contents: A glorious court/ Theodore C.Blegen.- Bound Fragments of item/James Ford Bell.

Standard Number and terms of Availablity

Give the standard Number of the book- International Standard Book Number (ISBN) or International Standard Serial Number (ISSN) either in continuation or in a separate paragraph. If it is to be written in continuation, the area should be preceded by full stop, space, dash, and space (.—). Give such number with the agreed abbreviation and standard spacing or hyphenation, viz., ISBN-0-04-418007-1.

Rule 1.BD1 Term of Availability

Give the terms on which the item is available. These terms consist of the price, if the item is for sale, or a brief statement of other terms if the item is not for sale

ISBN 0- 959 - 27588 - 3:$ 18.97

1.8E Qualifications

ISBN 0 - 959 - 27588 - : $ 6.97 (pbk.)

3. Call Number

The Call Number consists of Class Number and Book Number. The call number is provided by the classifier and usually recorded on the verso of the title page.

Location on the card

Class number is transcribed one line above the first horizontal line after leaving one space from the left edge of the card. Book number is transcribed on the first horizontal line after leaving one space from the left edge of the card.

4. Accession Number

The accession number is the serial number of the item acquired in the library and is transcribed in the catalogue entry. This is for the use of library staff. Library may not transcribe the accession number in added entries. This is usually recorded on the verso of the title page.

There is no rule prescribed for this purpose. For the sake of uniformity, the accession number may be written 4th line or 5th line from the red horizontal line of the card.

5 Punctuations

While describing all the areas and the elements, we also been discussing the use of punctuations. Punctuations prescribed in the code should be followed as it is.

6. Tracing

ACCR II defines tracings as "the record of the heading under which an item is represented in the catalogue, and the record of the references that have been made to a name or to the title or subject or series of an item that is represnted in the catalogue. For easy understanding this tracing section is divided into two sub-sections and it should be recorded in a paragraph, starting from the second indent. First sub-section is indicated by indo Arabic numerals in the natural sequence and the second sub-section is indicated by using Roman capital Numerals (I, II, II, IV...) In the first sub-section, we have to generate the subject heading according to Sears List of subject heading. There is no minimum number or maximum number of subject heading to be prepared, all the possible approach of the user group for want of subject of the documents should be statisfied. The second sub-section will be for the other approaches such as title, series collaborator etc.

TYPES OF ENTRY

When a reader wants a book, he approaches the catalogue to look under the name of the author, joint author, title, subject, series, etc. These are called access points. A number of entries are prepared to satisfy different approaches. The number of access points should be statisfied. The second sub-section will be for the other approaches such as title, series collaborator etc.

TYPES OF ENTRY

When a reader wants a book, he approaches the catalogue to look under the name of the author, joint author, title, subject, series, etc. These are called access points. A number of entries are prepared to satisfy different approaches. The number of access points (approach points) depend upon the nature of the document or item to be catalogued or approach of the users. There may be two or more entries prepared for each item.

The catalogue entries can be catagorised into two types:

1. Main entry
2. Added entries

Besides, there may be reference entries as;

see reference

see also reference

name title reference

Subject added entries are prepared with the help of Sear's list of subject headings and its principles.

Main Entry

AACR II defines main entry as "the complete catalogue record of an item presented in the form in which the entry is to be uniformly identified and cited. The main entry includes the tracing of all other headings under which the record is to be presented in the catalogue".

In a dictionary catalogue the main entry is prepared generally under author of the document as heading. If the authorship is diffused or not known the main entry is prepared under its title as heading or under the corporate body. Thus main entry contains maximum information about the whole book. All the other entries relating to a book are called added entries, which are usually derived from the main entry.

Added Entries

The purpose of added entries is to enable a catalogue user to find a particular item by some name or title other than the item used as the main entry heading. The number and kind of added entries required depends on the nature of catalogue use in each information centres. The following points should be considered when establishing a policy for added entries.

(i) An added entry policy should be applied consistently to book and non-book materials.

(ii) The policy should be in keeping with the chosen level of description.

(iii) Only names, titles, and series listed in the catalogue record are traced. Added entries may be made for any one or all of these if the cataloguer believes that a patron may search for an item under a particular heading (s).

There are different types of added entries.

a. joint author(s)
b. editor (s)
c. translator (s)
d. compilers (s)
e. illustrator (s)
f. subject
g. title
h. series etc.

There is a general provision to make an added entry under the heading for a person or a corporate body or under a title of some catalogue user might suppose that the description of an item would be found under that heading or title rather than under the heading or title chosen for the main entry.

Rule 21.30 and its subdivisions provide specific rules to prepare added entries under

(i) joint author
(ii) collaborators
(iii) writers
(iv) editors and comilers
(v) corporate bodies and other related persons or bodies if the

satisfy the needs of the subject approach to information, every library is expected to provide some sort of alphabetical subject catalogue. A number of methods have been developed by the library and indexing experts to provide subject approach to reading materials by manual and mechanical. Among them the standard list of subject such as the Library of Congress List of Subject of Headings (LCSH) and the Sear's List of Subject Heading (SLSH) are very popular in use in the English speaking countries of the world.

Reference Entries

Reference entries are prepared to provide access to names or forms of name not used as heading and to connect related headings in the catalogue. The references are also called as crosss reference, Chapter 26 of AACR II contains rules for making reference, because refrrences are directly associated with the choice of names and forms used in heading. Chapter 26 complements chapters 22-25. These may be :

1. See Reference

A see reference directs the user from a name or title not used as a heading to the chosen as name heading or uniform title.

For example in a catalogue, document on women medicine and related topics may be entered under the subject heading WOMEN MEDICINE. But the reader may approach the catalogue with the subject heading "PAEDIATRICS" which is not used in the catalogue. To direct the readers to the used heading, see reference entries are prepared.

Example :

	Paediatrics	
		see CHILD MEDICINE

Example :

	Birds	
		see AVES

2. See also Reference

As see also reference connects related headings. The alphabetical arrangements of entries has its own problem. It scatters related entries at different places based on the alphabetical nature of the heading.

See also references are made between different heading for the same persons when the persons work have been entered under more than one heading.

	Clements, Samuel Longhorne	
		see also Twain, Mark, 1875-1950

	Stringed instruments	
		see also VIOLIN

3. Name- Title References:

When a see or see also reference is made from a title that has been entered under a personal or corporate heading, it is made in the form of a name- title reference beginning with the personal or corporate heading followed by the title concerned.

Example :

	Ashe,	Gordon
		The croaker *see* Creasey, John *(Title page reads:... by John Creasey as Gordon Ashe)*

4. Explanatory Reference:

This is a see also reference containing an explanatory note giving more detailed guidance to the user. For example :

	Creasey, John	
		For works written under his pseudonyms, see Ashe, Gordon Halliday, Michael Marric, J.J. York, Jeremy

For acronyms also we can provide explanatory reference.

	NATO	
		see North Atlantic Treaty Organisation

3

Brief History of Cataloguing of Non-Book Materials

Early years of Nonbook Cataloguing

There are sometimes conflicting and sometimes elusive clues in the search for the beginnings of nonbook cataloguing. For example, Arundell Esdaile, in his book the British Museum Library, states that the British Museum started cataloguing maps in 1841, but rules for these materials were first published in 1897 in the Britsh Museum's Rules for Cataloguing, which contained a brief summary of the rules for the cataloguing of maps. Obviously, cataloguers were struggling with what to do with "illustrative objects" in the early years of the twentieth century because in a book published in 1922, Dorcas follows recognized problems that were still being debated forty years later:

....If with the entries for books there could be included entries for illustrative objects also it would undoubtedly add greatly to the use... of available resources, both and illustrative objects.

The systematic cataloguing of sound recording began around 1937 in some of the larger U.S. public and university libraries.

Some libraries treated these matarials in the same manner as paperbackes. i.e., uncatalogued and house randomly; other libraries stored them uncatalogued in workrooms. There were many reasons for this neglegience. Many librarians were uncomfortable with nonbook formats. Patrons' demand for audiovisual services was not widespread. There was little catalogue copy or commercial cataloguing for nonbook materials, and the orginal cataloguing of nonbook materials was, and still is, a more time-consuming task than the similar cataloguing of books.

There were only a few guides and articles about the cataloguing of nonbook formats, so some libraries developed their own cataloguing rules for nonbook materials. As centralized and commercial cataloguing became more common, the need for standards emerged. School libraries developed their own standards. Unfortunately, each group worked in isolation, producing rules that differed from those developed elsewhere. Because commercial cataloguers were reluctant to adopt any particular standard, they developed their own rules.

One aspect of this bibliographic chaos was the difficulty of identifying nonbook materials for interlibrary loan. Librarians were aware that the bibliographic records in various catalogues might have had different criteria for the source of the title, which made the correct identification of a desired item problematic.

In 1952, the Library of Congress embarked on a project that was not completed until 1965-to draft rules for the cataloguing of the nonbook materials in their collection. Preliminary edition of Rules for Descriptive Cataloging in the Library of Congress: Phonorecords, Rules for Descriptive Cataloguing in the Library of Congress: Motion Pictures and Filmstrips, and Rules for Descriptive Cataloguing in the Library of Congress: Pictures, Designs, and Other two-Dimensional Representations were published. Between 1953 and 1965 these rules were tested by working cataloguers, seciond preliminary editions published and tested, and eventually final editions appeared. The final versions were approved by the American Library Association's Descriptive Cataloging Committee and the appropriate committees at the Library of Congress. Despite their official acceptance, these rules caused porblems for small libraries with nonbook collections, particularly libraries that wanted to list nonbook materials in the general publick catalogue. These rules were designed for use at the Library of Congress where each type of non book format was housed separately and was described in a separate catalogue. Because of this particular L.C. arangement, the three documents were developed by three different committees, that did not coordinate their work.

The first edition of the Anglo-American Cataloging Rules (AACR1), published in 1967, was a disappointment to nonbook cataloguers. Part III, which dealt with nonbook materials, was based on the Library of Congress rules mentioned above. AACR1 treated each medium separately without regard for integration in a general catalogue. For example, the rules for entry and description differed from medium to medium. If a Renoir painting was reproduced on a poster, the poster was entered under the name of the artist and was not given a medium designation. If the same painting was reproduced on a slide, the slide was entered under title and was assigned a medium designation. In addition, AACR1 did not cover all the formats found in library collections. As a result, Part III was used by few librarians and criticized by many.

The Department of Audiovisual Instruction (DAVI), a part of the National Education Association (later called the Association for Educational Communications and Technology), was also working on a manual for the cataloguing of audiovisual materials during the later years of 60s. Because this was an association of audiovisual specialists, they had no interest in integrated catalogues or multimedia collections. Subsequently, DAVI respresentatives participated in the work of several library-related committees, and the fourth edition of this work titled *Standards for Cataloging Nonprint Materials* became one of the primary sources for the development of rules for nonbook materials in *Anglo-American Cataloguing Rules*, 2nd edition *(AACR2)*.

Pierce Grove recognized the need for an intensive dialog about nonbook cataloguing. He organized an institute that met for two weeks in August 1969 in Oklahoma and two additional weeks in conjunction with the american Library Association midwinter meeting in Chicago in January 1970 and the Association for Educational Communications and Technology conference in Detroit in April 1970. The mixture of invited guest lecturers, who were noted authorities in their respective fields, and participants from the broad expanse of librarianship, all types of media centres, commercial cataloguing firms, and computer centres provided an impetus for several national organizations in the countries of the three AACR authors to establish committees to develop standards for the cataloguing of nonbook materials. The institute was especially valuable in introducing nonlibrarians to cataloguing cancepts. For example, the head of a large U.S. media centre that porduced "catalogue records" was amazed to learn of the existence of cataloguing rules. His subsequent actions turned the records in his databank into ones that could be used by the broader cataloguing community.

The preliminary edition of Nonbook Materials: The Organization of Integrated Collections was published by the Canadian Library Association in 1970. This guide enabled libraries to have an integrated catalogue because the rules followed those for books as much as pollible. Nonbook Materials was recommended by the Canadian Library Association Council and by the American Library Association, Resources and Technical Services Division, Cataloging and Classification Section Executive Committee ''as an interim guide for the cataloging of nonbook materials, with the provison that a permanent ALA/CLA committee be established to work on any necessary revisions for the final edition and its supplements. It was also officially adopted in Australia and unofficially by two South American countries.

Nonbook Cataloguing in the 1970s

Following the American Library Association's provison, the Joint Advisory Committee on Nonbook Materials was formed with representatives from the American Library Association including a Library of Congress representative, the Association for Educational Communications and Technology, the Canadian Library Association, the Educational Media Association of Canada, and the Canadian Association of Music Libraries. Dr. Margaret Chisholm, in later years a president of the American Library Association, was its chair. All the comments sent to them about the preliminary edition were examined and included those that were pertinent. One innovation in this edition of Nonbook Materials was the idea of entry under performer. The committee asked us to do this as a trial. It was a successful experiment, and this idea was later incorporated into AACR2. At the request of the Library of Congress representative, a sample card for a phonorecord that had been marketed in four different formats was included. The same bibliographic record could be used by a librar three, or all of the formats by deleting the description for the fomats missing from their col of Congress had found this an economical v varying formats of the same item and wished to is interesting to note that since the International Principles and Future of AACR, held in 199 single record for various formats is again being d Materials: The Organization of integrated Colle was one of the primary sources for the develo nonbook materials in AACR2.

The British also found Part III, "Non-book M inadequate, because of the time pressure menti were not able to give Part III the detailed scru devoted to Parts I and II. The British announce investigate rules for nonbook materials and "to cc of this work, alongside that of the Canadians, revision" of AACRI at a meeting convened b Cataloging Committee at the American Library A convention in Detroit in 1970. The Media C Committee was established in 1970 with membe and audiovisual professions, "The committee w other work and discussions on both sides of particular, information and ideas were exchange Weihs and her colleagues in Canada." No Cataloguing Rules: Integrated Code of Practice of Anglo-American Cataloguing' Rules, British in 1973 and was one of the primary sources for t rules for nonbook materials in AACR2.

In 1974, C.P. Ravilions completed A Survey o and Current Proposals for the Cataloguing and D book Materials Collected by Libraries, W Suggestions for Their International Co-ordi UNESCO's efforts to promote universal biblio UBC. Based on these findings, the Internatio Library Associations and Institutions (IFL committee, with Ravilious as its chair, to work o for nonbook materials. The work of this committee resulted in the publication in 1977 of *ISBD(NBM)*: International Standard Bibliographic Description: Nonbook Materials. This work had some specific rules that differed from those in *AACR2*.

The transition from *AACRl* to *AACR2* was eased for nonbook materials by the publication in 1975 of a revised and expanded version of chapter 12 (audiovisual media and special instructional materials) and in 1976 of a revised chapter 14 (sound recordings). The publication of *AACR2* in 1978 signaled the end of the basic development period for nonbook cataloguing rules because it provided rules for all types of materials, and bibliographic records for these materials could be integrated into a common catalogue if a library so desired.

Developments in the 1980s

A significant problem emerged in the 1980s-machine-readable data files. Official rules for machine-readable data files first appeared as chapter 9 in AACR2. These rules and the section on these materials in the first edition of Nonbook Materials: The Organisation of Integrated Collections were based on the work done by the American Library Association's Descriptive Cataloging Committee Subcommittee on Rules for Cataloging Machine Readable Data Files, originally established in 1970. For various reasons, the Library Association Media Cataloguing Rules Committee was unable to do a detailed consideration of the draft chapter of special rules for the cataloguing of computer records prepared by one of its members, Ray Wall of the American Subcommittee's draft. Therefore, rules for these materials were not included in *Non-Book Materials Cataloguing Rules*. When *AACR2* was published in 1978, machine-readable data files were found mostly in large research libraries and principally manipulated by main frame computers. Most libraries did not have such files and ignored chapter 9.

When computer software became part of library collections in the 1980s, cataloguers found it difficult, if not impossible, to apply the rules in chapter 9 to these materials. Their dissatisfaction resulted in action on both sides of the Atlantic. In the United Kingdom, the

British Library commissioned a study that resulted in Study of Cataloguing Computer Software: Applying AACR 2 to Microcomputer Programs. by Ray Templeton and Anita Witten. In the same year, an American Library Association committee produced Guidelines for Using AACR 2 for Cataloging Microcomputer Software.

Both these documents were criticized by working cataloguers, so the Joint Steering Committee for Revision of AACR (JSCAACR) and its constituent national committees went "back to the drawing board." Some of the JSCAACR representatives themselves conducted their own research. For instance, a large number of software disks were borrowed from the Ontario Institute for Studies in Education Library and catalogued them at home using title screens as chief source of information. The nonbook cataloguer at the Institute had catalogued the same items using only external sources, i.e., not booting them on a computer. In comparing with its bibliographic records, there were found differences in the information given on the title screens and on the labels, packaging, and/or accompanying materials. This experience, also noted by other JSCAACR members, led to the requirement for computer files that the source of the title and the edition statement, if different from the source of the title, be listed in a man-dated note.

The most heated disagreements encountered on JSCAACR were over the rules for computer files. Essentially two groups emerged: the "main frame group" whose members worked in large research libraries with main frame computers and the "software group" whose members were drawn mainly from public and school libraries and whose collections contained microcomputer software. The main frame group wanted the mandatory listing in the bibliographic record of the type of file and the number of records and/or bytes. The software group stated that this information was of no interest, and may even be confusing, to their users. JSCAACR compromised by establishing area 3, the "File Characteristics Area" and making it mandatory "when the information is readily available." JSCAACR believed that this rule would satisfy both sides of the controversy. The main frame group would be required to list the file type and the number of records and/or bytes: the software group could ignore area 3 because the information was not readily available on microcomputer software. When *Anglo-American Cataloguing Rules*, second edition, 1998 revision *(AACR2R)* was published, the Library of Congress interpreted this rule in a manner that do not believe JSCAACR intended. L.C.'s bibliographic records for microcomputer software generally included file type because their cataloguers believed that it was usually easy to determine whether a disk contained data or programs or both.

Because of the urgent need for rules for these materials now flooding into library collections, JSCAACR decided in 1987 to publish a preliminary draft of chapter 9 "to help bridge the gap between. ..the rules for the descriptive cataloguing of machine-readable files. ..[in] AACR2... and the eventual publication of the final version in 1988. This publication also provided an opportunity for input on the efficacy of the rules before they were embodied in AACR2R.

When AACR2R was published in 1988, JSCAACR anticipated that the rapid development of computer files would necessitate many rule revisions to chapter 9, but it did not foresee the advent of the Internet, a tale for the 1990s.

JSCAACR met in Toronto in March 1986 at the same time as IFLA Committee on Cataloguing's Working Group on the International Standard Bibliographic Description for Computer Files met in London, England. It was not totally successful to reduce the potential for conflict in these two sets of rules, due to the IFLA committee's need to harmonize its work with the other ISBDs and the somewhat different orientation between the IFLA committee's European members and the JSCAACR representatives. ISBD(CF): International Standard Bibliographic Description for Computer Files was published in 1990.

JSCAACR representatives recognized that AACR2 lacked rules for some materials. One of these neglected mdia was holograms. Predictions about their acquisition by libraries had surfaced from time to time. Some time in the first half of the 1980s Michael Gorman (in the United States) along with other tried to develop rules for the cataloguing of holograms but failed in this endeavour because the minds of physicists and librarians simply did not meet.

They were unable to elicit from the physicists the specific information about the bibliographic nature of holograms that would aid in the construction of cataloguing rules. Neither of them continued to pursue this inquiry because libraries did not add holograms to their collections. Marc D' Alleyrand had announced in 1977 that he was writing Rules for the Cataloging of Holograms, but it is difficult to ascertain that it had ever been published. In a recent search of bibliographic databases, staff at the University of Toronto Faculty of Infonnation Studies library failed to find evidence that this book had been published.

Brief mention might also be made of the Multiple Versions Forum Report, which "was convened. ..to arrive at a consensus on various aspects of constructing bibliographic records for items that are the same in content but differ in physical representation. The forum concentrated, for the most part, on two-tier and three-tier bibliographic formats for print materials. It is believed at the time that if its concepts had been accepted, the concepts must also have been applied to nonbook materials in order to maintain the integrity of the catalogue. However, the proposals did not progress beyond the discussion stage.

Cyberspace and the 1990s

The explosion in electronic publishing and networked information in the 1990s made the development of cataloguing rules for Internet resources the most important descriptive cataloguing activity in this decade. Many governments had ceased publishing some of their documents in paper copy and these were only available on the Internet, e.g., the twenty-five volume Treasury Board Manual. An increasing number of scientific reports could also only be found on a website. Research libraries felt a pressing need to make these resources available to their users through their public catalogue. Many individuals and groups were active in the developing rules for Internet resources. The most influential of these were OCLC, the National Library of Canada, the Association for Library Collections and Technical Services, and the International Federation of Library Associations and Institutions.

OCLC received two grants from the U.S. Department of Education to build a catalogue of Internet resources. Erik Jul was the manager of both projects. During the first grant (1991-1993) Guidelines for Bibliographic Description of Internet Resources were distributed to 100 participants, who catalogued items selected by the OCLC Office of Research. "The resulting bibliographic records were examined and evaluated by OCLC, and comments and suggestions were compiled as the final research report was prepared. Suggested changes to the cataloguing rules and to the MARC format were forwarded to the appropriate committees of the American Library Association for their consideration." The CC:DA Task Force on Cataloging Internet Resources submitted its report at the 1993 American Library Association Conference in New Orleans. At the end of this trial period the findings were edited by Nancy Olson and retitled Cataloging Internet Resource, 'A Manual and Practical Guide'. During the period of the second grant (1994-1996), OCLC staff solicited comments, held a symposium, and attended many meetings to learn how effective these rules were. The second edition based on these findings was published in 1997.

In June 1994 the National Library of Cainada established the Electronic Publications Pilot Project "to acquire, catalogue, preserve and provide access to a small number of Canadian electronic journals and other representative publications available on the Internet." The Electronic Collections Committee set up three teams, one of which was the Cataloguing Task Group. An interim report dated July 15, 1994, revised Aug. 29, 1994, states that the group catalogued "chiefly electronic publications, but also including CD-ROMs. ..For descriptive cataloguing the group studied chapter 9, computer files, of. ..AACR2, OCLC's Guidelines for Bibliographic Description of Internet Resources and a variety of other articles and MARBI discussion papers. The final report, published in 1995 on the National Library's website, was not a manual of cataloguing rules, but rather a statement of policy and future direction for electronic publications in the Library's mandate. However, the experience gained in this project was transmitted informally to cataloguers and appropriate committees, such as the Canadian Committee on Cataloguing.

The rapid development of electronic resources also convinced IFLA in 1994 that a review of ISBD(CF): International Standard

Bibliographic Description for Computer Files was needed despite its recent publication. The ISBD(CF) Review Group was formed with John Byrum, the cllairperson of the ISBD(CF) working group, also appointed chairperson of the review group. The draft prepared by the ISBD(CF) Review Group was distributed to worldwide review. ISBD (ER): International Standard Bibliographic Description for Electronic Resources, published in 1997, has had a greater effect on the Anglo-American cataloguing rules than its predecessor, ISBD(CF). ALCTS established the Task Force on Harmonization of ISBD(ER) and AACR2. JSCAACR has already accepted many provisions in the final report of the Task Force including the change in general material designation from "computer file" to "electronic resource."

Not all cataloguing concerns in the 1990s were devoted to cyberspace items. In the beginning, the development of guidelines for the cataloguing of items that eventually came to be called interactive multimedia was a grassroots effort. "The very first informal discussion took place at a luncheon table at the Online Audiovisual Catalogers' biennial conference in Rochester, New York, October 1990." In June 1991 Intner invited about twenty cataloguing experts to an all-day meeting at the American Library Association conference in Atlanta to discuss the possibility of devising rules. She contacted several producers who supplied materials that the group could examine, unfortunately without the hardware to view them. Intner drafted the first version of the guidelines in November 1991 and wrote the proposal to CC:DA about the formation of a Task Force. The Task Force on Description of Interactive Media was established with Ben Tucker as its chairperson. Its report was delivered at the American Library Association's 1992 annual conference. The Interactive Multimedia Guidelines Review Committee was formed in 1993, with Laurel Jizba as its chairperson, to test the guidelines before their final publication in 1994. Guidelinesfor Bibliographic Description of Interactive Media has been met with resistance in some quarters because it was argued that any item manipulated by a computer is interactive. JSCAACR has not as yet accepted interactive multimedia as a separate medium.

Nonbook Cataloguing in the Twenty-First Century

Many of the papers presented at the International Conference on the Principles and Future Development of AACR, held in Toronto in October 1997, discussed concepts articulated in the IFLA study, Functional Requirements for Bihliographic Records: Final Report Since the conference, JSCAACR has commissioned studies of the conference delegates' recommendations, and, it appears that the Anglo-American cataloguing rules may undergo substantial change.

The winds of these changes were already in evidence before the conference. In late 1996 some staff members in the Cataloging and Support Office at the Library of Congress met to discuss the cataloguing treatment of materials that L.C. was digitizing from its own collections. This was really an attempt to set a conceptual context and a common terminology for addressing electronic resources. Draft Interim Guidelines for Cataloging Electronic Resources appeared on L.C.'s website at the end of December 1997. It was based on the IFLA study, Functional Requirements for Bibliographic Records: Finl Report. The Library of Congress' draft interim document did not deal with the cataloguing of Internet resources because the collection development guidelines for remotely accessed electronic resources are only now beginning to be formulated. Recently David Reser states the L.C. cataloguers are primarily using the document to provide guidance on the data elements to be used when LC has digitized the contents of items in its collection and needs to represent this fact on records that represent the original items, but they do provide other guidance on when to create a separate record for the digital manifestation.

Metadata, a hot topic in the late 1990s, is undoubtedly have an effect on cataloguing rules in the starting years of this new century. CC:DA appointed the Task Force on Metadata and the Cataloging Rules in 1995. Its final report deals not only with metadata and cataloguing, but also with the TEI header and the cataloguing rules, Dublin Core metadata and the cataloguing rules, Encoded Archival Description, and cataloguing problems with websites. So, it can be said, many more discussions are needed and will be continued for finding a solid decision.

4

Cataloguing of Non-Book Materials

Apart from the traditional collection of books the libraries are gradually adding to their collection, materials in non-book format. Non-book collections have many distinctive features and require special equipments for use and for reproduction purposes.

Non-book media, though forming an integral part of library colletion have received lower priority in processing. Cataloguing of non book media can facilitate access to such material and also provide bibliogrephic control for them. Cataloguing of non-book media necessitates a thorough understanding of the media itself. The cataloguers should be familiar with the various physical formats and the sources of information for cataloguing purposes. The challenge for the cataloguers is to mater all information about the software and hardware of all non-print formats too. They should also be aware of the new hardware and also wide range of non-print materials that come in the market.

Though, non-book materials itself include non-print materials yet, we need to understand three basic terms: media, non-print and non-book. Media commonly refers to those items through which information is recorded and a library user can access information. For defining non-print material and non-book material, distinction, needs to be made between the two. Non-book materials are basically non paper based which would include databases, microfocus, aeidios etc. The non-print collection is differentiated mainly on technical ground having some authenitc aspect. The generic terms non-book includes two broad categories, print and non-print. The non-print media are those on which printed words or visuals are not directly represented, such as magnatic tapes, digital recordings, etc.

General Problems of Cataloguing Non book Materials (NBM)

Before librarian embark upon cataloguing non book meterials certain factor warrant serious consideration which may help to formulate policy regarding organization of special materials. The following questions should be asked and resolved:

(i) What type of community is to be served (staff, students, general public, researchers, etc.)?

(ii) what is the function of the material in terms of the goals of the instruction (reference, porgramme support, enrichment, teaching ends, etc.)?

(iii) What special storage, maintenance, and security problems does a particular medium pose?

Other important questions which beg the attention of the professional staff to take decision before starting cataloguing NBM include:

1. Do all NBM need to be catalogued and classified in the same way and to the same extent?
2. Is the experience gained in cataloguing book is applicable to NBM or is there need to devise new theory and method for the purpose?
3. Are the documents to be freely available for access by browser or are they stored on closed access? If a library has chosen closen closed access aystem, it must maintain integrated public catalogue with detailed descriptive information of each item.
4. In addition, storage by an accession number or numerical arramgement system relieves the catalogue of the need to consider helpful classification by browsing. Decision on an open access system requires less descriptive information from the catalogue as the clients have the opportunity to search through the documents themselves to and in selection.

A library in academic environment committed to the multimedia approach might choose to handle all materials uniformly shelving them together and interfiling catalogue cards so as to bring attention to all print and non print items on a given topic. A public library might include entries for all types of material in its central catalogue but house audio visual material separately to maximize security. Academic libraries might use the same classification system for books and non book material but public libraries maintaining separate collection could use two or more different systems, on the other hand a special library having single format material or mixed media collection might need to develop special classification and indexing schemes in order to provide a sufficiently detailed breakdown of the collection's contents.

An integrated catalogue is recommended by almost all the writers on the subjects. Fothergill considers the storage of the library materials completely integrated to allow the client to browse amongst the whole stock for a subject rather than have to search through separate form divisions. Standardized packaging may achieve this with sound recordings, slide sets and films; but charts, specimens and models will need to be arranged in parallel. Whatever type or size of the library may be, situation demands, that libraries must construct an integrated catalogue consisting of entries for both NBM and books held in stock. But storage of NBM should be separate from general book stock whether available for direct access by browser or put on closed access. Confusion or chaos in the use of integrated catalogue by the clients might pose challenge to the technical staff. The technical problems regarding the form or identification of the material can be overcome by the use of material designations (GMD), and by clear guidance on the use of catalogue. Library experience asserts that the clients benefits more from a catalogue that gives a complete record of all the documents in the Library collection.

Computer is now widely used in the libraries for the storage and retrieval of information. Computerizing of audio visual data on a large scale in quite manifest. Fothergill has pointed out that the publication of the British catalogue of audio visual material illustrated that it was possible to establish a single computerized system that gives access to a combined catalogue of the nation's output of documents in all physical forms whether printed or audio-visual. There are now large integrated computerized catalogues, such as

OCLC, which demonstrate the ease of use and are provided throughout academic and public libraries.

SPECIAL ISSUES OF NONBOOK CATALOGUING

General Material Designations

Before the days of integrated catalogues, there were separate catalogues for each type of material. This was the accepted norm because nonbook materials were generally housed in a different section of the library, frequently stored in workrooms. No mention was made of general-material-designation-like terms in the 1949 publication of Rules for Descriptive Cataloginig in the Library of Congress.The beginnings of what would eventually be called "general material designations" appeared in 1952. It is noted that in 1952 the Library of Congress embarked on three projects to draft rules for three types of nonbook materials: phonorecords, motion pictures and filmstrips, and pictures, designs and other three-dimensional representations. Each of the documents dealt with the designation of format in totally different ways. Rules for Description Cataloging in the Library of Congres: Pictures, Designs, And Other Three-Dimensional Representations contained no provision for designations. Conversely, Rules for Descriptive Cataloging in the Library of Congress: Motion Pictures and Filmstrips directed a cataloguer to follow a title with "the explanatory phrase 'Motion picture' or 'Filmstrip' enclosed within parentheses. Directions for the use of "germane terms for the physical medium of the work", were published in Rules for Descriptive Cataloging in the Library of Congress: Phonorecords, "in order to distinguish the aural from the visual forms of the same work.". These terms (phonocylinder, phonodisc, phonotape, phonowire, etc.) were to be listed in italics. No written directions were given for their placement. Presumably, cataloguers were to be guided by the examples, which showed the "germane term" placed after a uniform title without square brackets and, in the absence of a uniform title, placed after the title and enclosed in brackets. This is a clear demonstration of the lack of coordination between the three Library of Congress committees, probably a result of the segregation of different formats in the collection at the Library of Congress. Ronald Hagler noted that "the original purpose of the general material designation was not so much identification as file arrangement. It originated with the early rules for the cataloguing of sound recordings. Its position following the uniform title of a composition ensured that all entries for a recording would file in a group separate from the entries for the corresponding score or literary text.

During the 1960s when many libraries began to add nonbook materials to their collections and to see the advantages of having bibliographic records for all materials in a single catalogue, the lack of media designations for all materials became a problem. Many libraries developed a scheme called colour coding in which there was a band of colour at the top of the catalogue card to denote a particular format, e.g., red for filmstrips, blue for sound discs, green for maps, etc. However, these colours were not standardized; each library choose its own colour scheme. This scheme became untenable when the number of nonbook formats exceeded the number of primary colours. The integrity of the colour stock could not be maintained when shades of colours must be used. However, some libraries hung on to colour coding long after other methods of indicating format were introduced, only abandoning them when card catalogues were discarded.

Media codes were another method of designating media. These generally consisted of two-letter codes used as the first part of a call number, e.g., RD for sound discs, PS for study prints. For example, the call number for a filmstrip titled "Mammals of the World" would have been FS 599 MAM. This also proved to be unsatisfactory because catalogue users were unfamiliar with the meaning of these codes. As a response to users' complaints, some libraries decided to use the full name of the medium in place of the codes, e.g., FILMSTRIP 599 MAM. Both of these schemes were developed for segregated shelving; neither was useful in libraries that wished to intershelve all their materials in one sequence.

Since many libraries rejected colour-coding and media codes, various organizations developed their own lists of media designations causing some media designation chaos in the cataloguing world. While the publication of AACRl in 1967 standardized some terms, it was a disappointment in this regard because media designations were not applied to all types of materials and not all media were included.

It was in response to the criticism from libraries wanting to have integrated catalogues that the Library of Congress and the National Library of Canada decided to develop a complete list of media designations. The British, one of the three-nation planners to the creation and revision of the Anglo-American cataloguing rules, did not want to be part of the decision-making because they disapproved of the concept of media designations.

The first decision taken in library of Congress in 1947, was to develop a generic list of media designations that would minimize the disruption to library catalogues. This meant that the list of terms would be practical rather than theoretical or philosophical. Minimal disruption meant that all media designations currently in use (i.e., those listed in AACRl and terms commonly in use in the library profession as media designations for media lacking official terms) would be retained if they did not contravene the following guidelines that we formulated. General terms for designations should be selected to discourage a proliferation of terms when the technology of a particular type of material changed, but not so general as to be meaning- less (e.g., record, film). Trade names must be avoided (e.g., microcard), and the terms must be in the singular to denote type of material rather than quantity. The terms also must be as understandable as possible to the library user. This latter guideline caused the major problem. In the 1950s, Jack Cooperman at the Library of Congress invented the prefix "phono," which became library jargon fairly meaningless to many catalogue users. At the time of meeting, some audiovisual specialists were using the "prefix-audio." "Sound recording" was eventually selected because it was used by the U.S. Postal Service and a few other non library bodies, was acceptable to music librarians, and could be readily understood by the general public.

This list was fornlalized with the publication of AACR2 in 1978 in which media designations were renamed general material designations. This was an occasion where the British and North Americans agreed to disagree because of their different attitudes to early warning signals in the bibliographic record and the different meanings of the same word on different sides of the Atlantic. For example, in the United Kingdom "kit" was something one carried on one's back while hiking and "pack" was a multimedia set, the reverse meaning of these terms in North America. British agencies were directed to use list I and North American agencies list 2. General material designations were made optional at the insistence of the British representatives to JSCAACR.

The greatest general material designation battle occurred over the term "machine-readable data file." This term was the choice of people working with main frame computers, mostly in large academic libraries, and was included in the list of general material designations in AACR2. The British preferred "machine-readable file" which they thought was a more inclusive term. As school and public libraries began to collect and catalogue computer software in the 1980s, staff in these libraries complained that their users had no idea what "machine-readable data file" meant. They vigorously recommended that the general material designation be changed to "computer software" or to "software." This was adamantly opposed by the main frame people. Eventually, the JSCAACR decided on a compromise. The general material designation "computer file" was established by taking one word from each term supported by the adversarial groups-"computer" from the school and public libraries group and "file" from the main frame group.

Since that time there have been some additions to the list, mainly in the revisions packages published between AACR2 editions. "Art reproduction," "braille," and "toy" were added between AACR2 and AACR2R; "activity card" between AACR2R and Anglo-American Cataloguing Rules, 2nd edition, 1998 revision (AACR2R-98).

"Interactive multimedia," the general material designation recommended in Guidelines for Bibliographic Descriptipion of Interactive Multimedia, has not yet been accepted by JSCAACR. The choice of this term was a vigorously debated topic by members of the committees that worked on this document. The first suggestions included "interactive media," "interactive multimedia," "interactive materials," and the qualifier "(interactive)" added to an appropriate general material designation, e.g., "videorecording (interactive)." Eventually the choice was narrowed to the first two, and drafts of the guidelines listed the one or the other at different times. One criticism of this general material designation is that it is frequently difficult to establish interactivity, particuarly if a cataloguer is unable to play the item. The producers' descriptions on packaging are not reliable because producers believe that the word "interactive" on their products will increase sales, and many items are labeled "interactive" that prove not to be when used.

The cardinal principle on which all editions of AACR has been based, the requirement that the item in hand is the one to be catalogued, began to crack with the decision of the American Library Association, reflected in the Library of Congress rule interpretation, directing that the original book be described with information about the microform placed in the note area. This concept was reinforced with the publication of Guidelines for the Bibliographic Description of Reproductions in which a hierarchical description is made with the original item in the primary position and the reproduction described secondarily.

It may be that general material designations are slowly becoming more problematic as technology develops new formats and ways of manipulating infomlation. For example, the general material designation "game" does not cover all games in a collection. Games are split two ways: those played on a computer are designated as electronic resource," the others "game." A game can also be buried in the note area in flash card records because many flash card sets say "can also be played as a game." The same is true of other types of materials, such as technical drawings, which can be assigned the designation "'technical drawing" or "microform" or "electronic resource." The same work of art can be "art original," "art reproduction," "electronic resource," "filmstrip," or "slide." The items that comprise a kit can now be found on a single CD-ROM. Should the latter be designated an electronic kit? Indeed, anything that can be photographed, microformed, digitized, or otherwise reproduced faces cataloguers with the dilemma of assigning a general material designation that is useful to their public.

The first edition of ISBD(NBM) proposed the use of dual general material designations, e.g. (Visual projection + Sound recording), which was abandoned in the second edition. Some present-day cataloguers have expressed interest in this concept as a way of indicating to the catalogue user the nature of an item, e.g., for a computer game [electronic resource + game].

Despite the alternate list of general material designtltions in the various editions of AACR2 for British use, most British libraries have steadfastly refused to use these designations, maintaining that their patrons should learn to read the complete bibliographic record. On the other hand, North American librarians have insisted on the need for general material designations listed early in the bibliographic record because they say their patrons rarely read the record beyond the title. This argument has less force than it once did. For many items, a catalogue user must read the bibliographic description, as the British advocate, to discover whether and what type of equipment is needed for the effective use of an item. The North American position will lose further ground if the current discussions about the move to catalogue the original rather than the item in hand are adopted. However, the elimination of the general material designation would bring other problems in its wake. The naming of media would then become a MARC prerogative, possibly subject to the whims of automated systems designers and their customers. As new nonbook formats were developed, this lack of a standard list of terms would be a fertile field for a return to the terminology chaos of earlier years.

Main Entry

Before the 1970s there were sharp differences of opinion about how nonbook items should be entered. For example, Standards for Cataloging, Coding and Scheduling Educational Media mandated title main entry. While Anglo-American Cataloging Rules, North American Text, Chapter 12 Revised, Audiovisual Media and Special Instructional Materials allowed entry under author in some circumstances, the Library of Congress and, consequently, many cataloguers, interpreted this very narrowly. Their rationale was that, in general, the intellectual responsibility for nonbook materials was diverse. Whereas authors were obviously responsible for the intellectual content of a book, more than three people usually contributed to the intellectual content of nonbook materials: cinematographers, caption or script writers, set designers, actors, composers, singers, etc. It would be difficult to establish anyone of these as primarily responsible for intellectual content. Therefore, the rule of three, a long-standing principle found in A.L.A. Cataloging Rule for Author and Title Entries and in AACR I (now rule 21.6C2 in AACR2R-98), dictated title main entry for nonbook materials, with the exception of many sound recordings that were traditionally entered under composer.

Those that opposed title main entry as a general practice for nonbook items replied that there were many people who contributed to the intellectual content of a book that were not acknowledged in cataloguing because it was not the tradition in book publishing to highlight their skills. Editors, book designers, indexers, and foreword writers can all influence the accessibility of a book's content. Some people espoused the auteur theory of motion picture-making, stating that the practice of crediting everyone who had anything to do with the production gave a false impression of responsibility. These people claimed that the director was the person responsible for intellectual content, that the writers, cinematographers, etc., did exactly what the director told them to do. At one point. Shirley Lewis, along with others traveled around to various production companies to test the auteur theory. Staff in the production companies agreed that, indeed, one person was responsible for their products, but each company had a different idea who that person was. Most companies named either the director or the producer.

Title main entry advocates also argued that entry under title would also provide more economical cataloguing because a cataloguer would not have to spend time deciding on the person or organization responsible for the intellectual content of an item. By and large, the proponents of title main entry were also proponents of segregated shelving, i.e., each medium housed by itself in a different part of the library. Some libraries had separate catalogues for each medium, and did not have to struggle with the problems of an integrated catalogue.

The Library Association Media Cataloguing Rules Committee proposed a system it called "unit entry." In this instance, there would be no main entry record. A basic record would be produced to which all appropriate headings would be added to create a set of bibliographic records for an item. While this idea floated around the cataloguing community for a long time, it did not gain much support for its serious consideration by international bodies.

It was decided that unit entry, if applied to book as well as nonbook materials, could be an acceptable method. However, it is realized that libraries would probably reject the massive recataloguing this change would cause. It came to the very firm belief that the same rules of entry must apply to all materials in a collection. Many nonbook materials did have the intellectual responsibility for an item clearly attributed to one, two, or three persons or bodies on appropriate sources of information. Even the occasional motion picture was filmed, directed, written, etc., by three or fewer people.

Some nonbook materials had nondistinctive titles. Most librarians agreed that sound recordings of symphonies, concertos, etc., should be entered under composer and original works of art under artist. However, if such items were produced in another format, the title main entry rule was applied because it was considered that more people were involved in producing the intellectual content of the items.

This situation was especially frustrating to libraries that wanted to intershelve all their materials. These libraries wished to have all the items, nonbook materials as well as books, on the same subject by a particular person sit together on their shelves. These items would be given the same classification number but different Cutter numbers or letters depending on the first word of their titles. Consequently, the items would not stand together in the shelf sequence of a popular topic. The only remedy for this situation was for a library to develop a set of internal rules for applying Cutter numbers or author letters.

AACR2, published in 1978, put this controversy to rest when it mandated the same rules of entry for all materials. Even then, some cataloguers believed that all motion pictures and videorecordings were to be entered under title because it appeared that all Library of Congress records for these materials were entered in this manner. However, Ben Tucker stated that, although few in number, the Library of Congress did enter motion pictures and videorecordings under a personal name when appropriate.

Media Form Subdivisions

The application of media fonn subdivisions was another controversy, albeit less serious than some of the others because it did not concern the basic concepts of cataloguing.

Some libraries stated that their clientele only searched for subjects in a particular fonnat. For example, their catalogue users wanted to know what the library had in a motion picture fonnat about polar bears, not about any of library's resources on polar bears. Adding general material designations to appropriate subject headings was a convenience to these users because their search could be confined to contiguous records in the catalogue, thus saving users from the need to look through all the subject records for the main topic.

Other libraries were opposed to the addition of media form subdivisions because they wished to emphasize that information came in a variety of fornlats. They believed the subject headings with media form subdivisions might limit catalogue users, that looking through all the bibliographic records on a topic would expose users to sources of information beyond their perceived needs.

This controversy was resolved when the American Library Association Resources and Technical Services Division Board of Directors adopted "Guidelines for the Subject Analysis of Audiovisual Materials," which suggested the optional use of media form subdivisions and that these subdivisions should be taken from general material designations. This gave an official sanction to libraries, which either used, or did not use, media fonn subdivisions in their catalogues. These Guidelines were published in the second edition of Nonbook Materials: The Organization of Integrated

Collections.

Subject Analysis for Nonbook Materials

The application of subject headings and classification numbers to nonbook materials could also be difficult. While currency and precision can be problems for the subject analysis of all materials, they are greater problems for nonbook materials. Many nonbook formats can be produced more quickly than books. For example. a videorecording about a recent disaster can be on library shelves long before a book on the same topic. Standard lists of subject headings and classification schemes are slow to produce new terms and numbers, particularly in the days before the Internet. The subject content of some nonbook items can be very specific. For example, trying to assign classification and subject headings to a film loop that demonstrated how to throw a baseball. Subject heading lists and classification schemes were developed for books, and most books do not deal with single concepts.

Because many nonbook formats were not, and are not, easily browsed, it was and is, particularly important that appropriate subject headings be used. The subject analysis problems associated with nonbook materials have eased since the advent of sophisticated automated catalogues. Now the catalogue user is able to access information in the bibliographic recom that was much more difficult to find in the early days of nonbook cataloguing.

DESCRIPTION

Inspite of all above discussed limitations, AACR seems to be only the solution and it is being followed for cataloguing the NBM. The cataloguing of NBM with AACR is discussed here. AACR2 has recommended three levels of detail in description and prescribes the minimum set of elements to be included at each level.

The bibliographic description of printed material may be confined to the description of the physical nature of the material. But in the case of non-book material, it is essential to describe the content in full and with specific details. Generaly, the small libraries use first level of description in cataloguing of non-book materials. The second level of description suggested byAACR2 calls for more information on series and edition than in generally required for AV materials The description, however, of non-book item should tell enough about the format and content to enable the potential user to decide whether or not it is suitable. The physical description area must include sufficient detail to indicate what type of machine is required for playback, projection, etc. Content notes must be comprehensive enough to minimize the need for auditing or viewing the item in order to determine whether or not it will meet the need of the patron. Consequently, the physical description and not areas for AV material should be as specific as possible, while the rest of the description can follow the first level format.

NBM Rules in AACR2

The general rules for descriptive information given in chapter I of AACR2 apply equally to all kinds of non book meterials. Rules for specific kinps of materials are found in chapters 3 to 12: cartographic materials (chapter 3), manuscripts (chapter 4), music (chapter 5), sound recordings (chapter 6), motion pictures and videorecordings (chapter 7), graphic materials (chapter 8), machine-readable data-files (chapter 9), three-dimensional artifacts and realia (chapter 10), microforms (chapter II), and serials (chapter 12).

Source of Information

The chief source of information for printed monographs is the title page but with the NBM the case is unusual. AACR2 recognizes this problem, by using the concept of the chief sources of information in relation to specific NBM. The individuality of each type of NBM is recognized and guidelines are provided in AACR2 to determine which source of information should be given first preference. The categories include:—

(a) The material itself including the container where this forms an integral part of the item, for example a cassette, cartridge, or cartographic.

(b) The container where this is completely separate from the item for example; a box.

(c) Accompany data that is guides and other leaflets issued with the item.

(d) Other sources for example relerence work.

Table 1. lists chief sources of information for different types of materials.

TABLE 1

Chief Sources of Information

Type of Material	Source
Books, pamphlets, and printed sheets	Title page
Cartographic material	a. Cartographic item itself b. Container or case, the cradle and stand of a globe, etc
Manuscripts	Title page Colophon
Music	Title page
Computer files	Title Screen
Sound recordings	
Disc	Label
Tape (open reel-to-real)	Reel and label
Tape cassette	Cassette and label
Tape cartridge	Cartidge and label
Roll	Label
Sound recording on film	Container and label
Motion pictures and videorecordings	Film itself and its container (if integral part of item)
Graphic materials	Item itself including any labels and the container
Machine-readable data files	Internal user label
Three-dimensional artefacts and realia	Object itself with any acompanying textual material and container
Microforms	Title frame
Serials (printed)	Title page

If necessary information cannot be found in the sources mentioned above, the information is to be taken from the following in order of preference:

a) any other source that fonns part of the item

b) accompanying item

c) any available source

d) compose yourself

If any information is taken from outside the item, it is to be enclosed in square brackets.

Organization and the Levels of Description

The bibliographic description of Non-book media follows the similar norms as for books and other print materials. The main structure of the bibliographic entry comprises of the heading, the description area and the subject description. The description is to be divided into the following areas:

Title and statement of responsibility

Edition

Material (or type of publication)

Publication, distribution, etc.

Physical distribution

Series

Note

Standard number and terms of availability

Each of these areas are further divided into a number of elements. The structure of bibliographic description as per the AACR-2R rules are given below:

First Level of Description

Title proper/Ist statement of responsibility. — Edition Statement.— Material or type of publication specific details. — Ist publisher, distributor, etc., date of publication, etc.

Extent of item

Note

Note

Standard number

Example:

The Confederacy/produced by Multi-Media Productions.—

Multi-Media, c 1972.

4 film strips (ca. 37 fr. each)

Second Level of Description

Title proper [general material designation] = parallel title: other title information/Ist statement of responsibility; each subsequent statement of responsibility. — Edition statement/Ist Statement of responsibility. — Material or type of publication specific details. Ist place of publication, distribution, etc; — Ist publisher, distributor, etc., date of publication, etc.

Extent of item: other physical details; dimensions. — (Title proper of series/ statement of responsibility relating to series, ISSN of series; numbering within the series. Title of subseries, ISSN of subseries; numbering within subseries).

Note

Note

Standard Number

Example:

The Confederacy [filmstrip]: the lost cause revisited/ produced by Multi-Media Productions. — Stanford, CA: Multi-Media, c1972.

4 film strips (ca. 37 fr each): col.; 35 mm. — (The Basis of our beliefs).

Third Level of Description

All elements that are required by rule are to be included. Apart from that the optional elements, may also be included for the purpose. Third level of description is generally required by National Libraries and Research libraries. The National Bibliographics usually follow the third level of description.

Example:

The Confederacy [filmstrip]: the lost cause revisited/ produced by Multi-Media Productions. — Stanford. CA: Multi-Media, c1972.

4 film strips (ca. 37 fr. each): col.; 35 mm. + 2 sound cassettes (37 min. 40 sec.) + teacher's manual (6p.; 22 cm.). — (The Basis of our beliefs).

Sound accompaniment compatible for manual and automatic operation.

The difference between level one and level two for non-book material is the expended physical description in level two. The General Material Description (GMD) and artistic content of the material is included in the body of the entry rather than giving in the note section in the second level. The only drawback in the second level is that it does not provide for the accompanying materials statement.

Title Statement

The title usually poses few questions that are not answered by the rules stated in AACR2. There are three points that need attention.

(a) The use of Uniform titles: A uniform title is that by which a work that has appeared under varying titles is to be identified for cataloguing purpose. Cataloguer faces this problem in musical work and sound recordings. If a musical work has titles that vary in phrasing and language, a uniform title is used, AACR2 aims to bring together and organize a composer's work by mucial form, except where a composition is generally referred to by a distinctive title.

(b) Supplied titles. Often NBM have no title and one must be supplied. Such a situation is very common with illustrations, specimens and models. But the supplied title must be an appropriate description of the intellectual contents.

(c) Collective titles. An individual item may contain several works and there may be two or more titles associated with its description. Sound recordings in particular, often have two or more titles associated with a single item; for example, the Open University sound cassette which has the development of the social sciences paired with the Social scientist as work. If there is no collective title associated with the work: then it will be necessary to record the titles in the order in which they appear in the chief source of information.

General Material Designation (GMD)

This is an optional addition, The general designation indicates the broad class of material to which the item being catalogued belongs, For printed or book form material, the term text is used as the general matenal designation. But most libraries choose GMD for non book materials, but not for book-form materials.

For certain forms of materials, British and North American cataloguing agencies use different terms as the gereral material designation.

AACR-2R provides two such lists, List 1 for British agencies and List 2 for agenices in Australia, Canada and the United States (Rule 1.1C1)

Table 2 : GMD-The British and North American Terminology.

(AACR-II) British and North American Terminology

List 1 : British	List 2: North American
braille	art original
cartographic material	art production
computer file	braille
graphic	chart
manuscript	computer file
microform	diorama
motion picture	filmstrip
multimedia	flash card
music	game
object	globe
sound recording	kit
text	manuscript
videorecording	map
	microform
	microscope slide
	model
	motion picture

music
picture
realia
slide
sound recording
technical drawing
text
toy
transparency
videorecording

Cataloguing NBM: Selected Rules and Examples

This section serves as manual of practice for cataloguing non book materials. Each type is depicted separately and detailed descriptive information for individual item is given. To illustrate the rules specimen cataloguer cards have been made for each item of non-book materials. Here, only main entry is provided and cataloguers and readers of this book as an expert in cataloguing of books, are expected to prepare added entries themselves.

The section comprises of the following items

1. Cartographic materials
2. Sound recordings
3. Motion pictures and videorecording
4. Graphic materials
    (a) Art original
    (b) Charts
    (c) Filmstrip
    (d) Flash Card
    (e) Pictures
    (f) Study Prints
    (g) Slides
    (h) Transparency
5. Microforms
6. Computer Files

MANUSCRIPTS

The term 'manuscript' means anything written by hand and not printed. Previous to the innovation of printing technology, all literature was contained in manuscripts. Ancient days manuscripts are found written on parchment (animal skin), vellum, palm leaves, metal plates (engravings) paper etc. In modern days, we write letters, personal diaries, legal documents such as wills, deeds, legal agreements, mortgages, leases, warrants, commissions etc, by hand. Hence these are identified as manuscripts and treated as original documents.

According to glossary of AACR2 manuscript is defined as a writing made by hand (including musical scores) typescripts, and inscription on clay tablets, stone etc.

Sources of Information

The chief source of information for a manuscript text is the manuscript itself. Within the mannuscript prefer information found on a title pages, in the colophon, then information found in a caption, heading etc., and lastly the text itself. Prefer a source however, that is part of the original manuscript to sources that have been supplied later. If information is not available from the chief source, take it from the following sources in the order of preference.

a) another manuscript copy of the item

b) a published edition of the item

c) references sources

d) other sources

Note : For collections of manuscripts, treat the whole collection as the chief source.

Prescribed sources of information for Different Sections

The prescribed source(s) of information for each area of the description of manuscript texts is set out below. Enclose information taken from outside the prescribed source(s) with square brackets.

Area	Prescribed Sources of Information
Title and statement of responsibility	Chief source of information and manuscript or published copies
Date	Chief source of information or pubished copies of manuscripts
Physical description	Any source
Note	Any source

Description

1. Title and statement of responsibility area (1.1b) Transcribe the title porper exactly as to wording, order and spelling but not necessarily as to punctuation and capitalization.

e.g.

Iramayanavacanam;yutha Kandam

Bhasya Irudayam

Anmalingamalai

Rule 4.1B2

If a manuscript text or manuscript collection lacks a title or lacks some of the data prescribed for the material below.

1. In the case of literacy manuscripts, such as diaries, journals memorandum books, acount books etc., supply a brief title indicating the nature of the material.

e.g..

[Diary]

[Seventeen poems]

[Collected works]

[Selected poems]

2. For manuscripts and for oriental manuscripts lacking a title page, follow, when appropriate, the provisions for early printed monographs, otherwise, supply a title by which the work is known or a title indicating the nature of the material.

e.g

(Treatise on Arithmetic)

3. For letters, post cards, telegrams, radiograms, etc, supply a title consisting of the word 'Letter' (or postcard, Telegram, etc) the date of writing (expressed as year, month, day) the place of writing, the name of the addressee and place to which addressed. Enclose any details not taken from the letter etc, its envelope, or enclosures, in square brackets.

e.g.

[Letter] 1901 March 6, Dublin [to] Henrik Ibsen, Kristiania [Oslo].

[Telegram] 1889 Feb. 8, London [to] Janus McNeill Whistler, chelsea, London.

4. For speeches, sermons etc, supply a title for a speech, sermon etc., consisting of an appropriate word (speech, address, etc) followed by the place and/or the occasion of the delivery.

e.g

(Lecture, Royal college of medicine, London)

5. For legal documents such as wills, deeds, mortgages, leases, warants, commissions, etc. supply a title for a legal document consisting of a word or brief phrase characterizing the document, the date of signing (expressed as year, month, day) the document, and the occasion for the documents if it can be expressed concisely. Enclose any details not taken from the document in squarebrackets.

e.g.

[will] 1943, Feb.8

[Lease, 1937 Oct. 17, of shop in Bridge St., Harrow, Middlesex]

6. For collections of manuscripts the material formed by or around a person, family, corporate body or subject. The materials may be in their origial form or reproduction, and may include photographs and printed materials. Supply a title by which the collection is known or a title, indicating the nature of collection.

e.g.

(Letters)

(Records)

(Indian papers)

Rule 4.1C

Optional addition General material designation

Rule 4.1D

Parallel Titles as instructed for printed monographs.

Ruel 4.1.E

Other title information as instructed for printed monographs and statements of responsibility as instructed for printed monographs.

e.g. Three Sonnets of Shakespear (GMD)/written in the italic hand by Pamela Thomason.

Pandiar charithiram [GMD]/written by Ammani

Rule 4.1F3

If a manuscript lacks a signature or statement of responsibility, supply the name(s) of the person(s) responsible for it, if known

e.g. the waste land (GMD)/T.S. Eliot; (with ms. amendment by Ezra Pound)

2. Edition Area

This area is not used for manuscript texts.

3. Material (or type of publication) Specific Details Area

This area is not used for manuscript texts.

4. Date Area

Precede this section by fullstop, space, dash, space. Give the date or inclusive dates of the manuscript or manuscript collection unless it is already included in the title as with letters and legal documents.

Give the date as a year or year, and optionally the month and day (in the case of single manuscripts) in that order.

eg. Records (GMD)/ American Coloization Society.- 1816- 1908.

Correspondence (GMD)/ William Allen. - 1821-1879.

Rule 4.4B2

If the date of delivery of a speech, sermon etc differs from the date of the manuscript, record the date of delivery in a note, unless this date is part of the title information.

[Speech] Glasgow Labour Club [GMD]/James Maxton.-1928 Jan. 13.

Note: Delivered Feb. 8, 1928.

5. Physical Description

This section should be commenced from a new paragraph, starting form second indent, continuation from first indent, if any.

Single manuscript (4.5 B1)

Records Sequences of leaves or pages, whether numberd or not.

e.g. 23 leaves iv, 103 leaves

If the manuscript has been bound, and bound at the end of the paginations.

70 leaves bound

Add, to the pagination, etc., of ancient, medieval and Renaissance manuscripts, the number of column, (of more than one) and the average number of lines to the page.

26 leaves (2 columns 45-47 lines)

Other Physical Details (4.5C) (connecting symbol is colon)

If the material on which a single manuscript is not paper, record the name of the type of material.

eg.

12 leaves: parchment

Dimensions (4.5 D)

connecting symbol is semicolon

Rule 4.5 D1 Single Manuscripts

Give the height of single unbound manuscripts in centimeters to the next whole centimeter up. Add the width if it is less than half the height or greater than the height. If the manuscript is kept folded, add the dimension when folded.

12 leaves : ill.; 20 cm folded to 10* 12 cm

12 boxes; 40*15*10 cms.

6. Series Area

This area is not used for manuscript texts.

7. Note Area

Start a new paragraph for each note.

Ruel 4.7B1

Nature, Scope, or form of manuscript(s): Make notes on the nature of the manuscript or the manuscripts in a collections unless it is apparent form the description. Use one of the following terms, as appropriate.

Holographs(s)- for manuscript handwritten by the author

m._ for all other handwritten manuscripts

mss._ for all other collection of hand written manuscripts

Type Scripts(s)

If the items or collection being described is a copy or consists of copies, add (carbon copy), and (transcript) or the plural of these, as appropriate.

eg. Holograph (carbon copy)

ms. (photocopy, negative)

if the item is signed, indicate this

Holograoph signed

Indicate the scope or form of a manuscript

eg.

Poem

Journal and Account book.

Rule 4.7B2 Language

Give the language or languages of the item unless they are apparent from the rest of the description.

In English

In Tamil

Rule 4B7 Donar

Make notes on the donar or source of a manuscript or manuscript collection, and on previous owners if they can be easily ascertained. Add the year or years of accession to the name of the donar or source, and add the year of owndrship to the name of a previous owner.

Purchase, 1951-1968

Gift of Mr. wright, 1938-1954.

Previously owned by L.McGarby, 1951-1965.

Note

Any other information the cataloguer may think that is important to the user group can be given as a note.

Note

Choice of access points : as instructed in printed monographs

Added entries : as instructed in printed monographs.

Example :

Bhasya Irudayam

Brahmanana Venkateswara Swamigal
1949-50

The manuscript in leaf form
contains 28 leaves with 8 lines in
each leaf size 30x6 cm

The manuscript is available with Sri. C.Krishnamoorthy
Mirasdar, North car street,
Shiyali (Tanjore)

Other information:

Call No.181.4N2 Acc No. 59020

181.4 N2	Venkareswara Swamigal, Brahmanana.
59020	Bhasya Irudayam [manuscript]/ Brahmana Venkateswara Swamigal.-1949-50. 28 leaves (8 lines); 30X6 cm. ms. In Tamil Owned by C.Krishnamurthy Mudaliar, North Car street, Shiyali (Tanjore). 1. Indian Philisophy I. Title

Cartographic Materials

The glossary of AACR II defines cartographic material representing, in whole or in part, the earth or any celestial body at any scale; includes two and three dimensional maps and plans; aeronautical, navigational and celestial charts; globes; block diagrams, sections, arerial, satellite, and space photographs; stleases; bird's eye views etc.

The chief sources for information are: the item itself or the container. The structure of the bibliographic description for cartographic materials is shown below:

Call Number	Creator of the item
Acc No	Title [GMD]= Parallel title: other title information/1st statement of responsibility; each subsequent statement of responsiblity. - Edition statement/ 1st Statement of responsibility.- Statement of scale; Statement of projection. - 1st place of publication, distribution etc: 1st place of publication, distribution etc: 1st publisher, distributor etc., date of publication etc. Extent of item: other physical details; dimensions+ accompanying material.- (Series). Notes Standard number and terms of avilability Tracing

The terms maps and globes are designated for all types of cartographic material in the GMD section.

Maps

The most common veriety of cartographic material is a map which is a kind of graphich representation of any place in the universe, on the earth, or in the heavens, real or imaginary. Relief maps, globes, atlases, and the photographs and the surveys which porvide raw materials for conventionl maps are regarded as cartographic materials.

Sources of Information (3.0B)

The information for cataloguing purpose is obtained from the following sources in this order:

1. The item itself (chief source of information)
2. Container or case
3. Accompanying material.
4. Other sources.

Main Entry

AACR2 does not change Cutter's rule that "the cartographer is the author of maps", but it brings about changes in rules for corporate authorship which means wider provision is made to make main entry under title for maps. However historical maps and maps of technical nature are often entered under the name of cartographers. It is also easier to locate the item if the cataloguer provides appropriates subject headings to maps.

Title proper (3.1B)

Record the title proper for a map following wording and order exactly, but following conventional library rules for capitalization and punctuation as it done in case of books. If the title inclues scale of map, it will be transcribed as part of the title proper, e.g.

Bartholomen one inch map of the Lake District—

If the title infromation does not indicate a geographic area, supply as other title information a word or phrase in brackets stating the region covered in the map. (3.1E2) .

General Material Designation (GMD)

Although optional, the cataloguer should use the general material designation "map" or "globe" in brackets as appropriate immediately after the title proper followed by colon, e.g.,

Explore it [map]: Philadelphia style...

Parallel titles or other title information if any is recorded following general rules for monographs, etc.

Statement of Responsibility (Rule 3.IF)

The statement of responsibility includes names of all persons or corporate bodies that have some responsibility other than for simple publication or distribution of the item, as long as these names appear prominently in the chief source of information.

Sets of maps may be treated individually or as a unit depending on which approach will be more useful for library users. For a set lacking a collctive title, separate cataloguing records may be made for the part, and linked by notes.

Edition Area

If a cartographic item includes an edition statement, it is recorded following general rules for descriptive information.

Mathematical Data Area (3.3)

Following the title and edition area (if any) or other designation area, the cataloguer should record "mathematical data area". The data pertain to three elements: scale; projection; and coordinates and equinox. A statement of scale (exception apart) is a must even if it is already given in the title. The scale is to be expressed as a ratio (1:), and preceded by the word scale. For example

...Government of India, New Delhi..— scale 100 mile to an inch or 1:357439.

Give the scale even if it is already recorded as part of the title or other information.

The following method for converting graphic scales to fractions is suggested.

If scale is given in terms of miles to an inch, multiple the number of miles per inch. For example number of inches in a mile: 1760x3x2 = 63360. The number of 43 miles converted into inches: 43x63360 = 2724,480 inches. This can be recorded as statement in catalogue entry as scale 1:2724,480 (Akers).

Other ways to determine scale are to use a bar graph or a grid, or to compare with a map of known scale, and to show the result as approximated, e.g., "Scale ca. 1:63,360." When there is no way to approximate, use the phrase "Scale indeterminable". The "scale varies" or "Scales vary" are also given when appropriate. Use brackets when the scale has been derived from a source other than the chief'source of information. If desired additional scale can be given in note.

In three-dimensional items, such as relief models, the vertical scale is listed after the horizontal, but it is optional.

The Statement of projection is to be given when it is found on the item, container, an accompanying material. It follows the statement of scale, being separated from it by space-semicolon-space.

Publication, Distribution, etc.

Give the place of publication, distribution, etc., according to AACR2 rule No.1.4C.

(i) Place of printing, etc., name of printer, etc., date of printing, etc. If the name of the publisher is unknown and the place and name of the printer or manufacturer are found in the item; give that place and name as instructed in rule 1.4G.

(ii) Optional addition.

Give the place, name of printer, etc., and/or date of printing, etc., if they are found on the item or its container or case or accompanying printed material and differ from the place, name of publishers, etc., and date of publication, etc., and are considered important for cataloguing purpose. (AACR2-3, 4G2)

Physical Description Area (3.5)

(i) Instead of pages, the physical description area consists of the number of items and the appropriate terms, e.g.,

1 map	1 celestial chart
1 atlas (300p.)	3 plans
1 globe	5 map sections

(ii) it also consists of colour if any, e.g.

1 map: col.; 41x46 cm.

1 map: col.; 89x58 cm. folded to 23x15 cm.

(iii) This area also describes material (if other than paper), mounting (if any), and dimensions. For maps height x width of the face of the map between the neat lines are listed in centimeters. If the map is circular, list the diameter in centimeters followed by the phrase "in diam". If a map lacks lines or is in extremely irregular shape, give dimensions of the sheet.

Other information of this area include:

(i) Material

1 map:col., plastic

1 map:col., silk

(ii) Dimensions

1map:col,; 25x25 cm.

1ms.map;123.5.152.4 cm.

1wall chart; 40x23 cm.

1 map:col.; on sheet 45x33 cm.

1 wall map : col; 169x133 cm.

1 map on two sheets; 25x35 cm. and 30x35 cm.

(iii) Mounting

1 map; col., mounted on linen

1 globe : plastic, on metal stand.

Accompanying Material and Series Statements

Record accompanying material according to AACR2 (Rule 1.5E). In case of map it is usually recorded in physical description area or in note area. For example :

17 maps; 90x96 cm. + iv. (xvii, 282p.; 25 cm).

Record series statement if any in series area. For example.

(Climatolgoical studies; no. 10)

Note Areas (3.7)

General descriptive information rules are followed. AACR2 includes the following items:

1. Nature and scope of items
2. Language
3. Sources of title proper
4. Variation in title/parallel title
5. Statement of responsibility if not recorded in the body of the card.
6. Edition and history
7. Mathematical and other cartographical data if not already recorded.

8. Publication, distribution, etc.
9. Physical description.
10. Accompanying material. If accompanying material intended to be used with map is too complex in its nature to be given in the physical description area, it is appropriate to record it in note area.

Example :

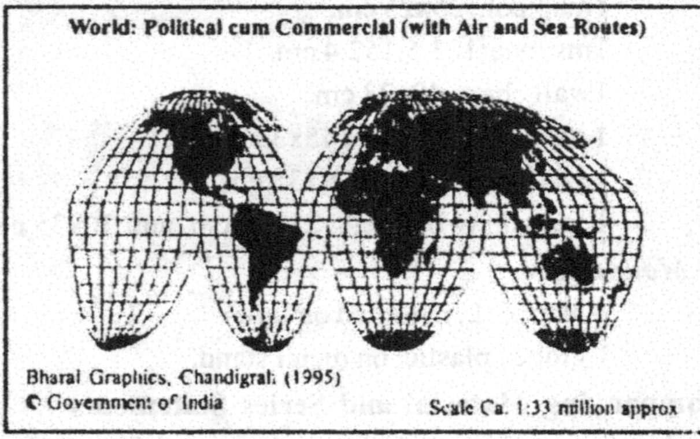

World: Political cum Commercial (with Air and Sea Routes)
Bharat Graphics, Chandigarh (1995)
Government of India Scale ca. 1: 33 million approx.

Other information:

Cull No. : 912 IND - Acc. No.	:	55381
Size	:	95 x64 cm.
Copyright	:	Government of India

Main Entry

912 IND	India	
55381	routes) [map] Government of India. - Scale ca: 33 million approx. - Chandigarh: Bharat-Graphics, 1995.	World: political cum commercial (with air and sea 1 map: Colour; 95X 64 cm. 1. World- Map I Title

In the above example here, the number of physical units and number of pages are given in description area. This is done according to rules 3.5B I and 3.5B3. Other physical details (viz., 133 col. maps) and dimensions are according to rules 3.5C and3.5D.

TOURIST MAP: NORTHERN REGION OF INDIA **Scale : 100 Miles an inch or 1357, 439** **Based upon Survey of the India maps** Produced-by the Directorate of Advertising and Visual publicity; Ministry of Information and broadcasting for the Department of Tourism, government of India New delhi. **and** Published for the Department of Tourism, Ministry of Transport and Communication, Government of India with the pemission of the Surveyor General of India 1992. **Published by and for the Government of India.**

Other Information
Call No : U8.445f K4
Acc No. : 50655
Size : 65 x 30 cm.
Note: References are given and the map is coloured

Main Entry

U8.445f N92	India. Directorate of Advertising and Visual Publicity.
50656	Tourist map northan region of India [map]/ produced by the Directorate of Advertising and Visual Publicity, Ministry of Information and broadcasting, for the Department of Tourism, Government of India, New Delhi.- Scale 100 mile to an inch or 1:357,439- New Delhi: Government of India, 1992. 1 map: col.; 65x 30 cm. Based upon: Survey of India maps. References are given. 1. India- Description and travel- Map I. Survey of India II. Title.

Globes

Globes represent the earth, celestial bodies, or the universe. General rules for descriptive infromation are also applied here. Certain additional information as described below is required for cataloguing globes.

Sources of Information : Information for the catalogue record is taken from the following sources in this order.

1. The item itself
2. Cradle and stand
3. Container
4. Accompanying material
5. Other sources.

Mathematical Data

This area follows the pattern adopted for maps. For example:

.-Scale 1: 31,680,000.-

Physical Description Area

This area comprises of the number of globes, celestial globes, or relief globes. Other physical details includes col., or b & w (i.e., colour, or black and white) the material from which the globe was made, if significant and the mounting detail. Diameter is given in centimeters followed by the phrase 'in diam'. This is the dimension of globe. For example:

1. globe: col.; 12 cm. in diam.

1. globe: col.; plastic, mounted on metal stand; 28 cm. in diam.

1. globe: col.; plastic, mounted on wooden stand.,

1. globe: col.; wood, on brass stand.

Globe with accompanying material and series note

Main Entry

Main entry is under title. If the globe does not have title of its own, it is provided by the cataloguer to indicate the area covered or the subject of the globe. If the title is supplied by the cataloguer, it is indicated by square brackets.

Geosphere Globe
Scale 1 :31, 680,000
Rand Mcnally
Chicago

Other Information :

1 Globe; colour, mounted on metal stand

41 cm. in diameter

Accompanied by one manual

Rand mark ;.iv/v

shows political and physical data

Title taken from manual

Cradle base has directions, hours, attached hemisphex ring, and half-circle arc.

Copy right year 1967

Call no 912 G298

Main Entry

G298 912	Geos	hpere globe [cartographic material].
		Scale 1: 31,680,000._ Chicago : Rand Mcnally, c
	1967.	
		1 globe: col., mounted on metal stand; 41 cm. in
49012	diam.	+ 1 manual ._ (Randmark;iv/v).
		Shows political and physical date.
		Title from manual.
		Cradle base has directions, hours, attached
	hemis	phex ring, and half-circle arc.
		1. Earth 2. Globe.
		O

Atlases

Atlases are the special materials which are described both as cartographic material and as a book.

Source of information for an atlas is, as for books, i.e., the title page. The difference is that for cataloguing atlases, the mathematical data area is included or it is recorded in note area.

Physical description area is included but shows volumes, pagination, visual data and tactile data (i.e., braille letters or other tactile systems), number of maps in atlas, colour. For example:

1 atlas (3v)

1 atlas (xvii, 37p., 74 leaves of plates)

1 atlas (100p., braille and tactile)

1 atlas (xvi, 97, 100p.): 35 col. maps.

1 atlas (339p.): 100 col. maps (some folded)

Most libraries choose to omit GMD for atlases, as an atlas is generally considered and handled like a book.

As stated earlier atlases are entered under title or as the statement of responsibility is indicated on the title page which warrants entry under author/compiler or corporate body according to prescribed rules of AACR2. For added entries they are treated like books.

Example :

Gem's School Atlas

*

Ratna Sagar
New Delhi
1995

Other Information:

Call No	:	912 IND
Acc. No.	:	5438
Pages	:	iiv, 80
Size	:	28 x 22 cm.
Contents	:	133 colour maps
ISBN	:	81-7070-248-0
Copyright	:	Govemement of India

Main Entry

912 IND		India.
		Gems' school atlas [map]/Government of India.-
		Scales vary.- New Delhi : Ratna Sagar, 1995.
		1 atlas (80 p.): 133 col. Maps; 28x22 cm.
5438		Audience : School children.
		ISBN : 81-7070-248-0
		1.World- Atlases I Title

Sound Recordings

According to the glossary of AACR II sound recording are described as "the recording on which sound vibration have been registered by machainical or electronic means so that the sound may be reproduced". Disc, rolls, tapes (open reel to reel, cartridge and cassette), sound pages, and sound recordings on film are included under this heading and designated by the term "Sound recordings".

Chief Sources of Information—The chief source of information for different types of material has been set out as:

Type	Chief Source
Disc	Disc and label
Tape (open reel to reel)	Reel and label
Tape cassette	Cassette and label
Tape cartridge	Cartridge and label
Roll	Label
Soundrecording on film	Container and label

Main Entry

Main entry for sound recordings is based on the same principles of authorship governing other types of library materials; entry will be under "the person chiefly responsible for the creation of the intellectual or artisitic content of a work". This means for most part, main entry will be under the name of composer of a musical work that has been recorded, or the writer of a book or other material that is being narrated (Rules 21.1 through 21.22 are applied). In some instances, an individual performer or performing group is regarded as the author of a sound recording and will be given main entry. It is only the types of material in the area of sound recordings that create difficulties for cataloguers. The problem of main entry is now analysed and elaborately explained below with corresponding examples.

1. Sound Recording of one work

The work(s) of one composer or author are entered under the name of that composer or author.

2. Sound Rccording-a Collection

A sound recording which contains musical or literary works composed or written by two or more persons is entered under the principal performer or group of performer as the case may be.

3. Sound Recording of no principlc performer

A sound recording which contains musical or literary works composed or written by two or more persons and has no principal performers or more than three principal performers is entered:

(a) Under the title, if the sound recording has a collective title for the component parts.

(b) Under the heading appropriate to the first work, e.g., that on side 1, band 1 of a sound disc, if the item does not have a collective title for the component parts.

4. Items without a collective title

These may be described in either of two ways:

(a) As a unit.

(b) In separate entries for each work.

These entries are linked by a "With" note.

Uniform Titles

Some classical music entered under composer are issued many a time under verying titles. In such cases, a uniform title is interposed between the author heading and the title proper. Such a title brings all the cditions translations, etc., of musical composition together in the same place in the catalogue.

Uniform title are formulated according to rules outlined in AACR2.

Title and Statement of Responsibility

If the title of a work is a non-distinctive word or phrase of musical work, the medium of performance, key opus numbers, etc., is listed as part of the title proper. If the title is distinctive, the medium of performance, key, opus number, etc., is listed as other title information.

Statement of Responsibility: If the persons or groups are the authors of spoken sound recordings, composers, collectors of field materials or who have contributed more to the recording than performance, are recorded like authors of books or corporate bodies in the area of responsibility. But exception to this rule for sound recording is that the names or narrators performers who solely function as musicians, are given in nóte area.

Publication, Distribution Area

If the item has both the name of the publisher and a subdivision with a distinctive name or trade name, give the subdivision or trade name rather than the Parent company. If no date of publication is available, the date of recording may be used instead.

Physical Description Area

List the number of sound cartridges, sound cassettees, sound discs, sound tape reels, or sound pages. List in parentheses after the specific material designation (SMD) the total playing time stated on the item, its packing, or its accompanying material.

Extent of Item (including SMD)

(i) Record the number of physical units of a sound recording by giving the number of parts in arabic numerals and one of the following terms as appropriate:

Sound cartridge
Sound cassette
Sound disc

Sound tape reel

Sound track film 1 sound cartridge 2 sound cassettes

(ii) Give the playing time of a sound recording

1 sound disc (50 min.)

2 sound tape reel (ca. 90 min.)

3 sound cassettes (40 min. each)

Other Physical Details

(i) Type of recording: Give, for a disc or tape, the type of recording.

1 sound disc (4.1) min.): analog

1 sound disc (56 min.): digital

1 sound cassette (90 min.): analog

1 sound cassette (60 min.): digital

(ii) Playing speed: Give the playing speed of an analog disc in revolutions per minute (rpm).

1 sound disc (45 min.): analog, 33 1/3 rpm

Give the playing speed of a digital disc in metres per second (m.per sec.).

Give the playing speed of an analog tape in inches per second (ips).

1 sound tape reel (16 min.): analog, 7½ ips

1 sound cassette (120 min.): analog, 5/16ips

Give the playing speed of sound track film in frames per second (fps).

1 sound track film reel (to min.): magnetic, 24 fps

(iii) Groove characteristic: Give the groove characteristic of an analog disc if it is not standard for the type of disc.

1 sound dis (7 min.): analog 78 rpm. microgroove

(iv) Track configuration: For sound track films, give the track configuration (e.g., centre track, edge track).

1 sound track film reel (10 min.): magnetic, 25 fps, centre track

(v) Number of sound channels: Give the number of sound channels, if the information is readily available, using one or more of the following terms as appropriate:

mono.

stereo.

quard.

1 sound dis (56 min.): digital, sterero.

1 sound tape reel (ca. 60 min.): analog, 7½ ips, 2 track, mono.

2 sound disc (66 min.): analog, 33⅓ rpm, mono., stereo.

Dimensions

Give the dimensions of a sound recording as set out in the following rules.

(i) Sound discs: Give the diameter of a disc in inches.

1 sound disc (20 min.): analog, 33⅓rpm, stereo.; 12 in.

1 sound disc (56 min.): digital, stereo.; 4¾ in.

5 sound discs: analog, 33⅓ rpm, stereo.; 10-12 in.

(ii) Sound track films: Give the gauge (width) of a film in millimeters.

1 sound track film reel (10 min.): magnetic, 25 fps, centre track; 16 mm.

(iii) Sound cartridges: Give the dimensions of a cartdge in inches if other than the standard dimensions (5¼ x 3 7/8 in). Give the width of the tape in fractions of an inch if other than the standard width (¼ in).

(iv) Sound cassettes: Give the dimensions of a cassette if other than the standard dimensions (e.g., the standard "dimensions of an analog cassette are 3 7/8 x 2½. in.). Give the width of a tape if other than the standard width (e.g., the standard width of an analog tape is 1/8 in).

1 sound cassette (85 min.): analog, mono.; 7¼ x 3½ in.,

(v) Sound tape reels: Give the. diameter of reel in inches. Give the width pf a tape in fractions of an inch if other than the standard width (¼ in.).

1 sound tape reel (60 min.): analog, 7½ ips, 2 tracks, mono.; 7 in., ½ in. tape.

Accompanying Material

Give the details of accompanying material if available.

Note Area

General rules for descriptive information are also applied here. Other important things to be recorded in the note area are as follows:

(i) If the medium of performance for a musical work is not clear from the title or the uniform title, it is given in notes; or if appropriate, these can be combined with contents note, e.g.,

The second work for violin and string orchestra.

(ii) Date of recording is given.

(iii) Source of title paper. e.g.

Title on container:—-

(iv) Names of the performers, if considered important, are included in notes.

(v) Duration time may be given for a multipart item without a collective title that has been described as a unit, e.g.,

Durations: 31 min.; 28 min.

(vi) A brief summary may be given for the contents of a spokcn sound recording, e.g.,

Summary: Storeis and poems, told by Miranda with booklet for the child to read along with the recording.

(vii) Contents: Titles of the individual works catalogued under a collective title, if considered important may be rccorded. If time is given for individual works, include this information.

(viii) Notes on publisher numbers: Serial album and record numbers are given as note. The number is to be preceded by the label name and a colon, e.g.,

K-Tel: NU 9580

Warner Brothers: J5A3139

RCA victor: LM 2268.

Example :

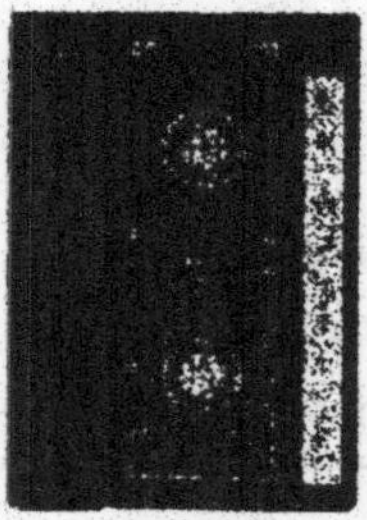

Mozart
Masterpiece
Classical

Midas
Delhi
1987

Other Information:

Call No.	:	782.1073 MOZ
Acc. No.	:	5942
Contents	:	1st movement- Allegro Molto 2nd movement- Andante 3rd movement- Menuetto;trio 4th movement- Finale; Allegro Assai

It is a 60 minute audio cassette with 2 tracks and stereophonic sound. The cassette is of standard dimension.

Main Entry

782.1073 MOZ	Mozart.
5942	Masterpiece classical [sound recording]/Mozart. -Delhi: Midas, 1987. 1 cassette (60 min.): analogue, 2 track, stereo. Contents: 1st movement- Allegro Molto - 2nd movement- Andante -3rd movement. Menuetto; trio - 4th movement. Finale; Allegro Assai. 1. Musicals I. Title

Example :

The Mills Brother's Great Hits
DOT
London
1958

Other Information :

Call No. : 784 Mil

Acc. No. : 67118

Dot Cs. : 25157

a castte

Ca. 60 minutes

Songs performed by the Mills brothers

Main Entry

(Under the performing group)

785 MIL	Mills Brothers.
67188	The Mills Brother's great hits [sound recording]. _ London: Dot, 1958. 11 Cassette (ca 60 min). Songs performed by the Mills Brothers. Dot : cs 25157 1. Music- popular (song etc) I. Title

Motion Picture and Video Recording

According to the glossary of AACR 2 Motion picture are described as "a length of film, with or without record sound, bearing a sequences of images that create the illusion of movement when projected in rapid succession". Loops, cartridges, Cassettes, Kinescopes, Strockshots, trailers etc., are included under this headings and designated by the term "motion pictures".

The following General Material Descriptions (GMDs) and Specific Material Descriptions (SMDs) are prescribed by AACR2.

GMD	*SMD*
Motion picture	film cartridge
	film cassette
	film loop
	film reel
Videorecording	videocartridge
	videocassette
	videodisc
	videoreel

Chief Source of Information

The chief sources of information for motion pictures and video recordings is the film itself (e.g., the title frames) and its container (and its label) if the container is an integral part of the piece (e.g., a cassette).

If the information is not avaiiable from the chief source, take it from the following sources in the order of preference accompanying textual material (e.g., scripts, shots lists, publicity materials), container (if not integral part of piece) and other sources.

Main Entry

Since the making of film or video entails collaborative effort, it is difficult to ascribe authorship to an individual or corporate author. It means, that as a general rule for most motion pktures, main entry will be under title in hanging indention.

If authorship responsibility can be attributed by definitions and rules of "Personal authorship" (Rule 21.1) then main entry will be under personal or corporate author. In case of animated films, there is one person who is clearly the creator. So the main entry will be under his personal name.

When the concept, art work, photography, editing, and sound track can all be attributed to an individual, the entry will be tmder the name of that person.

Title and Statement of Responsibilty

Record the title exactly as it appears on the title frames. Add in bracket "motion picture" or "videorecording" as appropriate immediately after title. Generally the producer and director are given in the statement of responsibility area. The animator and the writer may also be included in this area. Otnerpersons or bodies who have contributed to the work may be recorded in the note area.

Publication, Distribution, etc. Area

The publisher/producer, distributor, of releasing agent, etc., are given in this area. If the distribution date is not the same as the production date, the earlier date may be given in note.

Physical Description Area

This area is divided into the following three major elements.

(i) Extent of item: The number of physical units followed by one of the specific material designation is the first element. For example:

1 film cartridge	2 film loops
1 film cassette	2 videocassettes
1 film reel	1 videodisc
1 videoreel	

In the case of videorecordings, add the trade name or other technical specification in parentheses. If the item is available in the media centre in more than one video format, the technical specifications are listed in the note area.

If the exact playing time is mentioned on the item, on the container, or elsewhere, it is recorded following the extent of the item in parenthese.

For example:

1 film reel (27 min.)

1 videocassette (15 min.)

If duration is not stated, an approximate time, e.g. (ca. 50 min.) is given if it can be ascertained easily.

(ii) Other physical details: Following the duration, for all types of motion pictures, and videorecording, indicate whether the film is sound (sd) or silent, (si) and whether it is in colour or black and white and playing speed for videodiscs only and projection speed for motion pictures only. Note that revolutions per minute are given for videodiscs, and otfen projection speed in frames per second (fps) is needed for silent (si) film.

For example:

1 film reel (52 min.) Panavision; sd., col., 25 fps

The above description is for 1 film reel with a playing time of 52 minutes; Panavision is the special projection characteristics; the film has sound (sd) and in colour (col.); and the projection speed in 25 frames per second (fps).

(iii) Dimension: The dimensions are the width of a film (in millimeters) and the width of a videotape (in inches). A videodisc

dimension is the diameter in inches. Some examples are:

2 film reels (152 min.) Panavision; sd., col., 25 fps; 35 mm.

1 film cassette (15 min.) sd., b&w; standard 8 mm.

1 videoreel (32 min.) sd., col., ½ in.

1 videodisc (4i nun.) sd., col., 1500 rpm; 8 in.

Note Area

This area usually incorporates the following information.

(i) The name of person such as performers or other participants not included in the statement of responsibility but likely to be of interest. The names are prefaced by an appropriate term such as Cast, Presenter, Narrator, Credits, and if appropriate, a statement of functions.

(ii) Date of original producation if it differs from the date (s) listed in publication, distribution area.

(iii) Other titles under which an item has been relased, relationship to other version, and significant physical details not already given in the card. When a library owns a title in several formats, these are given in a note.

(iv) The videorecording system if it has not been listed in the physical description area. The notes "U standard" or "Beta" may be used in this area.

(v) A brief, objective summary of the content and intended use is necessary in order to judge the suitability. If appropriate, information on technique, cast, and audience level may also be included.

Example :

Other Information:

Call No.	:	920.2 GUY
Acc. No.	:	4331
Duration	:	25 minutes
Voice	:	P.C Ramakrishan

Credits: Videography- B. Saikumar, Editor- N. Chandrashekhar, Project coordinator: S.N. Kumar

---

Main Entry

920.2 GUY	Guy, Randor.
4321	S. R. Ranganathan: the man and his mission [videorecording]/ written, produced and directed by Randor Guy. - Bangalore: Kini Vista Kreation, 1992. 1 cassette (25 min.): sd. , col. Credits: Voice- P. C. Ramakrishna; Videography- B. Saikumar; Editor -N. Chandrashekhar; Project Coordinator- S. N. Kumar. Continued in the next card

920.2 GUY	Continued 1 Guy, Randor.
	S. R. Ranganathan: the man and his mission Sponsored by Sarada Ranganathan Endowment for Library Science. Video documentary. 1. Ranganathan- Biography I. Title

Example :

THE GREAT TRAIN ROBBERY
Writtten, Directed Photographed and Edited by Edwin S. Porter Blackhawk Films Lowa

Other Information:

Call No 353.0733 G7 year 1903a

Acc no. 12656

1 film reel

Silent

Black and white with colour sequence

Standard 8mm

Summary : One of the first motion westerns, using cross- editing techinques

Blackhawk : 865-35-1951

Main entry
under personal author

353.0733 G7	Porter, Edwin S.
12656	The great train robbery [motion picture]/ written, directed, photogrphed and edited by Edwin S.Porter._ Lowa : Blackwak Films, 1903. 1 film reel (10 min.) : si., b & w with colour sequences; standard 8 mm. Summary : one of the first motion picture western, using cross editing techniques. Black hawk : 865-35-1951 1. Motion picture, silent 2, Western films I.Title.

Example :

THE PERFECT [Motion Picture] Chopra Production Pankaj Film Distributors, 1993 80 min. sd B & W 75 mm Based on the Novel "The Perfect" by Johan Heed *Credits*: Producer—Raj Kumar Chopra Director—Ramesh Sehgal Music—Abid Noshad Film Editor—John Bloombcrg *Cast:* Bernard Shaw

Other Information :

Call No. : M N93

Acc No. : 29608

Main Entry

M N93	Chopra Production.
    29608	The Perfect [Motion picture]/Chopra Production, -[S.l.]: Pankaj Film Distributor 1993. 1. Film real (80 min): ed., B & W; 75 mm. Cast: Bernard Shaw. Credits: Producer, Raj Kumar Chopra; Direction, Ramesh Sehgal Music, Abid Noshad; -Film Editor, John Bloomberg. Based on the novel 'The Perfect' by John Held. Summary: The exploits of a country carpenter who perfect on building privies. 1. Carpentry I. Title.

Graphic Materials

According to the glossary of AACR 2, Graphic material are described as "a two dimensional representation whether opaque (e.g.. art originals and reproduction, flash cards photographs, technical drawings) or intended to be viewed, or projected without motion, by means of an optical device (e.g., filmstrips. stereographs, slides)'

Many of these materials are not catalogued and/ or classified in many libraries, because most of them cannot be physically shelved with corresponding monographic materials, hence book classification system is often not used. Rather use is made of a simple accession or serial number to keep them in order. Some libraries catalogue them fully and interfile catalogue card in public catalogue. Some libraries provide some identification method such as colour coding of catalogue records that represent the material listed above when they are interfiled in the main catalogue.

The following, GMDs and specific material designations (SMDs) are to be used:

GMD	*SMD*
art original	art original
chart	chart
	flip chart
	wall chart
filmstrip	filmslip
	filmstrip / filmstrip
	cartridge
flash card	flash card
picture	art print
	art reproduction
	photograph
	picture
	postcard
	poster
slide	study print
	slide

	stereograph, stereograph reel
technical drawing	technical drawing
transparency	transparency

AACR 2 allows the option of substituting from another category or adding more precise tenns to the above SMDs.

Sources of Information

The item itself including affixed labels, is the chief source. If the container is an integral part of the item, it can also be a chief source. If the item consists of several parts separately labelled, but only the container has collective itle, the container is the chief source. If the information needed does not appear on the chief source, it can be taken from the container, accompanying textual material, and other sources in that order.

Main Entry

Original works of art-paintings drawings, photographs, etc., are entered under the name of the artist. Reproductions are also entered under the artist responsible for the original, unless the reproduction is actually an adaptation of a work. However a slide or other mechanical reproduction would be entered under the name of the person who created the original work, just as the facsimile of a book would be entered under the author of the original book.

Filmstrips, study prints, and similar materials are almost always the result of collaborative effort between script writers, photographers, graphic artists, researches, and so on. Consequently, they are most often entered under title.

Title and Statement of Responsibility

Record the title from the chief source of information. If no title information is given there, the cataloguer must supply a brief title and describe it in square bracket and record the source (s) in note.

General Material Designation (GMD)

Give GMD immediately following the title proper as given above.

Parallel Titles/Other Title Information

These are recorded as instructed in AACR 2 (1.1D&E).

Record the statement of responsibility if there is a person or corporate body prominently shown on the chief source of information.

A word or phrase may be added if needed to clarify the relationship to the work of a peson or corporate body included in the statement of responsibility.

If a graphic item lacks a collective title, record the titles of individual parts.

Publication, Distribution, etc.

Art originals, unpublised photographs, and similar works will not have a "publisher". However the date of production should be given. Place of publication will be given only if it is a published graphic item. Statement of function of the publisher, distribution can be added; but it is an optional addition (Rule 8.4E). If the name of the publisher is unknown and the place and name of the manufacturer are found in the item, give that place and name as usual.

Physical Description Area

In short this area includes the extent of item (SMD), dimensions, colour and accompany material if there is any with the item catalogued.

Note Area

For graphic materials, the note area is used to clarify the artistic form when the physical description area does not do this adeqately; to give additional important title information; to list credits; to cite donors and previous ownership of original art; to clarify the history of an item and to describe the original work if the item being catalogued is a reproduction. Also to give physical details which are important but not readily fitted into the proper area. Intended audience, summary recorded in note area.

ART ORIGINAL

AACR2 (Appendix D) glossary defines art original as follows:

'An original two- or three dimensional work of art created by the artist (e.g. a painting, drawing or sculpture, as constructed to a reproduction of a painting, drawing or sculpture)'. Original paintings, drawing architectural renderings, and sculpture are included under this heading and designated by the term "art original". Art prints, two-demensional art reproductions, photographs, "picture", three-dimensional art reproductions are designated as model".

The physical description area indicates the materials used by the artist: the medium (acrylic, pastel, oil, etc.) and the base (canvas, paper, wood, etc.). Give the height x width of the work in centimeters, excluding the mounting and frame., e.g.,

1 art original: oil on canvas.

Note area includes the following information:

(i) The nature or form of the work, if that is not obvious from the description.

(ii) The source of title if not found in the chief source.

(iii) Name(s) of persons associated with the work.

(iv) Donor or source; previous owners, if any and the relevant date.

(v) Framed size; other physical details or importance.

CHARTS

A chart is an opaque sheet either flat or relief which presents information via graphs, pictures, tables, diagrams, or outlines. Wall Charts, and flip charts are included under this heading and designated by the term "chart".

Charts may be organized as ephemeral materials, in vertical file. Items of permanent value should be catalogued properly for their effective use. The physical description area includes the number of charts, flip charts, or wall charts. For flip charts, the number of sheets if opaque is given in parentheses. If appropriate, list double sides and also b & w or col. The chart's physical dimensions are given height x width in centimenters.

FILMSTRIPS

Filmstrip is a roll of film containing succession of images designed to be viewed on frame at a time. A short length of such film, sometimes mounted in rigid format is called a filmslip. Both are included under this heading and designated by the term "filmstrip".

The film is usually 35 mm, but may be 70 mm too and if cut apart and mounted could be turned into slides. Interdependent scripts or sound recordings accompanying the filmstrip are considered to be part of the cataloguing unit. Many filmstrips are issued as sets which are clearly meant to be used as set. However when each part of a set stands alone, each filmstrip may be entered separately, unless the sound accompaniment for several filmstrips is on a single disc or cassette.

The item itself is the chief source of information. Preference is given to title frames. If the container provides a collective title use this for entry. Filmstrips are usually entered under title with a name/ title added for the original book.

The physical description area includes the number of filmstrips, filmstrip cartridges or filmstrips and in parentheses the number of frames. The last numbered frame or, if applicable, the last numbered double frame is recorded. The frames in an unnumbered filmstrip are counted and added in square brackets.

In addition to general information as is usually given in note area, special equipment as project, etc., would also be recorded.

Flash Card: A flash card is printed with numbers, letters words, or graphics, and is intended for brief display (manual or mechanical) for drill purposes. The cards come in sets and may be coordinated with sound, in which case they may require a special audiocard players.

A flash card set will usually have a title main entry unless responsibility is clearly attributed one person.

The physical description comprises of number of cards, colour, size in centimeters and accompanying material.

PICTURES

A picture is defined by the AACR2 glossary as; a two-dimensional visual representation visible to the naked eye and generally on an opaque backing.

Pictures, art reproductions, art prints photographs, post cards, posters, reproductions of architectural renderings, and study prints are included under this heading and designated by the term "picture". The GMD [picture] is added immediately after the title proper.

A print is produced directly from a placte made by the artist. The plate, block, or screen prepared by the artist is an art original. It also falls under generic term "picture". Art reproduction are mechanically produced copies of art works usually by a photograpbic process. Posters have the characteristics of art reproductior or other kinds of graphic material. Their function is to send a message to announce or to advertise something. Photographs and postcards are usually incorporated into a vertical file, unless they are acquired as sets which are catalogued as units.

Source of Information

The item itself is the chief source of information. Preference is given to information on the picture rather than on the mount or frame. Other sources include container, and accompanying material.

Main Entry

The general rules for main and added entries as given in AACR2 also apply to all kinds of graphic material. For example, in cataloguing photographic material or other reproduction of art, main entry will be under the name of the original artist. However, if the work of an art is adapted from one medium to another e.g., an engraving is made from an oil painting, etc.) such a work will be entered under the heading (name) for the adapter.

Physical Description Area

The number of art prints, art reproductions, photographs, pictures, postcards, posters, or study prints are recorded here. Other physical detail follows :

Art prints: Give process and col.,.b&w, or sepia;a.

Art reproductions: Give method or reoproduction and b&w or col.

Photographs: If transparent, give "transparency".

Give negative (a positive print is not recorded)

Pictures, postcards, posters, study prints: List b&w or col.

Some example of this area are :

1 art print: lithograph, col.; 99x65 cm.

26 study prints: col.; 46x33 cm.

4 posters: col.; 92x61 cm.

1 art reproduction: photolith, col.: 36x38 cm.

50 photos.: col.; 9x9 cm. + 1 teacher note

Dimensions

Art prints, art reproductions : Height x width is given in centimeters but exclude mound or frame.

Photographs, pictures, postcards, posters, study prints: Give height x width in centimeters.

Note Area

Art prints and art reproductions: If known give information about original such as location and size. Record whether the item mounted or unmounted etc.

Study Prints: A study print is a graphic item that has been prepared specifically for teaching purposes. It is generally pictorial and it may or may not include text. The SMD is "study print". Sets should be catalogued as units while single itmes can go in the vertical file.

Slides: The AACR2 glossary defines a slide as "transparent material on which there is a two-dimensional image, usually held in a mount, and designed for use in a projector or viewer".

Sizes: Most commonly there are two formats i.e., 35mm and 110mm. A single frame slide of 35mm film in a 2" x 2" mount. The 110mm format is almost exclusively for domestic use. In addition, there is a 60 min square slide, which can be mounted and used in major lecturers, but is more widely used as a master for large colour prints. The dimensions of a slide may be increased to 250mm square, suitable for use with an overhead projector.

Kinds: There are speical kinds of slides such as stereographs, paired slides designed to be used with special viewers that create a three-dimensional effect, and sound slides, which allow brief commentary to be recorded on the slide mount, and also require special equipment.

Slides are designed to be used as a unit in sequence, as one would like to use filmstrip. Often they are stored in boxed sets, arranged in trays or magazines ready for projection or in plastic sleeves. When they are handled as a unit, each requires only one set of catalogue cards.

The slide sets are classified using the same system as chosen for other materials with the individual slides in the set identified by their number within the set. Slide sets that have accompanying sound are catalogued much in the same way as filmstrips with sound recordings.

The physical description area does not need to include slide size if it is the standard 2" x 2" or 5 x 5 centimenters. For modern stereographs, the number of reels and frames are given. Number of slides, colour, and accompanying material are listed.

In note area, the type of slide tray in which sets are mounted might be named, as a convenience to the user. If a projector of a special or unusual kind is need, this should also be stated in a note.

TRANSPARENCY

A transparency is a transparent image either mounted or unmounted, designed for use on an overhead projector or viewed over a light box.

Example :

Remodelling the Elementary School Library Indian Library Association, 1991 Produced by the Board of Education of Mukerjee Nagar, Town. 10 Kingsway Camp Committee on Planing School Library Building and Equipment Division Library Administration Division Indian Library Association Copyright 1991 by Indian Library Association Prepared Cooperatively by the Department of Library & Information Services, Engineering and Audio Visual Aids

Other Information :

The filmstrip contains 85 coloured frames, is silent, and the width of film is 90 mm.

Call No. : 231 N91

Acc. No. : 27788

Main Entry

231 N91	Mukerjee Nagar (Kingsway Camp). Board of Education.	
27788	Remodelling the elementary school of Education of Mukerjee Nagar, Kingway Camp; prepared cooperatively by the Department of Library and information Services Engineering, and Audio-Visual Aids. _ [S.1.]:Indian Library Association, 1991. 1 Filmstrip : si. col.; 90 mm. 1. School libraries. I. Title.	

Telematics for Libraries

John Reeves

University of California

Berkley

1998

Other Information :

This is a set of 8 coloured transparancies of 22x25 cm size and is meant for LIS learners. Accession No. 252 Call No.- 621.379

621.379 REE	Reeves, John.	
252	Telematics for Libraries [trnasperency]/ John Reeves.- Berkley: University of Calofornia, 1998. 8 transperencies : col.; 22x25 cm. Audience: LIS learners 1. Telematics I. Title	

Single transparency may be organized as ephemeral materials using vertical file, while longer boxed sets may be catalogued and stored as a unit.

The physical description area includes the number of transparencies and if applicable number of overlays in parentheses. It may give b & w or colour, etc.

Introduction to the card catalogue written by Charles Bergwall Sherwin S. Glassner Eye Gate Glive Bingley c1962

Other Information :

1.Film strip — Call no. 025.3 BER

35 Frames — Acc no. 81717

Colour

35 mm.

Series : library series;no.3

Main Entry

025.3 BER	Bergwall, Charles.	
81717	Introduction to the card catalogue [graphic]/ writen by Charles Bergwal [and] Sherwin. - S.Glassner._ Eye Gate : Clive Bingley, c 1962. 1 film strip (35fr.) : col.; 35 mm._ (Library services; No. 3). 1. Catalogue, card I. Glassener, Sherwin II. Title III. Series.	

Example (slides):—

THE DRUMHELLER BADLANDS OF ALBERTA Bob Jones Tornto Rinehart & Winston Ltd., 1972

Other Information :

12 slides

colour

Accompanying materials (1) 1 chart (2) Teacher's guide

Series: Holt geophotos resource kit; No. 12

ISBN 0-03-925788-6

Call No. 557.1233 J254

Acc no. 81718

Main Entry

557.1233 J254	Jones, Bob.
   81718	The Drumheller Badlands of Alberta [Graphic]/ Bob Jones._ Tornato: Rinehart & Winston Ltd., c 1972. 12 slides : col. + 1 chart + 1 teacher's guid (Holt geophotos resourcs kit; 12). ISBN 0-03-925788-6 1. Geology- Drumheller (Altas) I. Title II. Series. O

Example (Microfilm) :—

The Principles of Psychology

William James

Chicago
Library Resources
1990

Other Information :

Call NO. 150 JE37 Acc No. 81719

Microfiches

Sustrated

size 8x3 cm

Micro reproduction of original published in London: Macmillian, 1981.

23 cm

Main Entry

150 J237	James, William.	
81719		The principle of psychology [microform]/ william James._ Chicago : Library Resources, c1990. 2 microfiches L ill.; 8x 13 cm. Microreproduction of original published: London : Macmillan, 1981. 2v. : ill.; 23 cm. 1. Psychology I. Title

MICROFORMS

A microform may be defined as "a miniature reproduction of printed or other graphic material which cannot be utilized without magnification. Microfillns, microfiches, microopaques, and aperture cards are included under this heading and designated by the term "microform". The medium may be transparent or opaque. Among the transparent formats are microfilm, microfiche, and aperture cards.

Description

Microfilm is a strip of 35mm or 16mm film mounted on a reel or in a cartridge. Microfiche is a sheet of film, usually 3" x 5" or 4" x 6" containing reproductions reduced in ratios up to 90 items. Ultra-microfiche is a film sheet containing reductions 90 times or even greater. Aperture cards are computer cards (9x19cm) which contain key punched data and one or more openings. Opaque microforms includes microcards and microprints, which are cards or sheet containing printed reproduction of photograhically reduced material.

AACR2 treats microforms in a manner similar to facsilniles. In these cases, the cataloguer is to describe the microform item. Data about the original work, i.e., the chracteristics of the original book, periodical, etc., are given in a note.

Sources of Information

(i) Microfilm: The title frame at the beginning of the microfilm which gives data about the microfilm publication of the item, is the chief of cataloguing data for microfilm.

(ii) Aperture Card: The card itself is the chief source of information.

(iii) Microfiche: The title frame at the beginning of the microfiche serves as the chief source of information.

(iv) Microopaque : The title frame at the begining of the microopaque is the chief source. Eye-readable data at the top of the card may also be utilized.

Main Entry

Microformat (any form) does not effect or interfere in the choice of main entry. Generally it is always the same as for the original work. The nature, i.e., the type of format is indicated in the physical description area.

Title and Statement of Responsibility Area

This area is treated according to general rules for descriptive information. However, if the title of the microform is different form that the original, give the microform title in the title and statement of responsibility area.

Edition Area

The edition statement (if any) must be that of the microform and is recorded in the normal edition area. If the item also includes an edition of the original work, it is given in the note area.

Special Data for Cartographic Materials and Serials

If, the work is reproduction of a serial or map, the data about the original item should be given in this area.

Cartographic Material: Record mathematical data for a map reproduced in microformat as instructed to record in case of maps.

Seriais: Record numeric and/or other designation area as instructed for cataloguing of serials.

Publication, Distribution, etc., Area

AACR2 recommends that the information to be given here must pertain to the microform, not the original. Name of the original publisher be given in note area.

Physical Description Area

Give here the number of physical units of a microform item by giving the number of them in arabic numerals and one of the following terms as appropriate:

aperture card microfiche

microfilm

microopaque

Add cartridge, cassette, or reel as appropriate to microfilm. Add cassette if appropriate, to microfiche.

25 aperture cards

2 microfilm reels

1 microfilm cassette

3 microfiches

Add the number of frames of a microfiche or microfiches set if that number can be readily ascertined.

2 microfiches (147 fr.)

1 microfiche (120 fr.)

Dimensions

Give the dimensions of a microform according to the following rules.

Aperture card: Give the height x width of an aperture card mount in centimeters.

20 aperture cards; 9 x 19 cm.

Microfiches: If the dimensions of a microfiches are other than 10.5 x 14.8 cm, give the height x width in centimenters.

1 microfiche; 12 x 17 cm.

2 microfiches; 11 x 15 cm.-12 x 17 cm.

Microfilms : Give the width of a microfilm in millimeters.

1 microfilm reel; 16 mm.

1 microfilm cartridge; 35 mm.

Accompanying Material

Give the details of accompanying material as per AACR2 (1.SE).

1 microfilm reel; 16mm. + manual

1 nucrofilm reel;16mm + iv. (30p. ill; 23cm.)

Other Physical details: Microform is the typical positive. Black-and-white (positive) is not recorded. But negative or colour reproduction is given. Illustrations are also indicated. For example:

1 microfilm reel: negative, ill.

1 microfiche: all col. ill.

1 microfilm cassette: ill.

Series Area

A series statement pertaining to the microform will be given in the series area.

Note Area

Reduction ratio: Most microform readers in common use in media centres can accommodate materials with a 16-30 x reduction. A reduction ratio outside this range should be noted using the following terms:

Low reduction —uo to an inclusive of 15 x

High reduction —31 x to 60 x

Very high reduction —61x to 90 x

Ultra high reduction —above 90x. In this range the specific is also given, e.g.,

Ultra high reduction 150 x Reduction ratio varies

Reader: The name of the intended reader for cassette or cartridge containers is noted.

Any other information according to AACR2 rule for Note area can be recorded here in orderly way.

Example :

Indian labour Yearbook
labour Bureau, Ministry of labour

1978

Delhi
Manager of Publications

Other Information:

Call No. : 331 IND

Acc. No. : 43216

Filmed by IDC Camera Unil Washington D.C., USA

Produced by Inter Documentation Company (IDC), Leiden, The Netherlands. Reduction Ratio 1:19

1 microfiche containing 47 pages (frames), Negative

Main Entry

331 IND	India Ministry of labour. Labour Bureau.
43216	Indian labour yearbook 1978 [microform]/ labour Bureau, Ministry of labour. - leiden, The Netherlands: IDC, 1978. 1 microfiche (47 Fr.): Negative. Low reduction. Filmed by IDC Camera Units, Washington. 1. Working Classes- India -Staistics 2. labour Supply-India I Title II. Inter Documentaton Company, Leiden.

COMPUTER FILES

This includes files that are encoded for manipulation by computer. These files may comprise data or programs. The chief source of information for the computer file is the title screen. If title screen is not there then information may be taken from the internal source such as main menu, program statement, etc. If infonnation is not available from the internal source then it could be taken from:

The physical carrier or its label;
Information issued by the creator, publisher, etc.;
Information printed on the container.

In statement ot responsibility, give names of persons or bodies responsible for the content of the file. The names of sponsors etc. or the persons or bodies contributed in the production of the file are to be given in the, notes section. The material specific details area is used in the case of computer files. This is known as 'File Characteristics Area'. The following terms may be used to designate the file characteristics:

Computer data
Computer program(s)
Computer data and program(s)

If GMD isused then the term, computer may be dropped. Along with the file charactaeristics designation. the number of records, statements, etc. is to be given if the infoımation is readily available. The skeletal structure for Computer Files is given below:

Call No.	Creator of the item
	Title [GMD] = Parallel title: other title infrmationl 1st statement of responsibility; each subsequent statement of responsibility.-Edition statement 1st Statement of responsibility.-statement of file characteristics.-1st place of publication, distribution etc; 1st publisher, distributor etc., date of publication etc. Extent of item: other physical details; dimensions + accompanying material. - (Series). Notes Standard Number and terms of availability Tracing ○

In the physical dcscription thc following specific material designation may be givcn along with number:

Computer cartridge Computer cassette

Computer disk

Computer reel

Other physical details may include details on sound and colour. In the notes area, give details on the nature and scope and systcm requirements. Dimensions for disks. cartridgcs and cassctte are to be given. Dimensions for reels are not given.

The nature and scope of the file, systems requirement and languagc and script are given in the Notes Section.

Example :

The Internet for Absolute Beginers

Designed, written and produced by Mike Lloyd

ASLIB

The Association for

Information Management

Other Information:

Call No. : 621.385 LLO

Acc. No. : 4621

Contains 2 disks (double sided, double density: 3½ in. floppy disks)

System requirement: IBM compatible PC with Windows 3.1, 4MB RAM, 386 or above, 7 MB hard drive space, VGA or above and a Windows compatible mouse or other devices

Main Entry

621.385 LLO	Lloyd, Mike.	
    4621		The Internet for the absolute beginners [computer file]/ designed, written and produced by Mike Lloyd. - Computer program. - London: ASUB, 1995. 2 disks: double sided, double density; 3½ in. System requirements: IBM compatible PC with Windows 3.1, 4MB RAM, 386 or above, 7 MB hard drive space, VGA or above and a Windows compatible mouse or other devices. 1. Internet I. Title II. ASLIB ○

There are some physical characteristics such as number of sides, recording density sectoring. which are kept optional in the rule (Rule 9.5C2). If they are considered important and easily available, these may be included. In this Example, we have used the information double sided, double density accordingly. The dimension is to be given in inches to the next 1/4 inch.

Cataloging Internet Resources

The Internet although heavly use by researchers for almost three decades, was only introduced to the Public in the early 1990s when personal computer prices became very much affordable. It brought to public use an unprecedented wealth of information and became a factor in the way libraries organize and retrieve information. Libraries not only could not ignore its presence but also had to find a way to harness this new force and integrate it into their existing treasures of human knowledge.

Internet Cataloguing Projects

Aided by two grants from the U.S. Department of Education in 1991-1993 and 1994-1996, OCLC explored the possibilities of cataloging Internet resources. During the first project, cataloging guidelines using AACR2 were developed and published online. These guidelines were tested during the second project with a second edition of the guide being published and distributed, both in print and online form. The Internet database was established at OCLC to contain bibliographic records for Internet resources that we recataloged using the newly developed OCLC guidelines. Rule proposals were developed and presented to CC:DA as a result of these projects and proposals for changes to the MARC format were submitted to MARBI.

Problems with internet resources

For librarians, and especially cataloguers, whose main responsibility is to organize information for retrieval and use, the Internet has created both great excitement and grave concerns. The first concern was originated from the most important characteristic of the Internet: its dizzying growth speed. During the one-year period of the first OCLC Internet Project, from October 1991 to September 1992, the network traffic in bytes grew from

1.88 to 3.32 trillions. This pace not only has not slowed down but, on the contrary, has increased throughout most of the decade. The other concern was related to the characteristics of the materials available from the Internet, which were "poorly organized, and of variable quality and stability". Many papers published on the topic of cataloging Internet resources during this period had some discussion about the difficulties encountered with Internet resources. These difficulties included: a wide variety of types of materials to select; the materials are prone to changes (URLs, even file format, contents, etc.) with a huge potential workload for catalogue maintenance; difficulties in viewing of materials needed to do subject analysis; the cataloguing work will be extremely time-consuming since no derived records are available and that means potential backlogs will be created .

Should internet resources be cataloged?

It was quite obvious that the Internet needed organization. In fact, there have been various attempts to do that. However, all retrieval tools available now on the Internet have very limited capabilities, mostly because they rely on the directories and filenames assigned to the Internet electronic files, which contain incomplete, inconsistent and nonstandard data. Cataloguing is the invisible activity of libraries aimed at achieving order for effective information retrieval and use. Therefore, the first debate related to the Internet among librarians and other information professionals was focused on the viability of cataloging Internet resources. Some librarians considered Internet materials as too much unstable to be effectively catalogued. Others wondered if increasingly powerful search and browsing tools, automated indexing tools, and 'intelligent agents' would obviate the need for catalogues. Still other librarians came to the conclusion that, in spite of the many difficulties encountered in dealing with them, Internet resources should be catalogued like other types of traditional resources, believing that "The whole research (of Internet resources) process will be far more precise and efficient" in such a catalogue . By the later 1990s, cataloguers went even further in their advocating for cataloguing of Internet resources, believing that the "users more and more expect to have access to these resources, so the option of leaving them undescribed and thus excluding them from the catalogue is becoming indefensible". Some authors have even tried to look at Cutter's cataloging principles from the perspectives of Internet resources and found that these principles were still valid but concluded that catalogers needed new methods to achieve them. Another point in the debate was whether current cataloguing tools, such as USMARC format and AACR2R could be used to catalogue Internet resources. This debate ended with the findings of the OCLC Research Project in 1991-92. This landmark research project had two primary objectives: (1) to investigate the nature of electronic textual information available on the Internet; (2) to investigate the feasibility of creating MARC records for these objects using US- MARC format and AACR2R. The main conclusions drawn from the project findings were that, with a few modifications, US MARC computer files format and AACR2R Chapter 9 could be used to catalogue Internet resources. One of the modifications recommended was the creation of a new field in USMARC format for the electronic location and access of the Internet resources. This recommendation was subsequently approved and implemented with the creation of Field 856, Electronic Location and Access in the USMARC format by MARBI in 1994.

What Internet Resources should be Catalogued

Internet resources came in different formats, by different modes of access and of different contents/presentations. These could be a WWW site, or a Gopher site or an FTP site. They could be census data, or survey data, or bibliographic data. They could be library catalogues or databases or electronic journals. They could be news groups, discussion groups, or e-mail. Some authors tried to group them in broad categories as discrete files, databases and servers. The question is: What should be catalogued? Although individual librarians representing their own institutions might have different choices of types of Internet resources to catalogue, all agreed that no attempt should be made to catalogue the whole of the Internet, which, in fact, would ever be a "Mission Impossible." Most librarians. especially those working in an academic environment, agree that this is a collection development issue that requires a refinement of selection policy to include Internet resources. By and large, collection librarians believe that Internet resources should be selected based on the same criteria used for other traditional materials, namely valuable for the learning/teaching/research activities. For some academic libraries, "an interim decision was made to extend this policy beyond paid items to free Internet resources. With selection policy refined in this manner, the next question would be what specific types of Internet resources should be selected for cataloguing. Such resources should "include, but are not limited to: online journals and books; maps; graphical materials; and multimedia materials which may contain any of these objects". For Web sites, Web pages, those of corporate nature, thus more stable and reliable, might be more attractive for cataloguing purposes than those of personal nature. Data sets and Web sites providing useful statistical, census, and government information should also be considered as good candidates for cataloguing, especially for the main reason that many government agencies are now putting out their publications only electronically. So in short, it can be said that Internet resources should be selected based on their contents, merit, and warrant.

How should Internet Resources be Catalogued?

By the mid-1990s, for most librarians, the question was no longer "Should Internet resources be catalogued?" but rather "How should Internet resources be catalogued?" Again, part of the answer to this question came from another OCLC Internet research project. This second OCLC project, "Building a Catalogue of Internet Resources," 1994-96, involved, by the end of the project, 231 cataloguers representing almost all types of libraries, who volunteered to catalogue approximately 4,700 Internet resources. A manual, titled Cataloging Internet Resources: A Manual and Practical Guide, was developed by Nancy B. Olson to aid cataloguers participating in this project. The result of the project was an online catalog called InterCat Catalog, which has been steadily growing, and currently has more than 1.00,000 bibliographic records.

Cataloguing of electronic resources like computer disks, CD-ROMs, etc. is not something new. Cataloguers have been doing it for almost two decades. using AACR2 Chapter 9, but they were dealing with static objects. With the Internet resources available by remote access, cataloguers are dealing with very unstable materials.

Cataloguing of Internet resources, therefore, is mainly different in two areas: describing their changing characteristics and providing access information. In the first area, the most fundamental problem is a serious lack of cataloguing information necessary for description. Cataloguers cannot find needed cataloguing data from accompanying printed materials or containers, which are very much unlikely. The chief source of information for Internet resources will be the title screen or similar display from the terminal, which sometimes requires to be decompressed or processed in some manner. But even the title screen can change with time and with viewing means. Publication data (place, publisher, and date) and edition data are rarely provided. Physical description area should be omitted since there is no physical items availables. Designation of file characteristics (AACR2 Rule 9.3B and USMARC Field 256) is limited by AACR2 to just a few choices, namely Computer data, Computer program(s), and the combined Computer data and program(s) since the proposed expansion of the list of descriptors to include terms such as "Electronic journal," "Electronic document," "Bibliographic database" by OCLC after the first Internet project was deferred by MARBI. Because of all these difficulties, notes may be used more in bibliographic records for Internet resources than in those for conventional materials. In many cases, notes may need to be created for: source of title proper (MARC 500), variations in title (MARC 500), edition and history of file (MARC 500, 522, 567), publication/distribution (MARC 500), file characteristics (MARC 500, 516, 565), other formats available (MARC 530, 535).

In the second area, because of the remoteness of Internet resources, notes need to be created for: system requirements (MARC 538) and mode of access (MARC 538). Finally, and most important, at least one MARC 856 for electronic location and access should be provided. This field contains data for the Uniform Resource Locator (URL) for remote access and other kinds of data and can be repeated. The Library of Congress's Network Development and MARC Standards Office has issued Guidelines for the Use of Field 856. As URLs can change easily and frequently and this can create a huge catalogue maintenance problem, cataloguers need some working solutions. OCLC has developed a resolving system called

Persistent URLs or PURLs. PURLs are also URLs but they do not change. They are associated with URLs that can be changed as needed but this system, however, only works for URLs from registered users.

By 1997, many academic libraries have embarked on some sort of cataloguing Internet Resources Projects and we witnessed the publication of several project reports on the topic, a number of them dealing with cataloguing electronic journals. By now, some copy cataloguing for Internet resources has been made possible by source records available through the rapidly growing OCLC's Internet Catalogue.

In the meantime in 1994, the remoteness library community, through IFLA International Federation of Library Associations and Institutions), started reviewIng the Internal Standard Bibliographic Description for Computer Files (ISBD(CF)), which was first published in 1990. The whole process took three years to complete and the new International Standard Bibllographic Descnption for Electronic Resources (ISBD(ER)) was publishd in August 1997. Many important changes were incorporated into the new standard: Electronic Resource was replacing Computer Eile-as General Material Designation (GMD), the section on Type of Resource was completely reworked to improve its usefulness, with a total of 30 terms representing 3 levels of specificity, just to mention a few. The functionality of the new elements of the ISBD(ER) within the framework of the Functional Requirements for Bibliographic Records (FRBR) was examind and found adequate. The Joint Steering Committee for Revision of AACR (JSC) has decided to bring AACR2 into harmony with the ISBD(ER).

For cataloguing purposes, electronic resources may be treated in one of two ways depending on whether access is direct (local) or remote (networked). Direct access is understood to mean that a physical carrier can be described. Such a carrier (e.g., disc/disk , casselte, cartridge) must be inserted into a computerized device or into a peripheral attached to a compulerized device. Remote access is understood to mean that no physical carrier can be handled. Remote access can only be provided by use of an input-output device either connected to a compuler system or by use of resources stored in a hard disk or other storage device.

Cataloguing of Internet resources can be done by using a set of tools called ROADS, which stands for Resource Organization And Discorvery in subject-based services. It is a set of software tools designed to help to create information gateways on the Internet. At its simples, an information gateway can be just a simple list of links maintained by hand. The information gateway approach allows a subject based list of linds to be created and maintaine. ROADS allows, Internet resources to be fully described, allowing the end user to judge their relevenacy before trying to access them and it is properly organized. The organization and description of resources adds value to an information gateway. Roads allows to create a database of resource description. This is done via World Wide Web forms that have to be filled-in. This form is a data entry form containing aa number of fields, such as title field, keyword field, etc. Roads contains tools which will automatically create classified listing of the resources and a search machanism.

Monograph, Serial, or something eise?

The first decision that must be made when cataloguing an electronic resource is whether the item is a monograph or a serial-or a monographic set-or something like a loose-leaf publication. It is easy enough to spot a monograph-something published on a certain date and it is done. But monographs can be published in multiple volumes, over many years-but the set is designed to be complete at some print. These monographic sets have a rangc of dates. Each volume may have its own title and be catalogued separately, or all cataloged together on one bibliographic record, with or without a content note. Serials, on the other hand, continue when begun, there is no end planned. While the definition is being changed, in AACR2-there must be a chronological and/or numeric designation on an issue for it to be considered, and catalogued, as a serial. These are now being called "continuing resources" in the rule revision process for AACR2 chapter 12. Then there are those electronic resources that change over time. This includes web sites. home pages, dynamic databases (e.g.., OCLC online union catalogue), and online services (e.g., Autocat). They are updated or revised irregularly or frequently or minute by minute, but none of these changes results in a title page with a chronological and/or numeric designation. There may be a note: "Last updated Dec. 17, 2002" or "Intended to be updated regularly" with no indication that any updates actually occurred. No matter how much these may "feel" like serials, they are not serials by the current rules, so are to be catalogued much like the monographic sets.

So it is to first, decide what remote access electronic resource are for cataloguing. Is it a web site or something contained within a web site? Is it a serial, or a document from one issue of a serial? Is it a named column that appears regularly within a serial? Once you decided what you are cataloging, ignore all surrounding information unless or until needed for a note explaining where the document (or whatever) appears.

Is the item being catalogued a monograph, a serial, or something that is continuing but not a true serial? Once you make this decision be consistent in the treatment of the date in the 260, and notes about the item.

Remember a true serial carries a designation of volume and/or number and/or a chronological designation in a prominent position if no such designation, it may be a continuing publication, but it is not a serial. If the home page or list of items available on the web site contains something like "What's new" that is an indication of a continuing publication, as it is being updated with news regularly or irregularly. Again, if no numeric and/or chronological designation is present, it cannot be catalogued as a serial.

Sources of Informatsion

There is some change in the rule about chief source of information, which is quoted in part as follo vs:

9.B1. Chief source of information. The chief source of information for electronic resources is the resource itself. Take the information from formally presented evidence (e.g., title screen(s), main menus, program statements, initial display(s) of information, home page(s), the file header(s) including "Subject:" lines, encoded metadata (e.g., TEI headers, HTML/XML meta tags), and the physical carrier or its labels), including information that has been uncompressed, printed out, or otherwise processed for use. If the information in these sources varies in degree of fullness, prefer the source that provides the most complete information.

The rest of the rule is essentially unchanged.

Area 1

Title and Statement of Responsibility Area (MARC 245)

The major rule change made to this area is the change of the GMD to "electronic resource." There is a new provision to use the GMD "multimedia" or "kit," if the electronic resource "contains parts belonging to materials falling into two or more categories, and none of these is the predominant component."

For most remote access electronic resources, choosing the title proper is no more difficult than for any audiovisual or other special material. When the item has something that looks like a title page, the choices to be made for area are obvious. For most documents or home pages or web sites or newsletters or journals there is an obvious title. There may not be any other title information. There may not be a statement responsibility. If so, don't try to construct one; use what is in the chief source. Often titles are found in varying forms throughout a document sometimes with fewer words, other times with abbreviations. When there is conflicting information, or variation in title, choose the part of the item that gives the fullest information, and take the title and statement of responsibility information from that part. Give other forms of the title in 246 fields, if useful for retrieval.

Field 245 is to be an exact transcription of information found on the item.

> 245 Cataloging electronic resources $h [electronic resource] : $b OCLC-MARC coding guidelines I $c by Jay Weitz.

Remember we must always make a note stating where the title was found.

> 500 Title from caption of home page.

Serial cataloguing tends to be briefer than other cataloging, partly because other title information, responsibility, publisher, etc., tends to change over time. One may choose to include only title proper in area 1, and, if considered important, put other information in notes for serials.

Varying Form of Title (MARC 246)

Varying forms of the title are given in field 246 if they represent the entire work, in field 740 if they represent only a part of the work. Field 246 may be used to correct a spelling error in a 245 title, or to spell out numbers, to use the word "and" instead of the ampersand symbol, or to create a title from some part of the 245 that a user might remember as the title. Field 246 may also be used for a parallel title, caption title, or other form of the title found on the item. There are many indicators available for use with field 246, and MARC 21 bibliographic format or the OCLC-MARC format document can be referred for these. There is no period used at the end of field 246.

246 00 OCLC-MARC coding guidelines

AREA 2

Edition Area (MARC 250)

Rule changes to this area applicable to remote electronic resources include adding an example for "Interactive version" and adding the following:

9.2B8. If a remote access electronic resource is frequently updated, omit the edition statement and give the information in a note (see 9.7B7).

If the file contains any word(s) or phrase(s) indicating the same information was or is available in a different form, treat that word or phrase as an edition statement and transcribe it exactly as found.

250 English edition.

250 Electronic version.

AREA 3

Type and Extent of Resource Area (MARC 256)

This area will be revised together with area 5 in the final phase of revising chapter 9 of AACR2. Options being discussed range from expanding the list of terms to omitting the area altogether: watch for decisions.

AACR2 states the type of file is given "when the information is readily available." The revised chapter has dropped this statement. The only terms listed in the new chapter are:

Electronic data

Electronic program(s)

Electronic data and program(s)

CONSER has chosen not to use this area. CONSER cataloguers are required to use area 516 for similar information.

This area is required for remote access materials-if no physical description area is used, this area is to be used.

The list of terms in ISBD(ER) was modified for use in OCLC's Internet cataloguing guidelines-these terms may be used when cataloguing in OCLC until such time as final decisions are made to the area by JSC. The list below is from the Internet guidelines with the introductory word "computer" changed to the word "electronic."

- Electronic data
  - Electronic numeric data
    - Electronic census data
    - Electronic survey data
  - Electronic text data
    - Electronic bibliographic database
  - Electronic journal(s)
    - Electronic newsletter(s)
    - Electronic document(s)
    - Elcctronic image data
    - Electronic representational data
      - Elcctronic map(s) data
    - Electronic sound data
    - Electronic font data
  - Electronic program(s)
    - Electronic utility program(s)
      - Electronic application program(s)
      - Electronic CAD program(s)

Electronic database program(s)

Electronic spreadsheet program(s)

Electronic word processor program(s)

Electronic desktop publishing program(s)

Electronic game(s)

Elcctronic system program(s)

Electronic operating system program(s)

Electronic programming language(s)

Electronic retrieval program(s)

Electronic data and program(s)

Electronic interactive multimedia

Electronic online servicc(s)

AREA 3 (SERIALS)

Numeric and/ or Alphabetic, Chronological, or other Designation Area for serials (MARC 362)

This area is used for serial cataloguing when cataloging from the first issue. It is used in addition to the type and extent of resource area and is given following that area, according to rule 0.25 in the recent changes to chapter 9.

362 0 Vol. 1, issue 1 (Aug. 1999)-

If one is cataloguing from an issue other than the first, and if one knows when the serial began, that information is given in field 515, following the rule for note 12.7B8.

AREA 4

Publication, Distribution, etc. Area (MARC 260)

The new rules include the following instruction:

9.4B2. Consider all remote access electronic resources published.

One must always have a place of publication and the name of a publisher in area 4.

e.g. 260 [Washington, DC] : $b Library of Congress,

If the cataloger cannot find any indication as to who published or distributed a remote access electronic resource, one might questions whether the item is worth cataloguing. Sometimes the cataloguer finds reason to question the value of an item while searching for cataloging Information.

If, however, an item must be catalogued, but there is no place or name of publisher, follow directions in AACR2 1.4:

e.g. 260 [S.l. : $b s.n.],

Date of Publication, Distribution, Etc.

For all remote access electronic resources, a note must be used giving the date the item being catalogued was viewed. See 9.7B22.

e.g. 500 Description based on contents viewed Dec. 22, 2000.

Another new rule is:

9.4F4. If there is no publication, distribution, etc., date which applies to the item as a whole, and the item has multiple copyright dates which apply to various aspects of thc production (e.g., programming, sound production, graphics, documentation), transcribe only the latest copyright date.

Optionally, transcribe the other dates in a note (see 9.7B7) or in a contents note (see 9.7B18).

However, for a monograph, if the dates are given, but not as copyright dates, or as a mixture of copyright dates and publication or distribution dates, or as dates of updating, take the latest date as evidence of publication, distribution, etc., and use it in area 4 as an assumed date, in brackets.

e.g. 260 Dublin, Ohio: $b OCLC, $c (1999).

For a monographic set, or a continuing publication that is not a serial, an open date or a range of dates are given in area 4.

e.g. 260 Mankato, Minn. : $b Minnesota State University, $c 1997-

260 Washington, DC : $b Library of Congress, $c 1992-1998.

When cataloguing a serial, no date is given in area 4 unless cataloguing from the first issue. If one knows when the serial began, that information is given in field 515.

AREA 5

Physical Description Area (MARC 300)

At present, the physical description area is not used for remote access files. This may change.

AREA 6

Series Area (MARC 4XX)

There is nothing unique about the series area when cataloguing electronic resources.

e.g. 490 0 Project Gutenberg etext

AREA 7

Note Area (MARC 5XX)

There are about 30 possible notes, including some from the serials chapter and one from a recent LCRI. Notes may be combined if desired. Some additional examples of notes have been added in the revision to Chapter 9.

9.1B1. Nature and scope, system requirements, and mode of access

9.1B1a. Nature and scope (MARC 500 or 516)

This note is used to give brief information on the nature or scope of the resource unless this is obvious from the rest of the description. If fuller information is needed about the resource, use the summary note instead of this note.

This note is coded in MARC field 500 in all other chapters of M CR2, but CONSER users are directed to use field 516 for nature and scope; they must always use a field 516.

e.g. 500 Online auction site.

516 Electronic document.

9.1B1b. System requirements (MARC 538)

In the new chapter, an additional characteristic is added at the end of the list present in the 1998 AACR2: the type of any required or recommended hardware modifications.

Cataloguers are directed to: "Make a note on the system rquirements of the resource if the information is readily available.

Begin the note with *System requirements*. Give the following characteristics in the order in which they are listed below. Precede each characteristic, other than the first, by a semicolon. Many of these characteristics may be unknown for remote access electronic resources.

— the make and model of the computer(s) on which the resource is designed to run

— the amount of memory required

— the name of the operating system

— the software requirements including the programming language

— the kind and characteristics of any required or recommended peripherals

— the type of any required or recommended hardware modifications

e.g. 538 System requirements: Adobe Acrobat Reader.

9.7B1c. Mode of access (MARC 538)

The introductory phrase "Mode of access:" is now required.

e.g. 538 Mode of access: World wide web.

538 Mode of access: Internet.

12.7B1. Frequency for serials (MARC 310)

The frequency of publication of a serial is given in this note.

e.g. 310 Weekly.

310 Frequently updated.

9.7B2. Language and script (MARC 546)

Language and/or script of the spoken or written content is given in this note unless it is apparent from the rest of the description.

e.g. 546 Available in English and Spanish.

Programming language, if known, is given in the system requirements note.

9.7B3. Source of title proper (MARC 500)

This note is required.

e.g. 500 Title from title screen.

500 Title supplied by cataloguer.

9.7B4. Variations in title (MARC 500, 246)

Other titles such as the title in an HTML header, or a file name or data set name, may be given, as may any variation of the title proper that is found on the item. These will normally be given in field 246.

e.g. 246 1 $i Title in HTML header; $a American Birding Association home page

9.7B5. Parallel titles and other title information (MARC 500, 246)

Parallel titles in another language are to be given in field 246 if a separate added entry is wanted for that title; the parallel titles will, of course, already be recorded in subfield of field 245.

e.g. 246 13 Legende etrealite : les heros historiques et legendaires du Canada

Other title information not recorded in the title and statement of responsibility area, but considered important, may also be given here.

e.g. 500 Some sections carry subtitle: His life and times.

9.7B6. Statements of responsibility (MARC 500, 550, 536)

Names of people and/or corporate bodies not already named in area I, but considered to be important, may be included here.

e.g. 500 Copyright by Nancy B. Olson.

Information about the issuing body may be recorded in field 550.

e.g. 550 Issued by ALA Reference and Adult Services Division, Machine-Assisted Reference Section, Direct Patron Access to Computer-Based Reference Systems Committee.

Funding information may be recorded in field 536.

e.g. 536 Funded in part by the U.S. Department of Education, Office of Library Programs, under the College Library Technology and Cooperation Grants Program.

9.7B7. Edition and History (MARC 500, 522, 567)

Notes about the edition and/or the history of the item are given here in field 500.

e.g. 500 Originally available in print in 1993.

Geographic coverage of the item is part of the history of the file and may be given in field 522. A print constant is designed to display the introductory phrase: "Geographic coverage:".

e.g. 522 Country-level data from four Northwestern states (Idaho, Montana, Oregon, Washington).

Methodology used in preparation of the file may be recorded in field 567.

e.g. 567 Total civilian noninstitutional population of the United States.

12.7B7. Relations with other serials (MARC 580, etc.)

Notes can be generated from MARC fields 765, 767, 770, 775, 776, 777, 780, 785, and 787 about the relationship of the item being catalogued to other items. These linking entries may have print constants. These linking entries do not take the place of added entry fields, and do not generate added entries.

If a free-text note is needed about the relationship of the item being catalogued to other serials, use field 580.

9.7B8. Type and extent of resource (MARC 500, 565)

Information about the type and extent of the resource is the information considered to be important, and is not found elsewhere in the description. This note will probably change as areas 3 and 5 are changed.

e.g. 500 File in PostScript format.

Number of cases or variables making up the files may be recorded in ield 565.

e.g. 565 552 cases.

12.7B8. Numbering and chronological designation for serials (MARC 515)

Complex, irregular, or peculiar designations in serial numbering are given in field 515.

e.g. 515 Numbering irregular.

515 Additional issues on special topics are occasionally available.

9.7B9. Publication, distribution, etc. (MARC 500)

Information about publication, distribution, etc., not included in area 4 of the bibliographic record being created, but considered to be important, may be recorded here.

e.g. 500 Available commercially from: Oxford Text Archive, A-l300-A.

A date of release or transmittal may be recorded here.

500 "December 18, 2000."

9.7B10. Physical description (MARC 500)

For electronic resources available only by remote access, give details about color, sound, etc., here unless included in the summary. If the rules change to include area 5 for remote access electronic resources, this note will also change.

e.g. 500 Displays in color; with stereo sound.

500 Document formatted into 27 pages.

9.7B11. Accompanying material (MARC 500, 556)

Documentation may be in a separate remote access file, or available in print from the publisher or originator of the electronic resource. Information about such material is given here.

e.g. 500 Teacher's guide available in print from the publisher.

Documentation such as code books is given in field 556.

e.g. 556 Printed documentation available directly from the originator of the file.

9.7B12. Series (MARC 500)

Information about series not already included in the series area may be given here.

e.g. 500 Originally issued in series: American national election study series.

9.7B13. Dissertations (MARC 502)

The standard dissertation note is given as appropriate.

e.g. 502 Thesis (M.S.)—Minnesota State University,

Mankato. 2000.

9.7B14. Audience (MARC 521)

If the intellectual level of a resource, or its intended audience, is stated on the item, note it here.

e.g. 521 For ages 8 and up.

1.7B15. References to published descriptions (MARC 510, 524, 581)

A note indicating where a serial item has been indexed is given in field 510.

e.g. 510 0 Applied science and technology index.

The preferred citation of the materials being catalogued may be included in field 524.

e.g. 524 Jeannings M. Kent and Richard G. Niemi.

Youth-parent socialization panel study, 1965-1973. Ann Arbor, Mich: Inter-university Consortium for political and social Research, 1981.

Information about a publication based on the use, study, or analysis of the resource being catalogued is included in field 581.

e.g. 581 8 The adjusted 1990 numbers are used as a basis for title annual county population estimates published in Current Population Reports Series P-25 and P-26.

9.7B16. Other formats (MARC 530, 535)

Give details of other formats in which the content of the resource has been issued.

e.g. 530 Also available on CD-ROM.

The location of the original or duplicates may be recorded in field 535.

e.g. 535 Original document in archives of the Minnesota Historical Society.

9.7B17. Summary (MARC 520)

A brief objective summary may be given in field 520, unless enough information for the user is available elsewhere in the bibliographic record. Information normally given in other notes may be included here as part of the summary.

e.g. 520 Eight versions of a video game for 1-2 players. To survive, players use laser cannons to destroy flying demons.

9.7B18. Contents (MARC 505, 500, 504)

A formal contents note is given in field 505.

e.g. 505 0 1. Idaho — 2. Montana — 3. Oregon — 4. Washington.

This formal note may be enhanced with subfield codes for retrieval.

e.g. 505 00 $g 1. $t Idaho —$g 2. $t Montana —$g 3. $t Oregon —$g 4. $t Washington.

An informal contents note is given in field 500.

e.g. 500 Includes selected articles from print version; lacks illustrations.

A bibliography note is a type of contents note, given in field 504.

e.g. 504 Includes bibliographic references.

9.7B19. Numbers (MARC 500)

Numbers that may be important and are not recorded elsewhere may be included in this note.

e.g. 500 XY-2002

500 "RFCl251."

9.7B20. Copy being described, library's holdings, and restrictions on use (MARC 590, 506, 583)

Information about the copy being described or local holdings would be a local note so would go in field 590.

e.g. 590 Only available to patrons on first three terminals in Reference Area.

590 Not archived; only latest issue online.

Information about general restrictions on use is given in field 506.

e.g. 506 Restricted to users at subscribing institutions.

Notes about processing and reference actions may be recorded in field 583.

e.g. 583 Destroy $c September 1.

9.7B21. "With" notes (MARC 501)

If more than one work is contained in an online electronic resource, and separate bibliographic records are made for each, a "With'" note is made to connect these records. In note field 501, list the works other than those listed in field 245.

e.g. 501 With: Uncle Sam's jigsaw —U.S. Constitution tutor —Scramble.

9.7B22. Item described (MARC 500)

This note is added in the new rules with the directions that, for remote access resources, always give the date on which the resource was viewed for description.

e.g 500 Description based on contents viewed Dec. 17, 2002.

1.7B22. Combined notes relating to the original (MARC 534)

This note is used to describe the original item represented by the electronic resource being cataloged.

e.g. 534 $p Electronic text of: $a Sophocles. $t The Oedipus trilogy by Sophocles; English translation by F. Storr. $c Cambridge, Mass. : Harvard University Press, 1912. $f (Loeb Library) .

1.7B22. (LCRI) Combined notes relating to their production (MARC 533)

The Library of Congress rule interpretation gives the LC policy for describing an electronic reproduction of a book on the bibliographic record for the original. All the details about the electronic version are given in one note in field 533.

533 Electronic reproduction. $b Portland, OR. : $c PNW Publications, $d 1998. $n Mode of access: World Wide Web. $n System requirements: Adobe Acrobat reader.

MAIN AND ADDED ENTRIES

There are no special rules for choice or form of main and added entries for remote access electronic resources. These entries are chosen just as for any other type of material being catalogued.

One must be careful to check the online authority file for the form of a personal or corporate name before using it in a bibliographic record.

Subject Access

There are no special guidelines for choosing subject headings, genre headings, or classification numbers for remote access electronic resources. There has been some discussion in the literature and on AUTOCAT, the electronic listfCK cataloguers, about the need for giving classification numbers to materials not physically on shelves, but many agree that there is enough benefit for collection development to be able to group remote access works with other works available to students in a particular discipline to be worth the effort. Attaching holdings to such bibliographic records in OCLC may cause problems in a local system as with any other process. One must know how it does or doesn't affect the local system before beginning a project.

Subject headings and genre headings should be used just as for other items in a library's collections.

MARC 21 CODING AND TAGGING

Field 856, Electronic Location and Access

Field 856 was developed during the first OCLC Internet cataloguing project as a field to hold all information needed for access to the computer file being catalogued. It was hoped that this could eventually be a "button" that the user would push when viewing a bibliographic record that would take the viewer directly to the item being catalogued.

Every remote access electronic resource must have an 856 field in the bibliographic record containing the electronic address, usually the URL, for the item being cataloged. The 856 field is repeatable.

A typical URL appears in a bibliographic record as

856 40 $u http://lcweb.loc.qov/marc/856quide.html

Fields 006, 007, 008

A document from Network Development MARC Standards Office at the Library of Congress, Relationship of Fields 006, 007, and 008, explains that field was developed during the format integration process to solve the problem of field 008 not being repeatable. Field 007 had long been used for special materials to hold codes for characteristics not included in field 008. Field 006 was to include characteristics that could not be included in a single field 008. For example, a serial videorecording with field 008 coded for a videorecording has no provisions for serial characteristics. Those serial characteristics could be recorded in field in the same bibliographic record, and would become retrievable by local systems programmed to index the 006.

What Workform to Use?

The discussion was going on in some cataloguing communities about content versus physical format. Map people felt the "mapness" of their items took priority over the physical form; a map coded as an electronic resource was still a map and should be catalogued on a map workform, with its computer characteristics expressed elsewhere. And those handling computer journals at the Library of Congress had cataloged them on book/serial workforms, because their check in procedures and other internal processing steps could not handle bibliographic records on computer workforms. These problems and others led to a new solution-that of cataloging what are now electronic resources on workforms representing the content of the item rather than the physical form, and adding whatever fields 006 and 007 may be necessary to code all the physical characteristics necessary for retrieval under the possible searches.

A series of documents were produced for our use in deciding which workform to use for any given bibliographic record. The two current guidelines are:

Cataloging Electronic Resources: OCLC-MARC Coding Guidelines by Jay Weitz. Revised 2000 May 15 *www.oclc.org/oclc/cataloging/ type.htm*

Guidelilres for Coding Electronic Resources in Leader/O6. Network Development and MARC Standards Office, Library of Congress. July 1, 1999. *lcweb.loc.gov/marc/ldr06guide.html*

These documents explain that the descriptive cataloging of the materials covered has 'not changed; only the workform chosen for the bibliographic record is changed. Fields 006 and 007 are required in all cases. The GMD "electronic resource" is to be used for all these materials.

A new code "s" has been added to the list for "Form of Item" in byte 23 of field 008 (a fixed field in OCLC); and in field 006 as appropriate. Code "s" (Electronic) is defined as:

Item intended for manipulation by a computer. May reside in a carrier accessed either directly or remotely. May require use of peripheral devices attached to the computer. Do NOT use for items that do not require the use of a computer.

When cataloguing an electronic resource that is a monographic document of any type, use the workform for books with field 006 for the computer characteristics and field 007 for additional physical characteristics.

When cataloguing an electronic resource that is a serial document (journal, newsletter, etc.) that fits the current definition of serial by including a numeric and/or chronological designation, the serials useworkform is used, again with field 006 for the computer characteristics, and field 007 for additional physical characteristics.

The computer file workform is only to be used for computer software (including programs, games, fonts), numeric data, online systems or services, and computer-oriented multimedia. Fields 006 and 007 are added as appropriate.

Map items go on the map workform, music items on the music workform (scores or sound recordings as appropriate), visual materials go on the visual materials workform. In all cases fields 006 and 007 are added as appropriate.

Single Record or Separate Record?

Another practice under discussion is whether to catalogue an electronic manifestation of a title on a separate bibliographic record or on the bibliographic record for the print version. This is also discussed in the OCLC-MARC guidelines, with directions for both methods and discussion of other considerations. The CONSER guidelines permit the single record approach. OCLC prefers separate records, but permits single records. OCLC cautions users to check with your local system vendor and any network partners before choosing to use one approach or the other.

Monograph or Serial?

The OCLC-MARC guidelines also address the decision about coding an electronic resource as a monograph or as a serial. It is possible that the print form of a title will be catalogued as a serial, while the eletronic version may be catalogued as a monograph. The guidelines list the following types of material as currently being excluded from cataloguing as serials:

Databases (including directories, A&I services, etc.),

Electronic discussion groups (e.g., SERIALIST),

Electronic discussion group digests (e.g., AUTOCAT digest),

Gopher servers (e.g., LC-MARVEL),

Online public access catalogs (e.g., OCLC, RLIN),

Online services (e.g., America Online),

Web sites (e.g., the CONSER home page).

It is important that these and other decisions about creating bibliographic records for remote access electronic resources will change as the rules change. (See Appendix, Examples 1-3.)

Eletronic Book

There has been a great deal of interest in the cataloguing of electronic books, or e-books. The Library of Congress issued a rule interpretation for rule 1.11 A in Cataloging Service Bulletin no. 89 (summer 2000). This LCRI covers facsimiles, photocopies, and other reproductions, including electronic reproductions. It is reproduced below.

"I.IIA. Facsimiles, Photocopies, and Other Reproductions.

A reproduction is a manifestation that replicates an item (or a group of items) or another manifestation (e.g.. a reprint with no changes) that is intended to function as a substitute. The reproduction may be in a different physical form from the original. Reprodction is generally a mechanical rather than an intellectual process. The physical characteristics of the reproduction such as color, image resolution, or sound fidelity are influenced by the particular process used to create it, and therefore may differ from those of the original. Reproductions are usually made for such reasons as the original's limited availability, remote location, poor condition, high cost, or restricted utility. Cataloguer judgment will be required to distinguish electronic reproductions from electronic republications or simultaneous publication in analong and digital form (only reproductions are covered by the LCRI). For example, an electronic reproduction produced using scanning techniques that results in a facsimile reproduction may be easily identified as a reproduction. Other non facsimile electronic reproductions may also be considered under this LCRI when they purport to be a reproduction of the original and can serve as a surrogate for the original. Other cataloguing agencies choosing to follow this LCRI may need to develop their own criteria for distinguishing reproductions from manifestation judged not to be reproductions. In cases of doubt, or in cases where there is inadquate information about the original on which to base a description, do not consider the electronic manifestation to be a reproduction.

Non- Microform Reproductions

LC Practice : Follow these guidelines for reproductions of previously existing materials that are made for preservation purposes in formats other than microforms; non-microform dissertations and other reproductions produced "on demand"; and, electronic reproductions.

These guidelines identify the data elements to be used in the record for the reproduction, separate from the record for the original. For some electronic reproductions, however, LC may delineate details of the reproduction on the record for the original manifestation rather than create a separate record for the reproduction.

1. Transcribe the bibliographic data appropriate to the original work being reproduced in the following areas:

   title and statement of responsibility

   edition

   material (or type of publication) specific details publication, distribution, etc.

   physical description

   series

2. If appropriate, give in the title and statement of responsibility area the general material designation that is applicable to the format of the reproduction (cf- LCRI 1.1 C)
3. Give in a single note (533 field) all other details relating to the reproduction and its publication/availability. Include in the note the following bibliographic data in the order listed:

format of the reproduction

— dates of publication and/or sequential designation of issues reproduced (for serials)

— place and name of the agency responsible for the reproduction

Consider the "agency responsible for the reproduction" to be the agency that selected the material to be reproduced, arranged tor reproducing the material, exercised control over production formats, has overall responsibility for .. quality, etc. If the agency is unknown, give "[s.n.]"; if place and agency are unknown, use "[S.I.: s.n.]." Transcribe also the name of the agency from which to secure copies or the agency that made the reproduction if the agency is named in one of the prescribed sources tor the publication, distribution, etc., area of the reproduction.

— date of the reproduction

— physical description of the reproduction if different from the original series statement of the reproduction (if applicable)

— notes related to the reproduction (if applicable)

Other cataloging agencies choosing to follow this LCRI may have compelling local reasons (e.g., data manipulation) for recording notes relating to the reproduction in other than the 533 field (e.g., system requirements (538), restrictions on access (506)).

Apply rules 1.4-1.7 for the formulation of the bibliographic data in the 533 field note. Enclose cataloguer-supplied data in brackets. Omit the area divider (space-dash-space).

4. Use a physical description fixed field (007) applicable to

the reproduction. For elctronic reproductions, also supply information about the electronic nation and access (856 field) (See Examples 4-5).

EXAMPLE 1. Monograph

Type : a	ELvl : I		Srce : d		Audn : f		Ctrl :		Lang :	enq
BLvl : m	form : s		Conf : 0		Biog :		MRec:		Ctry :	ohu
	Cont :		GPub:		LitF :		Indx : 0			
Desc : a	Ills :		Fest : 0		DtSt : s		Dates:		2000,	

006 mfd

007 c $b r $d a $e n

100 1 Weitz, Jay, $d 1953-

245 10 Cataloging electronic resources $h [electronic resource] : $b OCLC-MARC coding guidelines / $c by Jay Weitz.

246 10 OCLC-MARC coding guidelines

256 Electronic document.

260 [Dublin. Ohio] : $b OCLC. $c 20CO.

538 Mode of access: World Wide Neb.

500 Title from caption. viewed Dec. 14. 2000.

500 "Revised 2000 May 15."

710 2 OCLC.

856 40 $u http://www.oclc.org/oclc/cataloging/type.htm

EXAMPLE 2. Continuing publication. Catalogued as open-entry monograph

Type : m ELvl : I Srce : d Audn : f Ctrl : Lang : eng

BLvl : m File : j GPub : 0 MRec: Ctry : nyu

Desc : a DtSt : m Dates : 1995,9999

006 a f 0000

007 c $b r $d a $e n

245 00 OLAC $h [electronic resource] : $b Online Audiovisual Catalogers, Inc.

246 10 Online Audiovisual Catalogers. 256 Electronic online service.

260 [United States) : $b OLAC ; $a [Buffalo, N.Y. : $b State University of New York at Buffalo], $c 1995-

310 Updated frequently.

538 Mode of access: Internet.

500 Title from home page; viewed on Dec. 14, 2000 (last updated: Aug. 12, 1999).

520 Web site for OtAC, an organization for catalogers of audiovisual and other special materials. Includes information about OLAC, its organization, officers, conferences, committees, and awards, rationale for cataloguing audiovisual and other special materials, book reviews and links to useful web sites.

650 0 Cataloging of nonbook materials.

710 2 On-Line Audiovisual Catalogers, Inc.

856 40 $u http//ublib.buffalo.edu/libraries/units/cts/olac/

EXAMPLE 3. Serial

Type : a	ELvl : I	Srce : d	GPub :	Ctrl :	Lang : eng
BLvl : s	Form : s	Conf : 0	Freq :	MRec:	Ctry : ilu
	Orig :	EntW:	Regl : x	ISSN : 0	
Desc : a	SrTP : p	Cont : 0	DtSt : c	Dates : 19uu,9999	

006 mfd

007 c $b r $d a $e n

022 1056-6694

245 00 ALCTS network news $h [electronic resource]

256 Electronic newsletter.

260 Chicago, IL : $b Association for Library Collections & Technical Services, American Library Association.

310 Irregular.

538 Mode of access: E-mail to subscribers.

500 Title from caption.

500 Available free to subscribers. Back issues available through ALCTS web site. Only available in electronic form.

500 Description based on vol.20, no. 9 (Dec. 15, 2000); viewed on Dec. 18, 2000.

710 2 Association for Library Collections & Technical Services.

856 0 ala.org $f AN2 $h listproc $i subscribe

EXAMPLE 4. [Given here in OCLC format rather than LC style]

007 cr

245 10 Introduction to United States government information sources $h [electronic resource] / $c Joe Morehead.

250 6th ed.

260 Englewood, Colo. : $b Libraries Unlimited, $c 1999.

300 xxv, 491 p. ; $c 25 cm.

440 0 Library and information science text series

504 Includes bibliographical references and indexes.

533 Electronic reproduction. $b Boulder, Colo. : $c NetLibrary, $d 1999. $n Mode of access: World wide Web. $n Access restricted to NetLibrary subscribers.

856 4 $3 Display record $u http://www.netlibrary.com/summary.asp?ID=11187

EXAMPLE 5

007 cr

245 10 Breeding design considerations for coastal Douglasfir $h [electronic resource] / $c Randy Johnson.

260 Portland, OR : $b U.S. Dept. of Agriculture, Forest Service, Pacific Northwest Research Station, $c [1998]

300 34 p. : $b ill. ; $c 28 cm.

500 Cover title.

500 "February 1998."

533 Electronic reproduction. $b Portland, OR : $c PNW Publications, $d 1998. $n Mode of access: World Wide Web. $n System requirements: Adobe Acrobat reader.

856 4 $u http:///www.fs.fed.us/pnw/pubs/qtr%5F411.pdf

METADATA AS A SOLUTION?

Although cataloging Internet resources is now a reality in many libraries, the problem of bibliographic control of the Internet remains far from resolved. The library profession efforts have been focused only on the output of the networked information flow. Some initiatives are needed at the other end of the flow. Metadata systems and schemes have been created for this purpose, i.e., providing Internet resource creators with a working mechanism to embed resource description elements in their prooucts. These elements will help in the discovery and retrieval of Internet resources. In fact, a study, carried out on nine Internet search engines, has found that "they commonly cover data contained in fields identified by the < HEADER >, < TITLE >, and < HREF > MTML tags". Among these various system, the Dublin Core (DC) has gained the most attention from cataloguers. The attraction to DC lies in its universality as a "switching language" and in the fact it has evolved with strong support and participation from OCLC. The library community has seriously looked into the applicability of the DC in cataloguing. A Dublin Core/MARC crosswalk (or mapping) was done by Library of Congress. The Committee on Cataloging: Description and Access of the Association for Library Collections and Technical Services (a Division of the American Library Association), has created the Task Force on Metadata and the Cataloguing Rules, to evaluate two metadata element sets (TEI-Text Encoding Initiative, and DC) as a source of cataloguing. The Task Force, in its Final Report, has recommended that ALCTS continue to monitor metadata developments, through the new Joint Task Force on Metadata with MARBI, for their potential impact on library catalogues and cataloging. The Nordic Metadata Project has gone a step further in creating the DC To MARC Converter, which "is capable of producing records in US MARC and all Nordic MARC formats from Dublin Core source data". The Converter is now available at this URL: *(hllp://www.bibsys.no/meta/d2m/)*. It could become a very important copy cataloguing tool in the future, if Internet resource creators embed DC elements in their products. Some authors have already started talking about a four-tiered Internet cataloging scheme, in which DC-based records will have some role. Taking one step further in this direction, one author has suggested the integration of the three tasks of cataloguing, indexing and markup editing at the creation step of the electronic documents so that "the cataloguing records exist with(in) the electronic source files". So metadata can be a solution in future for Internet Cataloguing.

5

Database Online Cataloguing

The database of an online public access catalogue consists of a number of files. The most important files from the perspective of subject access are the bibliographic file, the authority file, and the inverted file. The retrieval of subject or other information is the result of the interaction among these files. The heart of a public access catalogue is the file of machine-readable bibliographic records. The, bibliographic record is a surrogate for an actual document stored in the library or in an information centre.

The computer-manipulable bibliographic database is made up of bibliographic records which, in turn, are made up of fields, subfields, and characters. The author data for a book, for instance, is an author field, as for example is "Cutter, Ceharles A., 1837-1903". The birth and death dates of the author, then, are a subfield of the author field, made up of numeric characters and a hyphen. Generally speaking, bibliographic databases of online catalogues are expected to handle bibliographic records of variable lengths, consisting of a variable number of fields which may themselves be of variable lengths. In addition the fields may consist of a variable number of subfields.

A particular format of the variable-length bibliographic record, accepted as a national and international standard, is the MARC (Machine Readable Cataloguing) format.

The history of the MARC format goes back to the late 1950s, when the Library of Congress and other research libraries recognised that computer processing of bibliographic information had to be employed in order to solve problems such as cataloguing backlogs, and to provide better services to library clientelc. This realisation, coupled with financial support for conducting feasibility studies from the Council on Library Resources, eventually led to adoption of the MARC communications format for exchange of bibliographic data among libraries.

MARC bibliographic format, however, is really a family of bibliographic formats based on similar principles of record organisation but differing from each other in details. The first difference in the MARC formats is based on the country of adoption. Examples of MARC formats are US/MARC, UK/MARC, and CAN/MARC, indicating that these formats are accepted in the United States, the United Kingdom, and Canada. Another difference in MARC formats is based on the type of bibliographic information they contain. This is especially true in the US/MARC formats. There are currently MARC formats for books, films, serials, archival and manuscripts control, computer files, maps, music, and visual materials.

The Machine Readable Bibliographic Information Committee (MARBI) of the American Library Association recently initiated the process of integrating these multiple formats into one integrated MARC format. The descriptions of various bibliographic elements of MARC records that follow, therefore, are likely to undergo changes in the near future in view of this impending format integration. Nevertheless, the MARC format integration is unlikely to have major impact on the subject access to bibliographic records. The MARC format is identified by (1) its structure, (2) content designators, and (3) contents of the record.

The MARC format has three sections: a leader, a directory, and a data section.

Leader : The leader is the first twefity-four characters of a MARC record. The purpose of the leader is to provide information such as the length of the record, the type of bibliographic item, etc., which is necessary to begin processing the record. A leader looks like this:

00445nalnbb2200169lbb4500

The length of the record is given by the first five characters -

00445, and the length of the leader and record directory is given by the characters 00169. b in the example above represents a blank.

Record directory : The record directory is an index to the location of variable-length fields within the record. It consists of a variable number of fixed-length entries. Each of these entries is made up of three elements: a three- character field tag, a four-character field length, and a five-character starting character position, as shown below :

Tag	Field Length	Starting Character Position
008	0041	00006

Figure : Item in record directory

The tags or content designators within the record directory identify the fields occurring in the data section of the MARC record. For instance, the personal author main entry is identified by the tag 100. The field length gives the length of the field identified by the tag. The starting character position gives the location of the first character of the field relative to the first character of the first field. The first character of the first field, in turn, is given by the base address of data field in the leader. Entries for variable control fields (i.e., those fields whose tag numbers start with zero) appear first in the directory, followed by tags for other variable fields in ascending order by the first character of the tag.

Data fields : The variable fields that contain the bibliographic data follow the leader and the record directory. Control fields-that is, those fields whose tag numbers start with 00-precede other fields. The data fields, except control fields, may include indicators and subfield codes in addition to data and field terminators. The last field of the record ends with a record terminator.

US/MARC formats define over 170 variable fields. If one considers that most of these fields contain additional information in the form of indicators and subfield codes, one realises that these records consist of extensive information about the fields within the records as well as the data itself. All this coded and explicit information can be exploited at the time of subject retrieval. The MARC format for bibliographic records described above is called a communications format.

It is meant for exchange of bibliographic data among libraries and bibliographic networks. The bibliographic records of an online catalogue, therefore, need not be stored in MARC format. At the same time, there are advantages to storing the bibliographic data in MARC-compatible form:

> The compact record that suits today's circulation system will restrict access in tomorrow's online catalogue; the moderately complete record that provides access in tomorrow's online catalogue may restrict a library's capacity to offer sophisticated special retrieval or listings in the years to come. A short-term savings of lower-level compatibility may be paid for by long-term lack of flexibility. People who deal with full MARC become aware of the two fundamental roles of USMARC compatibility:

1. You don't need to process or display all the information just because it's there.
2. Once you discard information don't expect to restore it When it's gone, it's gone.

FIELDs FOR SUBJECT INFORMATION

A typical MARC record contains a vast amount of information that points to the topical contents of the bibliographic item it represents, as well as to other pertinent information such as the language of the publication. Much of this infonnation can be used in subject retrieval or in limiting retrieved sets of records. The following paragraphs identify the fields significant in this respect. In the list below, XX stands for numbers from 66 to 99.

The fields In the MARC records are grouped by function. They are, according to USMARC "The formats- Underlying principles" (1983):

00X	Control fields
0XX	Call number and control number fields
1XX	Main entry
2XX	Title, Title paragraph
3XX	Physical description
4XX	Series statement
5XX	Notes
6XX	Subject added entries
7XX	Added entries
8XX	Series added entries
9XX	Local-use fields

Some of the above fields explicitly deal with subject contents of the records while others only secondarily contain subject-bearing information. Each of these fields will be described from the perspective of subject access. For the sake of clarity, the description is limited to the USMARC format for monographs. It should be noted the other MARC formats do differ in detail. For instance, UK/MARC format has a provision for a PRECIS string, which does not appear in the US/MARC format.

Fields Intended for Subject Access (6XX fields)

Subject added entry fields (6XX fields) are explicitly intended for subject retrieval. These fields are:

600	Personal name subject heading
610	Corporate name subject heading
611	Conference or meeting subject heading
630	Uniform title subject heading
650	Topical subject heading
651	Geographic subject heading
69X	Locally assigned subject headings

Each of these subject heading fields contains two indicators and a number of subfields. The indicators provide additional information about the subject headings. The first indicator occurs in personal name, corporate name, and conference/meeting subject headings, and indicates the structure of the name, mainly for computer processing purposes. The second indicator shows the source of the given subject heading; for example, a value of zero in this position means that it is a Library of Congress subject heading.

Each subject heading consists of a main heading that may be followed by a number of subfields. The most relevant subfields for subject access are:

k .form subheading

x general subject subdivision

y chronological subject subdivision

z geographic subdivision

Personal name subject heading (600) : The 600 fields consist of subject headings that are personal names, names of families, names of persons used with the phrase "in fiction, drama, poetry. etc.", and titles of works that are entered under personal author. Examples of these headings are (Library of Congress 1980):

[600] 10#aKennedy, John Fitzgerald,#cPres. U.S.,#dI917-1963.

[600] 10#aShakespeare, WIlliam,#dl564-1 616.#tHamlet.

Corporate name subject heading (610) : This field contains names of corporate bodies such as governments, business firms, associations, churches, cathedrals, and ships. Examples are:

[610] l0#aVennont.#bDept. of Water Resources.

[610] 20#aUnited Nations#zAfrica.

Conference/Meeting subject heading (611): Names of conferences, meetings, religious councils, exhibitions, expositions, athletic events, etc, are entered in this field.

Examples include:

[611] 20#aNobel Conference,#n(ist:#dI965:#cGustavus Adolphus College).

[611] 20#aParis Peace Conference#d(1919-1920).

Uniform title subject heading (630): The uniform title subject heading of a work is a standardised title used when various editions, translations, etc., appear under varying titles. Uniform titles may be assigned to works such as radio and television programmes, motion pictures and video recordings. anonymous works, treaties, concordats, composite manuscripts or manuscript groups. Examples are:

[630] 00#aDead Sea Scrolls.

[630] 00#aBible.#pO.T.#pJudges V.

[630] 00#aTreaty of Utrecht#d(1713)

Topical subject heading (650) : By far, the most prevalent form of subject heading occurring in MARC records is the topical subject heading. Topical headings include general, terms such as does; chemistry; systematic names of families, genera, and species in botany and zoology; chemical compounds; names of events and holidays; names of fictitious or mythological gods and characters; and names or terms applied to individual objects or classes of objects.

Examples include:

[650] b0#aHeteroptera.

[650] b0#aAnimals#xFood habits.

[650) b0#aEnglish language#y20th century.

[650] b0#Mountains#zColorado.

Geographic name subject heading (651) : The geographic name subject heading includes natural features such as rivers, mountains, and deserts; names of continents, land masses and other geographic regions; archaeological sites; parks; and political jurisdictions (either by themselves or with subject subdivisions). Examples are:

[651] b0#aClear Lake (Iowa: Lake)

[651] b0#aUnited States#xHistory#y 1849-1877.

[651] b0#aCanada.#Statistical services.

Local-use subject headings (69X) : These subject headings are locally assigned by the libraries. Generally, they follow the patterns of 6XX fields. When local subject headings exist in MARC records, they complement the other subject fields. Likewise, there are other subject fields that may prove to be useful. These are:

653: Uncontrolled term (for use with technical reports)

655: Genre heading

Fields that may indicate subject

MARC records contain a number of other fields that, although not designed to be subject access points, do indicate the subject contents of the works they represent. The use of these fields in subject retrieval tends to improve the retrieval of relevant items and at the same time, results in the retrieval of more unwanted items. In general, these fields may not precisely identify the subject contents of the works they represent, but do provide a broad indication of the subjects covered by the corresponding works. The following are some of the fields useful in this respect.

Title fields **:** Next to the subject heading fields, title fields are powerful subject access fields in online public access catalogues. This is because at least in science and social science subject areas, titles of bibliographic items carry significant subject-bearing information. Such titles incorporate many keywords that refer to the subject content of the bibliographic item. However, accessing such titles for the purpose of subject access is relatively difficult in card catalogues, because the lead terms are not necessarily helpful. In online public access catalogues, on the other hand, access can be provided to meaningful keywords. Title fields include the following:

214 augmented title

240 uniform title

245 title statement.

The augmented title field (214) supplements the title statement field (245) by adding more descriptive terms to the statement. It is used only with technical report literature. This field, however, is not input by the Library of Congress. An example of this field is:

[245] 10#aDesign of a van-top low-profile HF antenna

[214] 00#aDesign of a van-top low-profile HF antenna; mobile communications

The uniform title field is a standardised title of an item. An example is :

[240] 10#aMass, Easter.#hFilmstrip

The title of this bibliographic item is:

[245] 04#aThe traditional Catholic Easter Mass.

The title statement field (245) is one of the most common fields in the MARC records, and consequently one of the most useful subject access fields. An example of title field is:

[245] 10#aBasic supervisory skills. #h Transparency/ #cPatrick M. Williams.

Series statement and series added entries (4XX and 8XX frelds): The publishers generally issue a variety of publications. For administrative convenience and other reasons; publishers may identify related publications by a common name; which is called the series name.

At least in some instances, the series names provide a clue as to the subject contents of the publications issued in the series. For instance, the series name "ACRL monographs", at least for the initiated, indicates that the publication may have something "to do with college and research libraries. Similarly, "US Public Health Service Publications" indicates publications likely to deal with aspects of public health. The 4XX fields encompass the following specific fields:

400 Personal name/title series

410 Corporate name/title series

411 Conference/meeting series

440 Title series

490 Untraced or differently traced series.

Examples are: —

[400] l0#aShakespeare, William,#d 1564-1616.#t Plays.

[410] 10#aUnited States.#bPublic Health Service. #tPublications, #vno .300.

[411] 20#aChicago Cartography Conference,#d< 1974) #tMap#vno.10#x0000-0000.

[440] b4#aThe John Dewey essays in philosophy. .

[490] 1b#aACRL monographs,#vno.8#x0000-0000.

Similar arguments apply to series added entry fields (8XX). These fields are:

800 personal name/title series added entry

810 corporate name/title series added entry

811 conference or meeting/title series added entry

830 uniform title series added entry

840 title series added entry.

Bibliographic notes : These fields contain information such as explanations about titles, editors, and these are of questionable value for subject retrieval; and are likely to become obsolete in the near future. Some of the note fields, however, are of potential use. For instance, field 502 (Dissertation Note) describes the form of the work, namely, a thesis or dissertation. Although this may not say anything about the exact content of the publication, it does indicate that the subject content is dealt with at a certain level of complexity, and such information may be used in controlling the retrieval. Similarly, field 505 (Contents Note), when it occurs, complements the subject heading fields. An example of a 505 field is:

Otb#av.l. Summary, master plan.-v.2. Subdivision regulations, town of Bridgewater.-v.3. Zoning regulations. town of Bridgewater.-v.4. Subdivision regulations. village of Bridgewater .-v .5. Zoning regulations. village of Bridgewater.-v .6. Subdivision regulations. town of Winfield.-v. 7. Zoning regulations, town of Winfield.-v.8. Subdivision regulations. village of West Winfield.-v.9. Zoning regulations. village of West Winfield.

The corresponding subject headings assigned to this record are::

[650] b0#aCitics and towns#xPlanning#zNew York #zBridgewater.

[650] b0#aCities and towns#xPlanning#zNew York #zWinfield.

(650] b0#aCities and towns#xPlanning#zNew York #zWest

Winfield.

Obviously, the 505 field above gives more specific information about the content of the publication than does the subject heading: "Cities and towns—Planning". Field 520 contains unformatted notes that describe the scope and contents of the work. This field, however, seems to be used more in juvenile publications than in other types of materials. Nevertheless, when such use occurs, it is quite informative. An example is:

bb#aRelates the events of the Battles of Trenton and Princeton which were part of the Christmas campaign fought during the Revolutionary War.

Its corresponding subject headings are:

[650] bO#aTrenton. Battle of, 1776.

[650] bO#aPrinceton,; Battle of, 1777.

1651] b1#aUnited States#xHistory#yRevolution, 1775-1783.

Main entry and added entry fields (lXX and 7XX) : The purpose of the main entry field is to provide the principal access point for the item. In most instances, authorship can be attributed to a personal author or authors. This type of authorship may not be of significant use in subject retrieval, although one can put forward arguments wherein a personal author is used as a starting point for a subject search. Other types of authorships, however, cannot be completely ruled out. In this respect, the following fields may be of some use:

110 Corporate name main entry

111 Conference or Meeting main entry

130 Uniform title main entry.

In many instances, the name of the corporate author provides some clues as to the subject content of the publications issued under its name. Again, as in the case of series entries, these clues are not necessarily specific to the publication in hand, but do nevertheless delineate the sphere of interest of the corporate body. For instance, consider corporations such as International Business Machines Corporation and Eastman Kodak Company. Without actually examining the publications issued by these corporations, one can speculate with some confidence that those publications are likely to deal with computers, programming languages, information retrieval, and the like, in the case of IBM, and photography, audiovisual equipment, techniques, information storage and retrieval, and so forth, in the case of Eastman Kodak Company. This type of natural specialisation on the part of corporatc bodies could be of significant help for subject retrieval. Examples of corporate or conference authors include:

[111] 20Vatican Council#n (2nd : #d1962-1965).

[110] 10Great Britain.#bHydrographic Office.

Examples of publications issued by these bodies and the subject headings assigned to those publications by the Library of Congress are:

Decree on ecumenism: With annotations, study outline and review questions (CATHOLIC CHURCH- RELATIONS, CHRISTIAN UNION-CATHOLIC CHURCH).

Paul, bishop, servant of the servants of God together with the fathers of the sacred council puts on permanent record the decree on ecumenism (CHRISTIAN UNION-CATHOLIC CHURCH).

More postconciliar documents (CATHOLIC CHURCH- CONGRESSES).

Port of Southampton. 1951; 1970 edition corrected to 1973. (SOUTHAMPTON (ENGLAND)-HARBOR, SOUTHAMPTON (ENGLAND)-MAPS).

Shetland Isles. 1884; corrected to 1973. (SHETLAND ISLES MAPS, TOPOGRAPHIC, NAUTICAL CHARTS- SHETLAND ISLES).

In the above examples, one need not explain which publications were issued by which corporate body. Similar arguments hold in the case of added entry fields, which are:

710 corporate name added entry

711 conference or meeting added entry

730 uniform title heading added entry

740 title traced differently

Examples of these fields are:

[711] 21#aWomen and National Health Insurance Meeting #d(1980:#cWashington, D.C.)

[730] 02#aOil, paint and drug reporter#p Buyers directory

Its title field is :

[245] 00#aChemical buyers directory

Example of a 740 field is :

[740] 01#aWhite backlash#hMotion picture

Its title field is :

[245] 00#aBlack power, white backlash#h Motion picture.

Classification number fields : The MARC format contains a number of fields that encode the subject of the bibliographic item in the form of classification codes. These codes are: Library of Congress one or more classification codes,which codes a classification (field 050), National Library of Medicine (field 060), Universal Decimal Classification number (field 080), Dewey Decimal Classification number (field 082) and government document classification number (field 086). Although the government document number's primary purpose is to identify the provenance of the bibliographic item. It nevertheless provides a clue as to the subject content of the item. For instance, it is reasonable to assume that a bibliographic item issued by the Department of Energy deals with energy resources. A combination of subject headings, keywords from titles, and classification numbers may prove to be quite effective in retrieving relevant items from the bibliographic file.

Control field 008 : Control field 008 is a fixed-length field of forty characters. This field contains a large amount of coded information, some of it duplicating the information presented elsewhere within the bibliographic record. Nevertheless, some of its codes could be exploited in relation to subject access.

The intellectual level code, which occurs in position 22 of the 008 field, describes the suitability of the bibliographic item for various audiences. For example, in code of *a* represents that the item is appropriate for preschool audiences, a code of *f* shows that it is suitable to specialised audiences, and so on. This code, clearly, can be used in selecting appropriate material at the time of information retrieval. For instance, the user who is interested only in professional-level material can reject material produced for elementary and high-school-level audiences.

In the case of books, the nature of contents code occurs in positions 24 to 27; that is, this code can be used four times in describing the contents of the bibliographic work. The nature of contents code indicates whenever the bibliographic item is a bibliography, a dictionary, an abstract, and the like. The code *n* represents a survey of literature, *e* an encyclopedia, and *w* law reports and digests. The government; publication code occurs in position 28 of the 008 control field. If the bibliographic item under consideration is a government publication, this code describes the level of the government that is responsible for the item's production. For example, the code *f* represents a federal/ national level publication, *i* intergovernmental bodies, and/ local governmental bodies. In the case of books, the biography code occurs in position 34 of the control field 008. A code of *a* represents an autobiography, *c* a collective biography, and *b* an individual biography. In addition to these codes, the 008 control field also encode whether the bibliographic item is a conference publication, festschrift, fiction, and the like. It also encodes the language of the bibliographic item.

Other fields

Other fields may also prove useful in bibliographic retrieval from online public access catalogues. These are the language code (field 041), the geographic area code (field 043), and the chronological code (field 045). If used carefully, even the GPO Item Number (field 74) could be used in delineating the subject content of a bibliographic item. The GPO item numbers are used in the distribution of depository publications by the United States Government Printing Office, and generally identify the types of publications being distributed (e.g., manuals, technical reports, and annual reports). Although an average user would not be aware of the significance of these numbers, reference and government documents librarians would be able to exploit them.

The MARC format for bibliographic records proved to be revolutionary. The development of bibliographic utilities in particular, and the growth of library automation in general, can be attributed to this bibliographic standard. There are, of course, criticisms on the format. One of the criticisms, for example, is that the format is too complex:, especially if one corisiders the entire family of MARC formats and the continual changes the MARC formats undergo. The criticism from the subject access perspective is that the format is bound too much to the printing of catalogue cards, and that not much thought went into making the MARC format more powerfu l in the online catalogue setting.

One critic be.moans the fact that the library community did not make use of the opportunity to have a separate field for indexing terms, in addition to the subject headings fields. Although he was mixing the notion of bibliographic formats with cataloguing policy, the fact is that MARC records do not contain index terms. Although one does not make, use of such terms in printing catalogue cards, they would be of immense use in subject searching. This deficiency is particularly glaring since other bibliographic retrieval systems, such as the National Library of Medicine's MEDLINE, contain terms that are searchable only online and other index terms which are both searchable and printable.

Whatever the format of the database, one should keep in mind that the database may contain typographical and other errors which may affect the retrieval of bibliographic records.

Authority File

The second file that forms a part of the online catalogue's database is the file of authority records. From the perspective of subject access, the subject heading authority records contain the authorised forms of subject headings, their synonyms, and their related headings. Maintenance of authority records and authority files is an integral part of cataloging work. The role of an authority record is summarized as follows:

1. It records a form of access point that is prescribed by the cataloguing code in effect and that is used to permit the

uniform application of this form for future additions to the catalogue which also use that access point for retrieval.

2. It ensures the collocation of records in a bibliographic file that have the same access point.
3. It ensures the issuance of standardised bibliographic surrogates.
4. It documents decisions taken with respect to the form of access point, so that the laborious and demanding task of determining the current form of entry is done only once, at the first occurrence of that access point in the catalogue.
5. It can record, as cross-references, variant manifestations of access points caused by natural occurrences as marriages, deaths, etc., different sets of cataloging rules, and local policy.

Obviously, the user of an online catalogue also benefits tremendously by the ability to access authority records. In the case of subject access, the user is normally expected to consult the latest edition of the Library of Congress Subject Headings, which is really an authority file, albeit in-complete, in paper copy format. The subject heading authority records are also available in machine-readable form. The authority records in machine-readable form are distributed by the Library of Congress in MARC communications format. Consequently, authority records consist of a leader, record directory, and data fields. The purpose and role of the leader and record directory are exactly the same as those of their counterparts in bibliographie records.

The data fields are divided into control and variable fields. Control fields of an authority record include:

Authority record control number (001)

Date and time of latest transaction (005)

Fixed-length data elements (008).

The variable data fields fall into five groups:

Bibliographic control numbers and codes (tags 01-09x)

Established heading fields (tags 100-151)

Tracings and references (tags 260, 360, 4XX, 5XX, 663 to 666)

Series treatment information (tags 64X)
Notes, (tags 667, 670, 675, 678, 680 to 682).

The structure of the variable fields is similar to that of variable fields in bibliographic records. Each variable field consists of indicators, subfield codes, data, and a field terminator. In the case of the last variable field of the authority record, the record terminator replaces the field termmator.

The established heading fields are 100, 110, 111, 130, 150, and 151. Every authority record must contain one of these fields. Examples of these fields are:

100 Established heading—Personal name, e.g., [100] 00$aGautama Buddha$xBiography$xEarly works to 1800

110 Established heading—Corporate name, e.g., [110] 20$aHarvard University$xHistory $yRevolution, 1775-1783

111 Established heading—Conference or meeting, e.g., [111]20$aPerdue Pest Control Conference$x Periodicals

130 Established heading—Uniform title, e.g., [130] b0$aBible$zFrance

150 Established heading—Topical subject, e.g., [150] b0$aArchitecture, Modem$y19th century

151 Established heading-Geographic name, e.g., [151) tbo$aUnited States$xBoundaries$zCanada

Tags 4xx provide see references to established headings from unestablished headings. For example, the following are the combinations of unestablished (tag 450) and established (tag 150) topical subject headings.

450 b0$aEnglish drama$xAfrican authors

150 b0$aAfrican drama (English)

Likewise, tags 5XX provide see also tracings from an established heading to a related established heading. An example is:

550 b0wgaIndians of North America$xWars$y1862-1865

150 b0$a$aand Creek, Battle of, 1864

Relationship of Authority File to Bibliographic File

The authority file of an online catalogue may be linked with the bibliographic file in a number of ways, depending on whether the authority file is machine-readable or not. These possible relationships are the following :

i. It may not be machine-readable; therefore there is no linkage with the bibliographic file. In such a case, the user has to consult the manual files, such as an authority file on cards or a printed file such as the Library of Congress Subject Headings for authority information.

ii. It may be machine-readable, but there may not be a link between the authority file and the bibliographic file. In such a case, the user of the online catalogue may not have access to the authority file. Even if he has access to the authority file, the system would not be able to display the corresponding bibliographic records.

iii. It is linked with the bibliographic file. This linkage is the most desirable one, both from the cataloger's and the user's point of view. From the user's perspective, he can search the authority file first, to locate the relevant subject headings, and then, once relevant headings are found, command the system to display the corresponding bibliographic records, without having to re-key the subject headings.

A number of articles explore authority control from the perspective of technical services.

Inverted File

The third file in the online catalogue database is the inverted file, which makes possible for the user to formulate complex queries and retrieve information rapidly. It is derived from the bibliographic file but is separate from it. User searches are carried out on the inverted file most of the time, and the bibliographic file is accessed only at the time of displaying or printing the bibliographic records.

The inverted file consists of information taken from selected fields of bibliographic records; this information is linked with identifiers that uniquely represent each bibliographic record. The information taken from the selected fields could include the entire information included in those fields and/or keywords derived from them. Finally, the Inverted file is sorted in some manner-for example, alphabetically—so that accessing of this file becomes easier. First, one decides which field should be represented in the inverted file. Then, one decides how each field is represented in the inverted file; for example, the entire field and/or keywords derived from that field. In the above example, it may be decided to include the author field as it is in the inverted file; the title and subject fields are represented as they are and by each keyword from them.

An	002
An introduction to computers in information science/T	002
and	002, 003
Artandi, Susan/A	002
base	001
bibliographic	003
Computers	002
Data	001
Data base management/S	001
data-base	001
Fayen, E.G./A	003
in	002
information	002, 003
information retrieval on-line/T	003
information storage and retreival systems/S	002, 003
Introduction	002
Lancaster, F. Wilfrid/A	003
management	001
Martin, James/A	003
of	001

online	003
on-line bibliographic searching/S	003
Principles	001
Principles of data-base management/T	001
retrieval	002, 003
science	002
searching	003
storage	002, 003
systems	002, 003
to	002

In the above example, /A, /S, and /T identify the fields which supplied the terms to the Index file. Likewise, 001, 002, and 003 are the Identifiers which uniquely represent corresponding bibliographic records.

The above inverted file allows a great latitude in searching. For Instance, one can issue the following search commands:

search for keyword= information

search for author= Martin, J. AND keyword= data-base

search for title= Information storage and retrieval systems

search for keyword= computer?

A question mark '?', represents truncation. For example, computer? stands for computer, computers, computersation, etc. Depending on the fields occurring in the bibliographic record, more than one field can be selected for keyword indexing. In the above example, both subject heading and title fields contributed keywords to the inverted file. If necessary, the source field of the keyword and the keyword's position within the source field may also be identified to improve the search flexibility.

Another file that is of considerable importance in the online catalogue is the detailed holdings files. The detailed holdings file, in the case of a union online catalogue, provides access to the holdings of each participating institution. It is evident from the discussion so far that all the files- bibliographic file, authority file, detailed hodings file, and inverted index file-work togethqr to provide subject and other types of access to the bibliographic records. Depending on the configuration of the online catalgoue, additional file- may be invovled.

An examination of the indexing policies of some online catalogues show that many of the fields described earlier in fact, used in subject retrieval. For instance, OLLI, the online catalogue of Georgia State University, indexes the following fields for subject retrieval.

Tag	Field name	Index type
110, 111	author	Keyword
130, 221, 427, 242, 420, 240, 241,		
242, 243, 245, 246, 247, 440	title	Title, Keyword
400, 410, 411	author (t-subfield)	Title, Keyword
600, 610, 611, 630, 650, 651, 690	subject	Subject,
691, 692, 693, 694, 695		Keyword
700, 705, 710, 711, 715	author (t-subfield)	Title, Keyword
730, 740, 780, 785	title	Title, Keyword
800, 810, 811	author (t-subfield)	Title, Keyword
830, 840	title	Title, Keyword
050	Call number	Call number

This example is presented from the perspective of subject access only. The index types subject and title mean that individual words in the fields are also separately indexed heading as units are indexed in the system. The index type keyword means that individual words in the fields are also separately indexed. The names of indexes in OLLI's terminology are: AU(thor), CO(mbination) T(itle), TE(rm), LA(nguage), and SU(bject). In addition, there are indexes for LC card number, ISBN, and ISSN.

Although some of the material presented here will probably be of greatest interest to developers of online catalogues and similar information retrieval (IR) systems, or to researchers trying to characterise and improve IR systems, the application of performance and usage data has a number of highly practical applications for librarians who have installed or are considering the installation of an online catalogue but the practical applications include the acceptance testing of commercial online catalogues, capacity planning, problem identification and diagnosis, and ongoing quality assurance.

To an extent, each library becomes an online catalogue developer. Even when a commercial system cannot be adapted by a client library the library's understanding of the strengths and weaknesses of the system's user interface and performance is a major asset in developing effective user training and support programmes and documentation.

Much of the discussion made here have drawn the experience gained over the last six years at the University of California Office of the President's Division of Library Automation (DLA), where a very large online public union catalogue called the MELVYL (registered trademark of the Regents of the University of California) system has been in production since the beginning of the decade. Since its initial deployment, the MELVYL system has undergone continuous evolution and refinement.

During the early 1980s, DLA staff added an elaborate data collection system to the MELVYL system. The data collected played a major role in a study of online catalogue use funded by the Council of Library Resources (CLR) and in several doctoral dissertations. In addition, the MELVYL catalogue development staff at DLA have used performance and transactional data continually in understanding system behaviour, improving the catalogue's user interface, validating changes and planning system growth.

In a real sense, performance-oriented analysis is a process of statistical data reduction, although recourse to detailed information is often useful in identifying and evaluating actual performance problems once they have been identified from summary statistics. Finally it is concentrated on the behaviour of users interacting with the online catalogue and the successes and failures encountered by these users. For these applications the focus shifts to the study of detailed session-related data and specific commands. Appropriate support systems for this type of analysis-currently a major research area-are discussed. Ways in which usage data can guide the ongoing evolution of an online catalogue are examined here.

Generally, three types of detailed data can be extracted from an operational online catalogue. These are:

Session scripts : The main goal of collecting script information is to allow the reconstruction of the entire dialogue between the user and the online catalogue.

Full session logs : Sessions can be thought of as time-stamped scripts. Collection of session data allows the replay of an interaction between the user and the online catalogue exactly as the user saw it. Consequently, session logging requires not only the recording of events, such as the display of a screen or the entry of a command, but also the time lapses between events.

Resource utilisation data : This is a finer level of detail that connects the measurement of various types of system resource utilisation with session logging Information. It can include summary figures like CPU time used, wait time, and disk read and write counts, or detailed audit trails of system components such as a database management system, the operating system or a telecommunications monitor that are invoked in processing a user command, along with entry and exit times and information on resource utilisation each time a system component is invoked.

There are substantial difficulties in collecting each of these types of logging data. Some of these difficulties are mechanical. For example, in a large-scale computer, a tele-communication monitor, an operating system, a database management system (DBMS) and an online catalogue are separate programmes that typically run independently and come from different sources. Most operating systems, telecommunications monitors and DBMSs incorporate extensive independent facilities for logging use and monitoring performance; data from all these sources must be reassembled, and information from external programmes such as a DBMS or a telecommunication monitor must be merged with session and resource utilisation data coming from the online catalogue application. Often this merging presents massive technical complexities owing to differences in the definition of an 'event' as viewed by the catalogue, the DBMS, the operating system and the telecommunication monitor, and owing to the massive amount of data generated from each of these sources.

One point that cannot be over-emphasized is the sheer bulk of the monitoring data that a large online catalogue generates. In the case of the MELVYL catalogue, for example, the amount of detailed monitoring data collected annually is on the same order of magnitude as the size of the bibliographic database being searched. The MELVYL catalogue services between four and five million queries and displays perhaps 50 million records to end-users per year. Each of these operations, in turn, produces multiple calls to the DBMS supporting the MELVYL catalogue and resource utilisation data is associated with each of these DBMS calls. The simple mechanics of storing, reducing and managing such a volume of data are daunting.

Other problem goes far beyond mechanical difficulties. In the case of collecting script information, recording user commands presents no problem, but recording system behaviour in response to these commands is much more difficult. The online catalogue's user interface can be expected to change over time; the response to a command entered today may not be the same as the response to the same command next week. Furthermore, the database being searched by the user is constantly growing and changing; a query that retrieves 50 records today may have retrieved five records a month earlier or may retrieve 500 a month later. Compromises on session reproducibility are required to keep the volume of the monitoring data within reason.

Another major issue in the collection of scripts is patron privacy. This has serious ethical implications, and may have, serious legal implications as well. The user's right to privacy must be balanced against the value of logging data to, the institution runing the catalogue. One must also consider the possibility that attempts may be made to employ data collected for logging purposes in other contexts; for example, library circulation records have been subpoenaed as part of criminal investigations. Over the years, different systems have adopted a range of approaches to this problem, including asking the user's permission to log his catalogue session in order to improve the system as part of the sign-on process, or replacing user IDs with anonymous session numbers in logging data to protect pattern anonymity. In the MELVYL system this problem is largely eliminated by the fact that the MELVYL catalogue is public access; where the, users need no ill to use the system in most cases.

For session data, system analysts are concerned most with response time as experienced by the end-user at the terminal. Most terminals access the system through networks, which may vary greatly in latency and thus yield great variations in response time as perceived by the end-user.

Network delays can easily exceed total processing time for short commands within the catalogue proper; they cannot be ignored and may cause significant changes in the way patrons interact with the catalogue. Since network delays take place outside the computer running the online catalogue, they cannot be measured by the catalogue itself. External monitoring; for example, by data-gathering micro-computers emulating terminals, is required to obtain information about delays generated by the network.

External monitoring, in turn, gives rise to several problems: it represents yet another data source that must be integrated to form a total picture of system behaviour, and this is made more difficult in most computer networks by the absence of a readily accessible global clock that allows distributed time stamping of events. Worse, external monitoring is a sampling operation that is typically performed by running pre-defined command sets on data collection microcomputers.

Data on network response cannot be collected for each user interaction in the same way that mainframe statistics can be collected query by query, unless the entire system employs intelligent workstations that support special performance measurement software facilities. In most environments, this requirement for specialised access workstations is an intolerable limitation on wide access to an online catalogue. Response time context is notoriously difficult to define in detail, particularly in the case of acceptance testing or guarantees of system performance that are part of a contract for a commercial system. For example, a specification may set limits on the maximum response time for a query, but a system message such as, 'The catalogue is working on your query', considered to be a response? Similarly, is response time to display a record-the-time until display of the first character of the response on the user's screen, or the time until the display of the last character of the response? In the latter case, the response time will be a function not only of the online catalogue's performance but also of the display speed of the end-user's tenninal. At 9,600 band, it takes about 1 or 2 secs. to fill a typical CRT screen running at maximum speed; at 300 band, the same screen will take about ½ minute to display.

For resource utilisation data, one of the greatest problems, aside from that of correlating and integrating data from multiple independent sources, is cross-user interference. Resource utilisation data are frequently non-repeatable since they measure what actually took place on the machine at the time that the data were collected. For example, the number of I/O operations necessary to complete a DBMS query may vary wildly, depending on the level of contention for space in the main memory cache maintained by the DBMS, and on what particular blocks from the database happen to be in the cache owing to previous commands or commands executing concurrently the DBMS query being measured.

An online catalogue may exist in one of three, environments: as a stand-alone system running on dedicated hardware as the MELVYL catalogue does currently; as part of an integrated system running on dedicated hardware as many commercial systems do; or as an application on a computer acting in the role of a service bureau. Each of these configurations has its own implications for interpreting resource utilisation data.

In the case of a stand-alone system, one can view the query optimisation problem for online IR systems not as minimum cost execution strategy for each query, but rather as determining the minimum response time execution plan for sets of queries subject to certain fixed net resources. There is nothing to be gained from keeping a fixed resource idle. This means that a really intelligent DBMS and online catalogue will actually generate variable resource utilisation for user queries based on aggregate smoothed system load. To make sense out of these data, it is necessary to log not only resource utilisation for individual commands but also periodic information about aggregate system utilisation.

When an application shares hardware with other applications (library or otherwise), one must consider the relative priorities and loads generated by these other applications in assessing online catalogue performance. This complicates all aspects of system measurement, tuning and evaluation, and may shift the focus of analysis away from the online catalogue *per se* towards the measurement and evaluation of overall computer systems perlormance.

Finally, in the situation in which an online catalogue is running as a service bureau, the goal often is not to minimise resource utilisation or response time but to minimise an accounting cost determined by some arbitrary algorithm devised by the service bureau. In such an environment, emphasis may be placed on minimising events that have little to do with system response time as perceived by the end-user.

AACR2 Principles in the Online Environment : Some Thoughts

The objectives of the catalogue are not clearly stated in AACR2. Nevertheless, it can be inferred that the code has the same underlying principles and objectives as stated in its predecessors, mainly Lubetzky's Code of Cataloging Rules and AACR I. In fact, the code is based on the Paris Principle's statement of functions of the catalogue and, historically, it follows Cutter's two objectives, the locational and collocational functions of the catalogue. The locational (i.e., the finding) function is predominant in the code, and this is apparent from the treatment of rules for description. The optionality of uniform titles is another indication of this approach.

With respect to the different capabilities of the online catalogue, therc arc a numbcr of questions regarding the objectivcs and functions of thc catalogue in thc new environment. A general question raised is whether the objectives and functions of the cataloguc as sct forth in the Paris Principles and adopted in AACR2 are still valid in the online environment. Another question which needs to be addressed in this regard is whether the catalogue in the online network environment should still maintain the same functions formulated for a premachine environment or should widen its scope to include new functions.

While the current objectives and functions of the catalogue continue to he valid in the new environment, the new technology may help fulfil them more comprehensively and accurately. Nevertheless, these objectives and functions are surely inadequate for the new environment. In addition to the finding and collocating functions, the online catalogue helps to better identify and characterise entities in terms of their nature, scope, and orientation through different data fields such as intellectuual level, document type, genre, language code, geographic area code, and additional notes. Similarly, a fuller description or the item helps the online catalogue to be used as a selecting aid for different users to choose one item over similar items. The locating of items is another function of the catalogue and, in this respect, online catalogues are far more capable of showing the location and status of the item(s) being sought.

In the following section, the function of the catalogue is analysed with regard to the impact of some of the major characteristics of the catalogue production technology and the online environment. These are: (1) the integration of library operations. (2) developments in networking and in global access to catalogues, (3) access to the virtual copy, (4) access to other types of bibliographic databases, and (5) online search/retrieval/display capabilities. The future AACR should consider all these factors.

(i) Intgration of different library operations

The integrated online library system has made it possible for different library modules to use the same bibliographic records within the same database management system. Acquisitions librarians, cataloguers, circulation librarians, document delivery librarians, serial librarians, and the reference librarians all have access to the same database and use it for different purposes. Also in an integrated system, the end user may have access to parts of acquisition status, circulation, and holdings information. In an integrated system it is, therefore, necessary for the catalogue record to fulfil the various bibliographic needs of different operations, from housekeeping functions to reference services. In this context, not only should the catalogue function as a finding tool as well as a collocating tool, but it should also help in the choice between one work and others.

The combination of approaches to an integrated online library system not only makes it necessary for AACR to expand the current objectives but also to put more emphasis on principles for the choice and form of access points as well as for description, i.e., data elements beyond author/title information. In other words, description, access points, and additional housekeeping elements should satisfy the needs of different users. For example, a reference librarian may need to find a specific item and at the same time identify different editions and manifestations related to that item to provide more help to the user.

(ii) Networking and global access to catalogues

The fact that the resources and bibliographic information of hundreds of libraries participating in national and international networks are now accessible to any remote user calls for a reconsideration of the functions and objectives of the catalogue. The question arises as to whether a catalogue should serve in the first place its local users, that is, to identify the holdings of a particular library, or to enable any user to access the collections of other libraries available through the network. In such an environment, consideration should always be given to the fact that the item in hand for cataloguing may be an expression or manifestation of another work known under a different title being held in another collection.

With respect to the network environment, there is some support for the pre[illegible]nce of the collocating function of the catalogue over it finding [illegible]ion. In a conceptual approach to a catalogue's functions as presented by Lubctzky to the Paris Principles, Wilson proposes that, with regard to the availability of different catalogues in an online network and with respect to the significance of "work" over "publication," priority should be given to the collocating objective. Dempsey points out that a lack of sufficient attention to the collocating objective of the catalogue has resulted in two problems in large shared databases: difficulty in authority control and an increase in duplicate rccord.

On the other hand, while in a large shared database the potential number of expression and manifestation of a work increase, it is more likely that access to a very specific bibliographic manifestation of a work, for example a partioular version, would be a common need for some end users and librarians. It is evident that in a shared system or network of catalogues there will be a good chance for the user to select those that suit his/her needs best among different representations of a work. Copy cataloguing through bibliographic utilities, which is usually a known-Item search, is another example of such a user approach.

With the availability of catalogues to different remote users, it is hard to give absolute priority to either of the two traditional functions of the catalogue. While catalogues should serve their local patrons well, they should also be useful to remote users.

(iii) Access to the virtual copy

With increasing developments in information technology it has become possible, in many online catalogues, to link directly to the worke i.e., online catalogues can also show virtual copies of an item. Access to full texts or digital reproductions through linking tags, such as USMARC field 856, has implications for the functions of the catalogue. In this case, through a useful description, the catalogue should help identify the characteristics of both the actual and virtual objects.

With respect to the volatility of electronic documents and the possible changes in the content of some of the fields, it is important to take a consistent approach in description and the basis for description. In terms of their contents, size of the file, date of updating, layout, links to other sources, and even the title, electronic documents may change over time without any indication. These changes have implications for the different functions of the catalogue. They also make the bibliographic control of such documents very difficult. The contents (i.e., data elements) in some fields need to be updated in order to describe and identify the document properly.

Another problem is how to help the searcher to differentiate between virtual copies of works, which may differ from one another just as printed editions differ. .

(iv) Availability of different types of bibliographic databases

With respect to the accessibility of different types of online and/or on-disk bibliographic databases (e.g., library catalogues, book trade bibliographic databases, national bibliographies, and A&I databases) to various users, a combination of approaches in terms of the functions of the catalogue should be considered.

With access to book trade databases, the catalogue goes beyond providing holdings information and becomes a gateway to explore what is newly published, what is to be published, and what is in print. In such an environment, emphasis is also put on functions such as the crucial choice of one item over another. This requires that, for further identification of the item, more descriptive elements, such as physical description, table of contents, and summary, should be provided in the bibliographic record. From a different point of view, the functions of the bibliographic database in the library world and book trade world are similar in many respects such as the finding function, the selecting function, and house-keeping function. Even the bringing together of works by a particular author and also collocation of series are functions wanted by the two communities. A major difference is in the collocation of different editions and manifestations of a work, which libraries appear to consider important enough to control by rules of entry. All these similarities and differences in the functions have implications for other principles such as the basis for description content of the bibliographic record, and the choice and form of access points.

(v) Search/retrieval/display capabilities and functions of the catalogue

Through its extensive capabilities the online catalogue can fulfil different functions more effectively than the card catalogue. For example, keyword searching on name of authors, co-authors, editors, titles, series, etc., not only facilitates the finding function but it can also help in the choice of one item over another. Boolean searching can, to some extent, facilitate both the finding function (e.g., ANDing the author's name with date of publication) and the collocating function (e.g., ANDing the author heading with the uniform title to assemble different editions of a work). Hypertext searching on any term or a combination of terms-as offered in the University of Toronto catalogue, the University of California catalogue (MELVYL), the Library and Information Services of Western Australia (LISWA), Hyper-Lynx, GoPAC (from DataTrek, Australia), OhioLink Central catalogue, and the Prototype Catalogue of Super Records—can extend a known-item search to other items which may be unknown to the searcher but may have some kind of relationship with the item first found.

AACR2 does not address the problems that resulted in response to queries for voluminous authors and works. For example, one of the major problems of the present online catalogues is that, in response to a search for voluminous authors and works, the searcher is presented with too many records to conveniently scan. This problem is exacerbated with keyword searching, in that too many records including less relevant and irrelevant data are retrieved. A search in large catalogues under "Hamlet" may retrieve too many records, for different editions and manifestations, for works about Hamlet, as well as works with the title Hamlet written by other writers. The problem becomes more serious when the user searches in a large shared catalogue such as a national union catalogue in which there will be a greater number of editions and translations or manifestations of a work held by different libraries. So the present approach in AACR2 toward the collocation of voluminous authors and works is not consistent with the search/retrieval/display capabilities of online catalogues.

Basis for description in the online environment and its implications for AACR

The shift in different codes of descriptive cataloguing from "work" to "item" and viceversa as the basis of description is, in fact, an indication of the relative importance of these two different approaches. In the networked online environment, the issue now requires a new look, where more than one catalogue is involved and also where catalogues are increasingly becoming a part of the global online environment there must, as a first principle, be consensus regarding the basis for the description of bibliographic entities, that is, what entity should be regarded as the basis for bibliographic description in an online environment.

The basic unit of description 'the cataloguing unit' in AACR2R is the physical item in hand (rule 0.24). This is also apparent throughout the statements of the rules in part 1 (the title page or its equivalent is chosen as the chief source of cataloguing data for description). To consider providing access to the "work," however, AACR2R maintains concepts such as main entries and uniform titles. AACR2R prescribes that, although the characteristics of if individual items are taken into account, the rules for choice and form of access points should apply to works and not generally to physical manifestations of those works. The following factors indicate the significance of both "works" and "items" and justify the need in AACR to maintain a hybrid approach when describing bibliographic entities:

(a) Users' needs vary a great deal. While some users may find any edition of a work useful others may require a specific edition with a particular feature. There are also users who look in the catalogue for a particular manifestation of a work or a work in a particular format.

(b) Many users do not know that a work may have several different editions and/or manifestations; the catalogue may contain more than the user may be expecting and it is an objective of the catalogue to display other works or items related to the sought item.

(c) Based on the users' familiarity with or knowledge of books as known or seen by them, the item and the cataloguing data on the chief source of information are usually more appropriate as the basic unit of description for most types of publication. However, the basis for the description of reproductions, e.g.. equivalent and near equivalent entities, is a different case; reproductions, particularly in microform, can be described as notes on the records created for the original item. This approach would make access to both works and their reproductions more consistent.

(d) For acquisitions, current awareness services, circulation, placing reservations on books and ILL (interlibrary loan), and for the purpose of importing and exporting records (for example, for cataloguing) that usually deal with specific manifestations, the work cannot be a good means of bibliographic data exchange. For this reason, libraries and bibliographic utilities catalogue the item representing the edition rather than the work.

(e) For national bibliographies and trade lists, which focus on newly published items, the description based on the item is considered more important.

Choosing the piece in hand as the only basic unit of description, however, does not apply to all types of publication. For example, a single issue of a serial does not provide sufficient cataloguing data for the description and also bibliographic relationships of the whole serial. Crystal Graham criticises AACR2 for its approach toward describing serials and states that there are structural, philosophical, and practical problems with that approach. Patrick Wilson proposes a redefinition of "work" to be taken as the basic unit of cataloguing. However, to base description on "work" has strong implications for AACR, in that it influences the choice and form of main entries and uniform titles, structure of the catalogue, and the ways in which the relationship of different entities related to a work should be treated and displayed on the catalogue record. As has been demonstrated in the Proto- type Catalogue of Super Records, it is possible to have a hybrid approach towards the basis for description in the online environment. While describing the item in hand can fulfil the finding, selecting, and locating-functions, a multilevel, super record for the description of and access to "work" and its different expressions and manifestations would fulfil the identifying and collocating functions in a more meaningful way.

Structure of the catalogue and the concept of multiple entries

The structure of the catalogue has an important role in the fulfilment of its functions. The principles underlying the structure of the catalogue and choice of entries in AACR2 include rules concerning the determination and construction of necessary entries for a linear, alphabetical catalogue of main entries, added entries, and references. An online catalogue based on such a linear approach has many problems in searching, retrieval, and display of bibliographic sources.

To overcome some existing search/retrieval/display problems, the future AACR should take a new approach to the structure of the catalogue and the bibliographic record.

(i) New approaches to the structure for the catalogue and the bibliographic record

In place of the single, unique, and self-contained main entry record, research has recently attempted to propose a new structure for the catalogue and catalogue record. Such new approaches imply that the existing cataloguing principles do not adequately address the retrieval and display problems of works that appear in many editions and manifestations. Reanalysing the nature of works and their publications, Heaney states that the major access to information is through the "abstract work" and that cataloguing rules and MARC formats should incorporate radical changes mainly in the content of the MARC tags, to address access problems of "works" and their manifestations.

The experimental prototype OPAC (i.e., the Bradford OPAC) uses a manifestation concept to group together sets of items that are manifestations of the same work. In terms of display, the Bradford OPAC avoids repetition of the author heading and title. What the user sees is an economical display of manifestations which makes clear their differences. However, the catalogue is more concerned with the general concept of manifestations and does not distinguish between different subcategories within each manifestation.

In the Prototype Catalogue of Super Records, a multilevel record structure is proposed which is more relevant to the online environment. Super records would provide a uniform access to different instances of a work. The super record for a work would contain the uniform title of the work and the author heading, if applicable, along with a categorisation for different expressions and manifestations being linked to actual records for items and copies available in the collection. This approach would result in a better syndetic structure. At its first level, the super record for a work expresses the abstract work only: it is not directly linked to any actual record for items or copies. This helps the searcher to identify and select the category to which an item may belong. With super records in place, online catalogues would be better able to reflect special subarrangements than are current catalogue structures.

Catalogue users will search and retrieve super records through name authority files and/or uniform titles authority files first, so that they can scan the record and decide on the type of edition or manifestation for which they are looking. The reverse is also possible: once a record for an item has been retrieved in response to a specific query, the searcher can move from that record to the relevant super record through an assigned link. This bidirectional approach makes the navigation of the bibliographic universe easier and more understandable. In those cases where an item belongs to more than one category, the linkage can be created between the item and the two categories to which the item belongs.

A major requirement of a multilevel record is to incorporate links between different records for different expressions and manifestations of a work. A hypertext technique is feasible in the online environment and could provide such links.

(iii) New ways to link records in online catalogues

In online catalogues it is also possible to provide different mechanisms for the retrieval and display of different types of relationships. This depends, to a large extent, on both the structure of machine-readable records and the software to allow strings of fields and/or subfields to be organised so that the computer can retrieve and display all related records in a user- oriented manner.

It is possible to link two or more fields or subfields in machine-readable records in such a way as to better identify relationships between entities.

Online catalogues and future computerised systems may provide new and more effective linking devices to help the searcher to navigate a catalogue. Using hypertext techniques for linking related records is a promising method in bibliographic databases for the enhancement of retrieval and access. This technique is developed through precoordination, in that the cataloguer consciously creates links between related records in user-oriented ways in order to maintain different kinds of relationships. Connecting related entities directly, hypertext links remove the burden of a further search (i.e.. having to return to an index and entering a new query) which may still fail to yield the desired results. Examples of such applications are: the University of Toronto catalogue, the University of California catalogue (MELVYL), the Library and Information Services of Western Australia (LISWA), HyperLynx, GoPAC (from DataTrek, Australia), OhioLink, and the Prototype Catalogue of Super Records.

As demonstrated in the Catalogue of Super Records, data elements in bibliographic records can provide links to a variety of sources, such as related records (for other works by the same author, other expressions, editions, manifestations, versions of the same work, other works about the same subject, other publications by the same publisher. etc.), name authority records (information about other forms of the author's name, author's affiliation, and field of expertise), subject authority records (related terms, broader terms, narrower terms, etc.), holdings and status information, reviews in electronic format, and full text and/or virtual copies available. For example, a link can be provided from the name of the author to the authority record for that author, to his/her other works, or to his/her homepage available on the World Wide Web. Another example: a link from the name of the publisher in the imprint area can be provided to the publisher's homepage, which provides information about other publications by that publisher. In a hypertext bibliographic record, notes will have a more important role in providing access to related documents, such as other versions, editions, or manifestations of a work. In a hypertext catalogue, record added entries can act as additional linking devices.

AACR should take into consideration the complex structure of the multilevel bibliographic record and the various implications which new linking mechanisms, such as hypertext linking; have for cataloguing principles and rules.

In the following sections some of the basic principles of AACR2 which relate to the structure of the catalogue are reexamined in terms of their relevance to the online environment.

Concept of main entry

Like its predecessors, AACR2 distinguishes between main and added entries. However, with the advent of computerised catalogues, the value of the main entry concept, which developed in the context of book and card catalogues, has been questioned, but no satisfactory and practical solution has emerged as to how its functions can be otherwise fulfilled.

A major justification for the concept often lies in its collocating function, in bringing together both different editions of a work and the works of an author. As a collocating device, the concept of main entry has been retained not only in multiple-entry card catalogues but also with the same justification in automated catalogues. In terms of collocation, main entry has two specific functions: (1) assembling and displaying works by an author, and (2) assembling and displaying different editions of a work. The following section is an analysis of the main entry concept in terms of its functions in an online environment to see what influences the different capabilities may have on this principle. The focus of this section is only on main entries for personal names.

(i) Online search/retrieval/display and the concept of main entry

Keyword searching : Keyword searching on names will retrieve only those records that match the term(s) keyed in by the searcher, whether the term appears in main entries, added entries, or any other significant word indexed from the text of the record. Keyword searching capability cannot replace the main entry in terms of its collocating function. It can, however, facilitate the collocating function: once access to one or more specific items has been provided through keywords, the searcher can extend the search by keying the exact form of the author heading or the uniform title found on the retrieved record(s) to search for related editions with the same terms only. With hypertext links, as demonstrated in the University of Toronto catalogue, the University of California catalogue (MELVYL), the Library and Information Services of Western Australia (LISWA), HyperLynx, GoPAC (from DataTrek, Australia), OhioLink, and the Prototype Catalogue of Super Records, any keyword in the bibliographic record can potentially be a link to related records which have similar information.

Boolean searching : Boolean search is another capability for bringing together different editions of a work. This can be done by keying in two or more data elements, such as the author heading and the title proper or the uniform title and by using the "AND" operator. Since the titles proper of different editions of a work may vary, titles proper in conjunction with author heading cannot be a useful element for the collocating function. The "author/title" search key, which many systems provide, is an implicit Boolean search which has the same limitation. Instead, a Boolean search on the author uniform heading and the uniform title, including relevant qualifiers, can achieve the collocating function more effectively. This approach is another justification for the main entry concept in a new form and structure.

Index browsing : In browsing, for example, the author index will display together all the works by an author irrespective of his/her type of contribution (e.g., primary author, joint author. editor, compiler). It can be seen that, even with browsing capability, a useful collocation of different expressions and manifestations of a work is not possible with the present structure of entries. Browsable indexes can help to solve the collocation problem if the author and the title indexes are precoordinated for meaningful arrangement and display of related entities. Also, for the uniform citation and display of entries in the browsable author index, we need to identify the primary author. To link works, however, the primary author's name should be in a uniform heading. This is again another justification for the concept of main entry in an online environment.

Online display and the concept of main entry : The display format in online catalogues is independent of the storage format. Therefore, when a number of records are displayed in response to a query, the retrieved titles need to be displayed in conjunction with a second primary identifier such as the author heading. Otherwise, not only is the identification of the retrieved items not complete, but different works by an author are also not distinguished and assembled. This primary element is necessary in online displays of related works. Online displays, for instance default listings in brief displays, require that, in addition to titles proper, another principal element must be displayed. The following example may help to make this idea clearer:

As the convention now exists in many OPACs, when a work is entered under title or under a corporate heading with an added entry for editor or compiler, this person's name would still need to be displayed in conjunction with the title proper in the brief display to uniquely identify the work and to differentiate between works with identicate titles. From another perspective, that of the catalogue user who does not understand what main entry is, an editor or a compiler may seem to be the primary identifier or access point which should be displayed in conjunction with the title in brief displays and in single entry listings.

(ii) Networks, access to other catalogues, and the concept of main entry

In shared cataloguing systems and networked environments, it is important that the same entity be catalogued under the same uniform entry. This is essential for different operations such as searching, checking duplicate records, copy cataloguing, adding new holdings, etc. A work and also different editions and manifestations of a given work should be presented under the same entry. Otherwise, different problems may arise for different users: inconsistencies between catalogues and difficulties in the identification of the relationship of different instances of a work, all leading to confusion for the librarian, and the end user. A uniform main entry heading, with variants appropriately linked, avoids such problems in networked environments.

As a concept, the main entry relates rather to the nature of relationships between entities (authors to their works or works to their expressions and manifestations) than to the physical medium through which those entities are to be described. Many works, particularly in the fields of literature, philosophy, religions, law, and music, require such a uniform construct for identification and collocation. Even if technology provides catalogues with sophisticated devices, such as hypertext facility, to link two or more related entities to one another, it does not help the user if catalogues do not show him/her the nature of these relationships. Without such a concept the catalogue, whether manual or computerised, loses its integrity and usefulness.

It can be concluded that online catalogues still need a construct to carry out some specific functions which cannot be fulfilled thoroughly through other devices. Of great concern is the fact that the main entry concept is not meant to be a single function element but rather a concept that is essential to fulfil several functions. If the concept is to be retained in the future *AACR*, it is therefore in need of a redefinition that will focus on its rationale and multiple functions: main entry is a uniform construct for the naming and identifying of works and also for the useful collocation and arrangement/display of the different expressions and manifestations of a work.

In addition to the identification of the primary author, the concept of a uniform mode of identification, citation, and collocation is dependent on two key identifying elements which are emphasised in *AACR2*: uniform titles for works and uniform headings for authors.

Uniform headings for titles

Any work can potentially be produced in different expressions (e.g., editions, translations) and/or in a variety of physical formats. This concept is intrinsic to the bibliographic universe and its control has been an essential principle for catalogues. In this context, the name of the work, i.e., the "uniform title," has been devised in descriptive cataloguing to collocate different editions and manifestations of a work. *AACR2R* has devoted a full chapter to this concept; however, the use of uniform titles is optional in this code.

The functions of uniform titles are: (1) to standardise the original title of a work, (2) to standardise the form of the main entry heading for anonymous works, (3) to group together all editions and manifestations of a work under one particular title, and (4) to identify the relationships between an edition and a work. In the 1993 amendments to *AACR2R*, a new provision for uniform titles has been added to the functions of the uniform title: "for differentiating between two or more works published under identical titles proper" (rule 25.1 A). The rationale for the principle of uniform titles, however, rests mainly with two functions: (1) the uniform identification of a work and (2) the assembling of entities derived from or related to the same work. From a different point of view, uniform titles support at least four types of bibliographic relationship: equivalence, derivative, whole-part, and sequential relationships.

The rationale and the functions of uniform titles is examined in the context of the online environment as to see whether the structure and content of uniform titles, as formulated in AACR2, are appropriate for the catalogue's functions and are compatible with the different capabilities of online catalogues.

Online search/retrieval/display and the concept of uniform titles

A major problem in searching online catalogues is that in response to a query through the name of works, such as Hamlet, Bible, or an anonymous classic like the Arabian Nights, the searcher is presented with too many records to conveniently scan. This is an indication that in their present state uniform titles are not suitable for useful retrieval and display. In other words, uniform titles as access points or collocating elements are not useful for the effective retrieval and collocation of different expressions and manifestations of a work, and they should be reformulated for such functions in accordance with the capabilities of online catalogues. Without the uniform title associated with the main entry heading, one can see that different editions of the same work are scattered among the retrieved records for other works by the same author. This problem is highlighted in online catalogues: they may need a number of screens to list all retrieved items and the searcher may have to spend considerable time to identify the relationship of a sought item to a work and find what he/she is searching for.

While the occurrence of editions of the same work with different titles and different works with similar titles increases in large catalogues and union databases, the concept of uniform titles can help control this problem. With regard to the catalogue's collocating function, uniform titles can play a more important role in the online catalogue. While uniform titles alone increase the search results (i.e., recall), the addition of other data elements (i.e., qualifiers), such as version (i.e., the physical format), language, date, and part of the work, to the uniform title will narrow down the search results and will increase precision. *AACR2* can prescribe additional qualifiers which would be functional in the meaningful retrieval and collocation of related entities.

In an electronic environment with hypertext facility, uniform titles are needed to provide links between different occurrences of a work and to collocate and display, in a meaningful order, all the available expressions and manifestations of a given work, as has been demonstrated in the Prototype Catalogue of Super Records. Through the uniform title approach in super records, separate records for different versions of a work are grouped and linked to one another. As can be seen, since a uniform title approach is used as a uniform identifier and a collocating device wherever a work has more than one edition and/or manifestation in the catalogue, the concept of multilevel records, in general, reinforces the principle of unifonn titles. In hypertext catalogues, a browsable uniform-title index or uniform titles authority file with the name of the author(s) of each work could provide easy access to works.

Uniform headings for persons

Another principle that is essential to the fulfilment of the collocating function and for the integrity of the catalogue is a uniform heading for each person. An examination of this principle in light of different capabilities of online catalogues reveals that the concept is still valid in the online environment but that the new technology may influence the content and form of name headings, as well as the scope and extent to which it would be possible to achieve collaboration in their standardisation.

(i) Online search/retrieval/display and the principle of uniform headings

Keyword searching : Keyword searching facilitates the finding function of the catalogue through the form of an author's name that appears on the title page or in information sources, i.e., the form which is usually familiar to both the book world and the searcher. However, with keyword searching it is only possible to search names under the form in which they have been recorded in the bibliographic record. Keywords, not being subject to authority control, naturally do not always collocate all the works by or about an author if there are variant forms of name. However, keyword searching facilitates the collocation of an author's works: once access is made to a record through any form of the name, it is possible to assemble works by or about a particular author through a further search on the uniform author heading.

Truncation : With right-hand truncation, the online catalogue is able to retrieve those names which begin with the characters defined by the searcher. In other words, names must be entered uniformly, at least for the few beginning characters, to retrieve all the works by a given author. Obviously, however, truncation also allows the searcher to retrieve records which are not relevant to his/her needs. Therefore, the more complete the input heading is, the more chance there will be for retrieval precision. Thc closer we can get to "natural" forms of names, the more efficiently successful will our catalogue searches be.

Authority control systems : In an online catalogue utilising name authority files, access to the works of a given author by variant forms of the name can be as effective as access by the uniform or preferred heading. The distinction between the established form of a name and any cross-reference to it is invisible to the searcher. This apparent ease of consultation may render catalogue users and library administrators unaware of the professional effort which goes into collocating the various works by and about an author. In fact, more emphasis must be placed on this in the online environment than with previous forms of catalogue.

Adherence to the principle of uniform heading is a means of

maintaining the one-to-many relationship (i.e., one name to many works) in bibliographic databases and, thus, to achieve the collocation of all works available by a given author in the catalogue. Even in authority control systems there is still a need to establish one form of a person's name as the uniform heading and others as references. In fact, uniform headings are still considered to be an important principle in authority work.

Index browsing : In systems allowing the browsing of name indexes, it is necessary, in general, that any name be presented in a uniform manner in the list to avoid confusion. It is also necessary that works by an author be retrieved through and assembled under a single form of name in browsable author-title indexes. More effective display could result from uniform indexing in browsable indexes. In systems which do not repeat the main heading on every line in brief displays, uniform headings are essential. The browsing capability thus reinforces the need for the principle of uniform headings.

Online displays and the principle of uniform headings : With regard to differences in the physical forms of the manual catalogue and the online catalogue, the very rigid ideal in the card catalogue of assembling in *one place* all the works a library has by a given author has shifted, in the online catalogue, to the ideal of the system's ability to retrieve all the works of an author through any searched form of his/her name and to display them together under one uniform heading for the author. Under whatever form of name the works by a given author have been searched, the default listing of those works, particularly in brief displays, requires that the name of the author be presented in a uniform manner. Similarly, in catalogues with a hypertext interface, links can be provided from any form of a name to the records, but the name should appear under a uniform heading when records are displayed; otherwise, the catalogue may lose its integrity and the searcher may think that the works displayed are by different authors.

(ii) Networks, global access to catalogues, and the concept of uniform headings

The communication of bibliographic records for cataloguing purposes: reference services, interlibrary loan, and document delivery services depends to a large extent on the uniformity of headings. An important factor concerning the value of uniform headings is the ever-increasing use of bibliographic utilities, such as OCLC and RLIN, and national bibliographic agencies, such as Library of Congress. Most libraries attempt to be consistent with the Library of Congress for headings and contribute to the Name Authority Cooperative Project (NACO) initiated by that library.

In searching the different catalogues accessible in a network, the patron, the technical services librarian, and the reference librarian usaually expect to find the works of a given author under one form of heading. Except for differences in user interfaces, a first requirement is to conform to the concept of uniform headings at the national level. Links to national online name authority files, such as the Library of Congress Name Authority File (LCNAF), would be a most desirable answer to differences in authors' names and can provide consistent access to catalogues and other bibliographic lists.

(iii) Availability of different types of bibliographic databases

A major problem in the online environment is that there are many different types of bibliographic databases and a wide variety of users. A difficulty in searching different databases is that, while there is a uniform approach in library cataloguing in relation to uniform headings, other communities such as the book trade and A&I services are less concerned with this principle, so that in many bibliographic databases the same person may have been entered under a variety of unlinked names.

Content and form of name headings in an online environment

As emphasised in the Paris Principles, the content and form of names in headings, as well as the principle of uniform headings, should be agreed upon nationally and, to some extent, internationally. Over the last one hundred years the Anglo-American cataloguing codes have formulated necessary rules concerning the form of personal and corporate headings.

In the following sections the content and form of personal and corporate headings will be reexamined in light of the searching/retrieval/display capabilities of computerised catalogues and with respect to searchers' expectations of an integrated online environment.

(i) Content and form of personal name headings

According to the general rule (rule 22.1), the name by which a person is commonly known should be chosen as the basis for the heading for that person.

The form of a name is an important factor in searching and retrieval, particularly in online systems in which the searcher has to key in the name as a search string. It is seen that users often enter personal names in a form and sequence different from those prescribed for *AACR2*. A rather different approach form that adopted in a manual environment is possible, in that searches under the names of authors no longer need to be phrased in the exact form and order of the author's name headings in online catalogues, such as Okapi (Online Keyboard Access to Public Information, developed at the Polytechnic of Central London), MIRLYN (Michigan Research Library's Network, the University of Michigan's Online Public Catalog), and SULIRS (Syracuse University Libraries Information Retrieval System). Cross-references and/or keyword access offer the possibility of entering the search names in any order. Keyword searching also reduces the need for complete "surname+initials+(full forenames)+dates" headings as in AACR2R. With keyword searching, the inversion of surnames and rules for the choice of entry element in compound surnames and names with prefixes become unnecessary. The most useful form of name is the fullest form. The German code (RAK), which is being revised for online catalogues, takes a similar approach and strongly rejects any substantial reduction in personal name entries.

There are other factors, such as the need for default listings of the works of an author and the needs of the book world, citation traditions, and international exchange of bibliographic data, which require the standard order of "surname, forename" in full form for personal headings. There is at present no consensus on the content and form of headings among the different creators of bibliographic records. There are, however, to some extent similarities between library cataloguing and the book world: both tend to use the best-known form of name with library cataloguing more inclined to use the complete form.

Truncation of headings, especially automatic right-hand truncation, can help to retrieve works by authors whose complete heading (i.e., surname, forename, or initials) is not familiar to the searcher. Variations in the fullness of forenames seem unimportant in systems with a truncation capability. An online catalogue with keyword searching of headings and automatic right-hand truncation needs rather different rules for the formulation of headings and references. It should be noted, however, that searching names through truncation may retrieve too many records to scan easily. Another problem with personal name headings is that initials often cause searching and retrieval problems in online catalogues. The middle names or initials users include in their queries for personal names are sometimes counter- productive in helping them find the heading used in the catalogue.

Differentiation between identical names : The differentiation between identical names is an important requirement, particularly for large files and shared databases in which the frequency or such headings increases as files grow or merge. The use of dates of birth and death, as in *AACR* may not always be particularly useful to searchers, who might have no idea of when a particular author was born. Differentiation of author by discipline can be a more useful approach. The field of expertise at least lets the searchers guess which author they want to look at.

Another element which can help in the consistent association of a person with a given work is his/her role in the creation/ production of the work. This approach, has been practiced by a number of A&I services for a relatively long time. It would help users if such differentiation were to become a principle associated with assigning name entries. *AACR* should address this issue in association with the principle of authorship.

(ii) Content and form of headings for corporate bodies

The issue of corporate headings was one of the problems on which there was considerable debate at the Paris Conference but the decisions made have not all proved to be entirely workable.

Even today different national codes have different approaches toward the form of corporate headings. In terms of names of jurisdictions forming the entry word of some government headings, *AACR2R* uses the English language form, while in the RAK a name in the official language of the country is preferred.

Searching, retrieval, and display of corporate names in online systems are often frustrating to the user. Many of the problems concerning the searching of corporate bodies publications relate to the content and form of headings for these bodies. *AACR2* prescribes that, in general, corporate bodies should be entered under the name by which they are commonly identified, except when other rules provide for entering them under the name of a higher or related body or under the name of a government (rule 24.1). Some of the problems concerning with the searching, retrieval, and display of corporate headings in online systems are:

(1) It is particularly difficult to search under the exact form of corporate headings in online catalogues because the user has to key in the search string. How much of the heading should be keyed in by the searcher to initiate the search, since corporate names are usually long, often similar to one another, and appear in different forms, such as acronyms, initials, and subordinations (e.g., World Health Organization, WHO or W.H.O.)?

(2) In some cases, headings for subordinate bodies associated with the same parent body do not follow a uniform approach. While the "World Health Organization" appears as the heading for this body, a number of subordinate bodies incorporating the acronym "WHO" are treated as headings in the catalogue; for example, "WHO Collaborating Centre on Environmental Pollution Control," "WHO Commission on Health and Environment," "WHO Expert Group on Pesticide Residues. The same problem exists with the "Food and Agriculture Organization of the United Nations" and some of its subordinate bodies beginning with "FAO:"

(3) Entering corporate bodies under the name of the higher body would often cause inconvenience for the searcher,

especially in large catalogues and shared systems. The use of indirect corporate headings can somctimes appear meaningless to catalogue users. Names can be considerably distorted because of rearrangement of the elements of the name and, in many codes, by translating the name of thc jurisdiction.

(4) The addition of a geographic name to the beginning of headings for corporate bodies often does not make sense in the online environment. Exact searching and truncation on headings beginning with the name of a jurisdiction or geographic name often result in too many hits. Headings likc "Australia, Australian Parliamentary Observer Group," "Canada, Canadian High Commission," and "Canada, Canadian Armed Forces," which are problematic for searching, could be more straightforward if "Australia" and "Canada" were omitted from the heading.

(5) In most cases truncation on corporate headings does not make sense because of the similarity in the first few words at the beginning of such names, particularly when corporate bodies are entered under a higher or government body or heading beginning with geographic names. Also in brief displays, because of screen limitation, the name of the parent body alone may fill the allotted space. A possible approach, which depends on the software used, is to avoid repeating the name of parent body but to display the name of subordinate bodies for better differentiation.

(6) Clustering of all the publications of different departments and divisions of a corporate body is not usually sought by searchers. Also, it does not make sense in brief displays where, because of screen limitation, only the first few elements of the heading are displayed, thus obscuring the name of the actual issuing body. Consider, for example, how frustrating the retrieval of publications of different subordinate bodies of the United Nations would be in an online catalogue.

So, it is concluded that direct headings, i.e., subordinate bodies under their own heading, would lessen these problems, provided that the heading for the subordinate body is self-sufficient. There are a number of factors that also justify this:

- direct headings form a shorter string and are more suitable for online displays, especially for brief displays;
- most searchers are usually looking for the publications of a given subordinate body and are not interested in the parent body;
- truncation on direct headings (name of subordinate bodies) is more useful than on indirect headings (name of parent bodies);
- alternative approaches could be provided by means of authority control. As with advanced name authority files linked to the bibliographic file, it is possible to search names in different forms; considerations should also be given to any form which may be looked under by catalogue searchers;
- the addition of geographic names or a general designation to corporate headings for their further identification or differentiation should be re-examined with regard to the difficulties of searching such names. The present approach in *AACR2* rule 24.4, in that a general designation or a geographic name is added in parenthesis to the corporate heading for further identification or differentiation, should be followed in other cases.

In general, while a fuller form of personal names seems more useful in the online environment, corporate names need a simpler approach in that, for example, direct headings for subordinate bodies are more responsive to the search/retrieval/display capabilities of online catalogues. Nevertheless, the problems of corporate headings in online catalogues such as the form and structure (e.g., official name versus name most frequently used; most frequently used versus conventional or modified name; language; transliteration; punctuation and display problems) require further research.

Principles for online display of bibliographic information

Since cataloguing codes basically deal with providing description of and access to bibliographic entities, it is reasonable that they should also give guidance for data representation and identification, i.e., record displays and arrangement. Description and access are most effective if the information on the catalogue record is clear, useful, and adequate for different users. This is in line with the objectives of the catalogue, in that the catalogue should help in the better identification of works/items. While one of the major differences of online catalogues from card catalogues is their extensive ability for displaying bibliographic information in a variety of formats, *AACR2* does not provide any guidelines for online displays, and many problems in online display stem from the treatment of its rules. Also, many problems in online display could be attributed to lengthy headings prescribed in the code.

Problems in online displays

The ways in which bibliographic information is displayed online have often been criticised by cataloguers. One of the difficulties faced by the user of online catalogues lies in the wide variations in possible format. This is largely due to the fact that, unlike card catalogues which had a fixed storage/display format and usually presented the same level of information, online catalogues differ from one another both in display formats and in the levels of information displayed. These variations may often confuse the user, particularly when moving from one catalogue to another, for example in searching different remote catalogues through the Internet.

A common problem in online displays is related to the brief display, where the information is often the one-line record, which is inadequate or confusing for identifying items. For example, in response to a query for a voluminous work by a given author (e.g., Hamlet by Shakespeare), the brief display may show the author heading and the title repeated on every line, the only element being the date of publication. This sort of brief display does not make sense to the user. To increase clarity and save -space, it is desirable to include the author statement (main entry heading) once only, where it applies to multiple retrieved records. The display of long corporate bodies also has implications for online catalogues, especially for brief displays: not only may the heading displayed not be distinct enough to identify the body conclusively, but also the title probably cannot be displayed completely.

Library materials are different in terms of their nature and the data elements necessary for their description and access. The case of serials is a notable one: the author/title/publication/date approach generally useful for monographs is not applicable to serials; they are rarely entered under author, and the date of first publication can often be more confusing than helpful.

Sumarizing, it can be said that the matching of some of the basic *AACR2* principles against individual search/retrieval/display capabilities of the online catalogue revealed that, while a number of fundamental principles, such as the main entry, uniform titles, and uniform headings, remain valid in the online environment, current principles are not entirely adequate for online search/ retrieval/display requirements. There is a need for additional principles so as to secure more effectiveness in the searching, retrieval, and display of bibliographic data, e.g., concerning the basic unit of description, bibliographic relationships, and online display of bibliographic data.

The following conclusions are derived from the examination of a number of *AACR2* principles carried out in the light of the various capabilities of the online environment.

(i) Functions of the catalogue

Conceptually, the objectives and functions of the catalogue are independent of its physical form and arrangement. Technology can, however, influence the way in which these functions are carried out: the more developments there are in the technology of catalogue construction and in the online environment, the more possibilities there are of achieving those objectives and functions.

Due to the wide and varied use of bibliographic records in the online environment, the scope of catalogue functions should be expanded in *AACR* to encompass additional functions. The two basic functions i.e., the finding function and the collocating function remain valid, but the catalogue also can serve to further identify entities, to choose one item over similar items, to locate items and copies of items, and to maintain databases in terms of record updating. The collocating is of particular importance in the online environment with hypertext facility.

(ii) Basis for description and the structure of the catalogue

In terms of the basis for description, AACR should consider all the different functions of the catalogue and should take a hybrid approach, in that both the work and the physical item should be taken into account. The multilevel record structure, as demonstrated in the Prototype Catalogue of Super Records, can incorporate this hybrid approach without the need for radical changes to the MARC bibliographic format. To avoid online retrieval problems for works appearing in different editions and manifestations, as well as for a more useful collocation and display of such works, the concept of super records for works could be applied, particularly in those catalogues which consider the collocating function as being equally important to other functions. To achieve this, principles are needed concerning the structure of super records; categorisation of entities in the bibliographic hierarchy, the data elements associated with the entity at each level, particularly for uniform titles, and also principles for establishing and maintaining bibliographic relationships.

AACR should provide guidelines for the construction of different files for example, bibliographic, authority, and holdings and also the links between them; and also for the indexing of different fields and sub fields concerning access to required elements in the record. The principles should also suit the structure of a hybrid system including both MARC records for access to items and super records for providing a multilevel approach to works, their expressions, and manifestations. In such a catalogue, different indexes are needed for both string searching and browsing. A possible approach would be to provide guidelines for the construction of (hypertext) browsable indexes for names (personal and corporate) and titles (titles proper, uniform titles, and series). It is also useful to provide name authority files and a uniform-title authority file for searching and browsing.

(iii) Concept of main entry

Rather than being the locus of complete information for the bibliographic record or the primary access point, main entry is an important concept that maintains some basic functions of the catalogue—that of identifying and collocating, in a uniform way, difterent expressions and manifestations of a work. In other words. if a major function of the catalogue is to identify and collocate works as well as their editions and manifestations, there is a need for a concept such as main entry. It is particularly needed in the online environment for the useful retrieval, display and arrangement of search results. Unless we devise new mechanisms for the uniform identification and collocation of the different manifestations and editions of a work, it would be unwise to abandon the concept of main entry.

Nevertheless, in order to delineate the concept more clearly and to avoid confusion as to its functions, main entry is in need of redefinition. The new functional definition should address the validity of the concept in terms of its various functions, irrespective of the catalogue's physical environment.

(iv) Concept of uniform titles

Similar to the concept of main entry, uniform titles are needed in online catalogues to perform some basic functions, such as providing links between different expressions and manifestations of a work and to distinguish among works with identical titles proper. Because of present problems in the online retrieval of the various expressions and manifestations of works, a concept such as a standardised form of the title of a work can serve to identify and collocate them. In online catalogues, particularly with hypertext facility, the content and structure of uniform titles need to be simplified in order to avoid online retrieval problems. *AACR* should prescribe more natural qualifiers which would be functional in the useful retrieval and collocation of related entities.

(v) Principle of uniform headings

It is difficult to maintain the integrity of the catalogue and to fulfil its collocating function without maintaining the principle of uniform headings. Uniformity of headings for authors is especially important in network environments, where different catalogues and other bibliographic databases are accessible to the user through the same terminal. This is also of particular significance in shared cataloguing systems and union databases. Library cataloguing, book trade bibliographic databases, and A&I services should at least be consistent or compatible in certain areas such as uniform headings. In effect, standardisation or compatibility in the form of headings, which has long been recognised as a highly desirable requirement for universal bibliographical control (UBC), becomes more critical in the global online environment.

(vi) Content and form of name headings

In terms of the form of personal and corporate name headings for effective searching, retrieval, and display, online catalogues need a simpler approach. The form of headings needs to be reconsidered in terms of its suitability for different searching patterns and for display. But searching under single letters, such as initials, is still a technical problem for many library systems. For corporate bodies, direct headings are usually more responsive to online search/retrieval/displays.

Cataloguing concepts are derived mainly from elements that represent the nature of bibliographic entities. In general, it can be concluded that there is not such a close relationship between the conceptual foundations of *AACR* and the technology of catalogue construction. Nevertheless, just as the physical limitations of paper or card technologies imposed some practices, such as the "rule of three" limiting the numher of access points, the search/retrieval display capabilities of online catalogues require that some principles and rules should be modified to take advantage of the new technology whereby computers are able to manipulate, modify, and organise or reorganise bibliographic data more effectively than was possible in the manual environment.

STANDARDS FOR CATALOGUING

The effective exchange of bibliographic data between agencies can be accomplished only if the records confrom in respect of : (1) the structure, (2) the content designators, and (3) the data element definitions. The Universal Acceptance of the ISO 2709 record structure (International Organization for Standardization ISO 2709-1981 Documentation: format for bibliographic information interchange on maganetic tape, 2nd ed. General, ISO, 1981), as a basis for exchange formats, addresses the first issue and thus has enormously benefited the information community. There are equivalent national standards too.

The second componet relates to the content designators which are represented in most bibliographic formats by tags, indicators and subfield codes. There are several bibliographic formats many of them come from the Marc family, viz. MARC, UKMARC, INDIMARC, and so on.

Since the early 1970s, an extended family of more than 20 MARC formats has grown up, whose paths have diverged owing to the different national cataloguing practice and requirments. The differences in these formats mean that editing is required before the records can be exchanged. One solution to this incompatibillty was to develop an international MARC format, known as Universal MARC (UNIMARC) which would accept records in one national format and porvide a mean whereby records in one national format could be converted first into UNIMARC and then into another national format. This would in effect require each national agency to wirte two conversion programs: one to convert from the national MARC format into UNIMARC, and another to convert from UNIMARC into the national format, instead of having to wirte a separate porgram for each other national format with which the records were to be exchanged.

The First version of UNIMARC was published by the International Federation of Library Association and Institutions (IFLA) in 1977. This was followed by a second edition in 1980 and by the Unimarc Handbook in 1983. All of these focused primarily on the cataloguing of monographs and serials and reflected international progress towards the standardization of bibliographic information as represented by ISBDs

The MARC record format was designed by the Library of Congress and the British Lbrary to communicate a bibliographic description in machine-readable form. This MARC I format was tried around 1966 but was superseded by MARC II or MARC in 1968.

MARC II

It was a one-format structure on the machine- readable medium capable of containing bibliographic data of all forms of library materials, such as books, monographs, serials, maps, music etc., and related records. The structure or the physical representation of the machine-readable medium, the content designators, such as tags, indicators, and subfields codes used to identify the data elements; and the content or the data itself such as author, title and bibliographic descriptions are the three components of the LC MARC format.

MARC II officially, began in March 1968, 1960 and its distrubution began for all English Language material providing a weekly magnetic tape of zonal 1000 records. Thereafter, other documentation began to be issued, including formats for other materials over the period 1970-73. In 1972 films records were distributed, by 1973 records for serials, maps and French books, by 1975 German Spanish and Portuguese materials.

MARC II is a subscription service; by subscribing to this service a library can acquire, in machine readable form cataloguing data for American and other foreign publication as described above. In fact, the Library of Congress catalogues the documents, i.e., books and non-book materials, records the data on magnetic tape and supplies copies of the tapes to various interested libraries. The libraries which get the copy of magnetic tape, can than porduce printed catalogues of their colloections entries on cards and various kinds of bibliographies (author or subject, etc.) bu using a computer. Most libraries obtain access to MARC data through products and services developed by publishers computer system developers, time-sharing services and other intermediaries. At present a growing number of vendor supply the MARC database on CD-ROM disks or digiital optical videodiscs accompanied by software which supports the retrieval of specific cataloguing records and the printing of card sets. A specimen of LC catalouge card (MARC) is given on next page:

Bedford, Richard

Perceptions, past & present of a future for Melanesia/ Richard Bedford. - Christchurch, N.Z. : Dept. of Geography, University of Canterbury, c1980.

73 p. : ill., maps; 21 cm. — (Macmillan Brown lectures, ISSN 0464-2767 : 79) .

Bibliography: p. 66-73.

$5.00 (pbk.)

1. Melanesia—Politics and government—Addresses, essays, lectures, 2. Melanesia—Economic conditions,—Address, essays, lecturers. 3. Melanesia - Social conditions—Addresses, essays. lectures. 4. Melanesia—Poupulation— Addresses, essays, lecures, I. Title. II. Title: Perceptions, past and present, of a future for Melanesia. III. Series.

DU490.B43 1980   993-dc19   81-196414

AACR 2 MARC

Library of Congress

Library of Congress Catalog Cards (Full MARC)

Uses of MARC :

MARC tapes are being used for various purposes. Following are some of important uses:

1. A centrally prepared catalogue can be distributed to the receiving libraries in a machine-readable form.
2. In spite of increasing acquisitions, the catalogue can be kept up to date without employing additional staff.
3. The production cost of card catalogue on the computer (MARC System) is lesser than that of purchasing the Library of Congress catalogue cards.
4. The MARC tapes can be utilized for acquisition functions, i.e., selecting, ordering and claiming unsupplied books without any additional cost. They can be used to produce spine labels, book pockets, etc.
5. The MARC tapes can be used for producing conventional

card catalogue by the subscribing libraries.

6. The MARC data can also be used for producing book catalogues as demonstrated by the Washington State Library.
7. The MARC tapes can besed for computerised SDI service.
8. It automatically perfoms resource-sharing functions.

Mini or Microcomputer-based MARC is commercially based cataloguing system. Practically a microcomputer is housed in the Library and a set of floppy disks is provided which contains the entire MARC database. It is then quicky retrieved and edited as needed.

Limitations

The following are few limitations of the Machine-Readable catalogue system:

1. The MARC record for any title is almost similar to the conventional bibliographic record, as such it inherits all its limitations.
2. The MARC format will be limited, at least for the next few years, to the English language books because the MARC character set is severally limited in respect of special characters.
3. The time gap between the creation, of MARC record and a catalogue record copy by the participating library, which is inherent at present in the existing card production methods of the Library of Congress, will not be removed until and unless both the cards and tapes are prepared from the same machine-readable record.

MARC records are no longer created only by LC. but also but many other agencies, and are available through bibliographic utilities and from commerical services.

Several additions and improvements took place in MARC and other standard formats. This has happened to cope with the various new types and formats of information sources, and also to cope with the cahging needs of users. For example, CCF came out as two sets of standards, one for bibliographic records (called CCF/B) and the other for factual records (called CCF/F). Recent additions to MARC have also included fields for creating hyperlinks among various documents. All the Marc formats, such as USMARC,

UKMARC, UNIMARC, etc., have included a field (Field 656 Electronic location and access) to hold data on electronic resources; for example, such as web page. A number of fields have also been added to link records; for example, in the USMARC fields 760, 762, 765, 767, 770, 772, 773, 775, 766, 777, 780, 785, 786, and 787 have been added as various linking entry fields. Similarly field 536 has been created to hold finding information note, field 561 for holding information on ownership and custodial history, and so on.

The world Wide Web is becoming an integral portion of life in today's society. A big part of the web's allure is the availability of vast amounts of information and entertainment. The fact that potential library users have discovered the web is not lost on library administrators, many of whom are aggressively incorporating digital resources into their information offerings.

The marketplace also plays an important role in librarian's choice of what is offered to the user community. Product developers are aware of the web's ubiquitous presence and, as a consequence, are creating many new products or new versions of previously developed products that are designed specifically for use through web browsers. This begs the question of what role digital information will play in the evolving library marketplace. In particular, will information in the MARC 21 communications format' continue to have relevance to library systems and patrons, or will XML replace MARC as the standard for library information?

AN XML SOLUTION

It should come as little surprise that there are many different visions for libraries' digital future. Some of these future digital library visions assume that the MARC communications format will continue to be an essential building block. Others reject in whole or in part the continued relevancy of MARC 21 and urge library systems development based on other information standards.

One such iconoclastic approach is being advanced by Dick R. Miller, Head of Technical Services and Systems Librarian at Stanford University's Lane Medical Library. Mr. Miller and his staff are researching the extensible markup language (XML) to see if this offers a suitable replacement for MARC. In presentations made to the Medical Library Association (MLA) in 1999 and the Machine-Readable Bibliographic Information Committee (MARBI) in 2000, Miller observed that with the "burgeoning web development, we felt that our 'library Information was under-utilized due to its segregation from mainstream web resources, and in danger of becoming marginalized." Lane Medical Library staff projects that there will be a sionificant decline in the use of traditional library resources since, in their view, MARC-encoded information can not be used in the web environment.

IS MARC DEAD?

Lane Library staff examined the MARC 21 bibliographic format and found that, in their view, "the MARC formats hamper bibliographic data's effective integration in web interfaces." In particular, since MARC employs a mark-up language and structure different from XML and HTML, both standards more closely identified with web development, the continued use of MARC will guarantee that some library information will be useful on the web (e.g., XML) and some will not (e.g., MARC). Dick Miller calls this "Bibliographic apartheid."

Particular problems that Lane Library staff noted with MARC 21 include:

* Information is recorded in a variety of (sometimes inconsistent) ways in a variety of (sometimes inconsistent) places. This can be seen in how date information is recorded. Dates for example are found in the MARC 21 record in the 005, 008/00-05 - 008/07-10, 008/11-14, and 260 $c in four distinctly different formats.
* There are inherent complexities in the format that are handled inconsistently across the formats. For example, fixed field type information is embedded in 4XX, 5XX. and 7XX $w subfields in authority records, and in 76X-78X $w subfields in bibliographic records.
* MARC records include some information recorded in coded form that, can not be justified in today's computing environment with much cheaper storage media. Examples of information are needlessly recorded in encoded form

include: government publication (008), language (008,041), country (008, 043), and relators ($4).

* Finally, the MARC format is seen as "flat, with limited support for hierarchy" and, in his view, does not support web linking well.

IS AACR2 DEAD?

Equally troubling in the view of the Lane Library staff is that current cataloging standards place far too much emphasis on physical description and not nearly enough emphasis on access to intellectual content. Additionally, a major problem with current cataloging practice as seen through the lens of AACR2 is what they see as its inadequacy in describing bibliographic relationships.

Lane's observations include:

* There is no need to worry about consistency of access points since keyword searching in the new web access environment obviates the need for spending time of this issue.
* Headings should not employ more than a single language (e.g., Germany, Bundesamt fur Naturschutz.). Multiple language headings serve as an impediment to the internationalizion of the catalogue.
* No effort should be made in regularizing the order of headings (e.g.. Dept. of. ..) since web-based keyword searching takes care of finding the heading and sorting out inconsistencies. The telephone book is cited as an example of how inverting corporate names enhances retrieval.
* Variation in headings ought to be recorded in authority records rather than trying to sort them out in bibliographic records. Additionally, some types of information are presently recorded in bibliographic records such as publishers' names and places of publication but might be migrated to authority records with merely a link to the authority record to avoid duplication of data entry.

SO WHY XML?

Having reached the conclusion that MARC is not adequate to provide access to library information over the web, and similarly feeling that it was counterproductive to try to maintain library information in more than one format, the Lane Library staff set about looking for alternatives.

In looking for a data structure that would support library information on the web and also address what were seen as problems in current bibliographic description, Lane Library chose XML. Miller observes that the "significant aspect of XML may be its separation of content, presentation, and linking, so that each may be handled optimally." Additionally, XML was seen as "inherently hierarchical" and "advanced and web-oriented." He further notes that there is a widespread adoption of XML in the business world because it works well with e-commerce web applications.

Other considerations that led to Lane's selection of XML included:

* XML is characterized as the "universal Web data format," a "simplified SGML, using HTML syntax, with added web efficiencies."
* XML employs a single character set, Unicode; to represent all data.
* A current problem is that there is no agreed-upon standard for XML library applications. This could be addressed as the library community gains familiarity with working with XML bibliographic information on the web.

XML MARC SOFTWARE

To test whether XML is suitable for recording and communicating bibliographic information, Lane Library staff developed software that maps MARC data into XML markup. The MARC bibliographic structure was analyzed and DTDs were developed to optimize data structures and minimize what was seen at Lane as needless duplication of similar data types. For example, the several places for recording language information in the MARC 21 bibliographic format (e.g., 008/35-37, 040$b, 041, 242$y, 546) were compressed into a single code. The conversion software was designed to take the MARC 21 bibliographic data to XML but not back, since Lane Library staff believe that the MARC format is not relevant now nor will it be in the future. Although Miller reports that the software works well, he believes that it requires considerable additional work, particularly to account for data types less common at Lane Library. He also notes that documentation for the program as it currently exists needs to be enhanced so that the program can be applied more consistently.

THE END OF MARC?

The impetus for this discussion, as well as for a joint meeting of MARBI and CC:DA, was a column in the American Library Association's (ALA) journal, American Libraries. In the April 2000 issue, David Dorman reports Dick Miller as saying, "We need to replace MARC as soon as possible with an equally rich, but unencumbered format that facilitates, rather than impedes, our ability to experiment."

Dorman goes on to assert that "That unencumbered format to which he was referring is, of course, XML." He concludes that "The $64,000 question is: Will ALA or another professional group lead a standard effort to adapt the rules of AACR2 cataloging to XML so that the profession can settle on a single successor to MARC? Or will we backslide into an environment in which there will be multiple ways to encode AACR2 bibliographic data on the Web?"

In MARBI's view, as related to development of standards for digital libraries, XML and MARC do not represent an "either/or" choice but rather an "and/with" choice. MARC is a communication format that has several uses: input, storage, processing, communication, and display. XML is being considered as a standard for use in library systems in other areas such as the emerging NCIP circulation protocol. XML is a meta language, and the use ofXML will require significant standardization and process training just as MARC currently does. Significantly, XML can be used as a wrapper for carrying MARC encoded information. There is a need, however, for building a set of standardized library-related XML style sheets.

In CC:DA's view, XML presents new opportunities and extended life for MARC. XML retools the carrier but not the content. XML may suggest a different relationship between libraries and publishers and other content creators by communicating metadata along with the content. The apparent difficulty in expressing bibliographic relationships in the current AACR2 may be improved by experimenting with ways to describe relationships such as using URLs for linking.

FUTURE WITH XML

XML will play a significant role in the future of online delivery of library information. Web browsers are being developed today with XML in mind, and product developers are working on many new applications geared to the creation, retrieval, and manipulation of XML information.

So if XML is so great, this is the right time just to switch to it rather than some time in the future? Here are a few observations:

* Tens of millions of dollars have been invested into the current worldwide aggregation of hundreds of millions of MARC cataloging records. The MARC format is well understood within the library world, and it is the only format that approaches universal application. Additionally, there is a broad range of software built to use MARC data, and a marketplace commitment to enhance it. Additionally, there is widely available software that enables the effective searching of MARC data over the internet.
* Given that library technical service resources are limited and that tools to quickly and easily convert MARC information into XML do not as yet exist, it is likely that MARC data will be in use well into the future. It should be noted that there is no broad-based agreement that such a transition should indeed happen. Without such agreement or the required standard adoption, a piecemeal switch to XML will cause the information balkanization that Mr. Miller anticipates if the MARC status quo persists.
* Experimentation with XML markup coding of library information has taken place over only the past year or two. It will be instructive to analyze the successes and failures that this experimentation has engendered to determine the need for standards and tools (e.g., DTDs, stylesheets, etc.). It is likely that a detailed, unbiased study of this experience will contribute to a universally acceptable XML mark-up

standard.

* There is no broad-based agreement that current cataloging rules are inadequate. Indeed, although the cataloging community has a long-term commitment to the revision and expansion of the descriptive cataloging code, there is, if anything, an abhorrence of anything approaching a new edition of AACR.
* Use of XML for library information does not enjoy widespread acceptance in the past 2 years. This is driven by the near total lack of data creation, management, display, and searching tools, the lack of broadly accepted standards for XML encoding and display of library information, and the very low level of understanding of XML within the library community. Nevertheless, all of these problems will probably be resolved in time.
* XML support on web browsers available in 2000 ranges from marginally adequate to non-existent. This is especially important in comparing Internet Explorer to Netscape Navigator.
* It is by no means a given that data in multiple markup conventions can not be searched efficiently within a single search session. Many of the internet searching programs currently available or in development can perform meaningful searching without being tied to specific markup conventions.

WHERE DO WE GO NOW?

The MARC format is a mature and broadly accepted mark-up language for recording library information in machine-readable form. It is likely that the huge investment in data creation and software will guarantee its use long into the distant future.

XML seems to have the potential for fostering a commercial market- place much broader than the library market and as such, will in time have considerable financial resources devoted to it to create the "user friendly" data creation tools and other related management and retrieval software that will ensure its acceptance.

As knowledgeable consumers of information, librarians are in a particularly strong position to influence the development of XML software applications and systems. It is not too early to consult with library automation vendors to inquire about their future plans vis-a-vis XML. Similarly it is not too early to insert our expertise in the extra-library world to move software and standards development in directions best attuned to appropriate information management.

So it can be concluded, is MARC dead? Certainly not. Does XML have a future in managing library information? Absolutely! The journey is just beginning.

On the next page , Marc-21 code list as used by INFLIBNET for its soul software is provided that can be used as a model list for developing any software for library cotaloguing.

MARC21 Code List INFLIBNET for Its SOUL Software

MARC21 Taj No.	Descriptions	Books	Theses	Serials	Remark
001	**Control Number (NR)**				
003	**Control Number Identifier (NR)**				
005	**Date & Time of Latest Transaction (NR)**				
006	**Fixed Length Data Elements - AMC(R)**				
007	**Physical Description Fixed Field (R)**				
008	**Fixed Length Data Elements -GI (NR)**	(NR)			
013	**Patent Control Number (R)** $a Number (NR) $b Country (NR) $c Type of Number (NR) $d Date (R) $e Status (R) $f Part to document (R)				
015	**National Bibliography Number (NR)** $a National bibliography number (R)				

016	**National Bibliography Agency Control Number (R)** $a Record control number (NR) $z Canceled or invalid control number (R) $2 Source (NR)				
020	**ISBN (R)** $a ISBN (NR) $c Terms of availability (NR) $z Canceled/invalid ISBN (R)				
022	**ISSN (R)** $a ISSN (NR) $y Incorrect ISSN (R) $z Canceled ISSN R			Serials	
027	**Standard Technical Report Number(R)** $a Standard technical report number (NR) $z Canceled/invalid number R				
028	**Publisher Number (R)** $a Publisher number (NR) $b Source (NR)				For electr-onic items

030	**CODEN Designation (R)** $a CODEN (NR) $z Canceled/invalid CODEN (R)				
033	**Date/ Time Place of Event (R)** $a Formatted date/time (R) $3 Materials s ecified (NR)				
034	**Coded Cartographic Mathematical Data (R)** $a Category of scale (NR) $b Constant ratio linear horizontal scale (R) $c Constant ratiolinear vertical scale (R) $d Coordinates—westernmost longitude (NR) $e Coordinates —easternmost longitude (NR) $f Coordinates —northernmost latitude (NR) $g Coordinates —southernmost latitude (NR) $h Angular scale (R) $j Declination —northern limit (NR) $k Declination —southern limit (NR) $m Right ascension —eastern limit (NR) $n Right ascension —western limit (NR)				For Cartographic Material

	$p Equinox (NR) $s G-ring latitude (R) $t G-ring longitude R				
036	**Original Study Number for Computer Data files (NR)** $a Original study number (NR) $b Source (agency assigning number (NR)				For Computer File
040	**Cataloguing Source (NR)** $a Original cataloguing agency (NR) $b Language of cataloguing (NR) $c Transcribing agency (NR) $d Modifying agency (R) $e Describing conventions (NR)				
041	**Language Code (NR)** $a Language code of text/sound track or separate title (NR) $b Lanuage code of summary or abstract/overprinted title or subtitle (NR) $d Language code of sung or spoken text (NR)				

	$e Language code of librettos (NR) $f Language code table of contents (NR) $g Language code of original and/or intermediate translations of text (R) $h Language code of original and/or intermediate translations of text (R)				
043	**Geographic Area Code (NR)** $a Geograhic area code (R)				
045	**Time Period of Content (NR)** $a Time period code (R) $b Fonnatted 9999 B.C. through C.E. time period (R) $c Formatted pre-9999 B.C. time period (R)				
080	**UDC Number (R)** $a UDC number (NR) $b Item number (NR) $2 Edition identifier (NR)				
082	**DDC Number (R)** $a Classification number (R) $b Item number (NR)				

	$2 Edition number (NR)				
084	**Other Classification Number(R)** $a Classification number (R) $b Item number (NR) $2 Source of number (NR)				
086	**Government Document Call Number(R)** $a Classification number (R) $z Canceled/invalid classification number (R) $2 Number source (NR)				
088	**Report Number (R)** $a Report number (R) $z Canceled/invalid report number (R)				
100	**Main Entry -Personal Name (NR)** $a Personal name (NR) $b Numeration (NR) $c Titles & other words associated with a name (R) $d Dates associated with name (NR) $f Date of work (NR)				

	$k Form subheading (R) $l Language of a work (NR) $n Number of part/section of a work (R) $p Name of part/section of a work (R) $q Fuller form of name (NR) $t Title of a work (NR				
110	**Main Entry- CorporateName (NR)** $a Corporate name or jurisdiction name as entry element (NR) $b Subordinate unit (R) $c Location of meeting (NR) $d Date of meeting or treaty signing (R) $f Date of work (NR) $k Form subheading (R) $l Language of a work (NR) $n Number of part/section of a work (R) $p Name of part/section of a work (R) $t Title of a work (NR)				
111	**Main Entry -Meeting Name (NR)** $a Meeting name or jurisdiction name as entry element (NR)				

	$c Location of meeting (NR) $d Date of meeting (NR) $e Subordinate unit (R) $f Date of work (NR) $k Form subheading (R) $l Language of a work (NR) $n Number of part/section of a work (R) $p Name of part/section of a work (R) $q Name of meeting following jurisdiction name entry element(NR) $t Title of a work (R)				
130	**Main Entry —Uniform Title (NR)** $a Uniform title (NR) $d Date of treaty signing (R) $f Date of work (NR) $k Form subheadin (R) $l Language of a work (NR) $m Medium of performance for music (R) $n Number of part/section of a work (R)				

	$o Arranged statement for music (NR) $p Name of part/section of a work (R) $s Version (NR) $t Title of a work (NR)				
222	**Key Title (R)** $a Key title (NR) $b Qualifying information (NR)				
240	**Uniform Title (NR)** $a Uniform title (NR) $d Date of treaty signing (R) $fDate of work (NR) $k Form subheading (R) $l Language of a work (NR) $m Medium of performance for music (R) $0 Arranged statement for music (NR) $p Name of part/section of a work (R) $s Version (NR)				
245	**Title Statement (NR)** $a Title (NR) $b Remainder of title (NR)				

	$c Statement of responsibility, etc. (NR) $f Inclusive dates (NR) $g Bulk dates (NR) $h Medium (NR) $n Number of part/section of a work (R) $p Name of part/section of a work (R)				
246	**Varying form of Title (R)** $a Title proper/short title (NR) $i Display text (NR)				
247	**Former Title or Title Variations (R)** $a Title proper/short title (NR) $b Remainder of title (NR) $f Date or sequential designation (NR) $h Medium (NR) $n Number of part/section of a work (R) $p Name of part/section of a work (R) $x ISSN (NR)				
250	**Edition Statement (NR)** $a Edition statement (NR) $b Remainder of edition statement (NR)				
254	**Musical Presentation Statement (NR)** $a Musical presentation statement (NR)				

255	**Cartographic Mathematical Data (R)** $a Statement of scale (NR) $b State: ment of projection (NR) $c Statement of coordinates (NR) $d Statement of zone (NR) $e Statement of equinox (NR) $f Outer G-ring coordinate pairs (NR) $g Exclusion G-ring coordinate pairs (NR)				For Maps
256	**Computer File Characteristics (NR)** $a Computer file characteristics (NR)				For Computer File
257	**Country of Producing Entity for Archival Films (NR)** $a Country of producing entity (NR)				
260	**Publication, Distribution, etc (Imprint) (NR)** $a Place of publication, distribution, etc. (R) $b Name of publisher, distributor, etc. (R) $c Date of publication, distribution, etc. (R) $e Place of manufacture (NR) $f Manufacturer (NR) $g Date of manufacturer (NR)				

270	**Address (R)** $a Address (R) $b City (NR) $c State or province (NR) $d Country (NR) $e Postal code (NR) $f Attention position (NR) $g Attention name (NR) $i Type of address (NR) $k Telephone number (R) $l Fax number (R) $m Electronic mail address (R)				
300	**Physical Description (R)** $a Extent (R) $b Other physical details (NR) $c Dimensions (R) $e Accompanying material (NR) $f Type of unit (R) $g Size of unit (R) $3 Materials specified				

306	**Playing Time (NR)** $a Playing time (R)				For Music
307	**Hours, Etc. (R)** $a Hours (NR) . $b Additional information (NR)				For electr- nic items
310	**Current Publication Frequency (NR)** $a Current publication frequency (NR) $b Date of current publication frequency (NR)			Serials	
321	**Former Publication Frequency (R)** $a Former publication frequency (NR) $b Dates of former publication frequency(NR)			Serials	
340	**Physical Medium (R)** $a Material base and configuration (R) $b Dimensions (R) $c Materials applied to surface (R) $d Infomlation recording technique (R) $e Support (R) $f Production rate/ratio (R) $h Location within medium (R) $i Technical specifications of medium (R) $3 Materials specified (NR)				

351	**Organization and Arrangement of Materials (R)** $a Organization (R) $b Arrangement (R) $c Hierarchical level (NR) $3 Materials specified R				
362	**Dates of Publication and/or Volume Designation (R)** $a Dates of publication and/or sequential designation (NR) $z Source of information (NR)				
440	**Series Statement/ Added Entry-Title (R)** $a Title (NR) $n Number of part/section of a work (R) $p Name of part/section of a work (R) $v Volume/sequential desgination (NR) $x ISSN (NR)				
490	**Series Statement (R)** $a Series statement (NR) $1 Library of Congress call number (NR) $v Volume/sequential designation (R)				

	$x ISSN (NR)				
500	**General Note (R)** $a General note (NR)				
501	**With Note (R)** $a With note (NR) $5 Institution to which field applies (NR)				
502	**Dissertation Note (R)** $a Dissertation note (NR)		Theses		
504	**Bibliography, Etc. Note (R)** $a Bibliography, etc. note (NR) $b Number of references (NR)				
505	**Formatted Contents Note (R)** $a Formatted contents note (NR) $g Miscellaneous information (NR) $r Statement of responsibility (R) $t Title (R)				
508	**Creation/Production Credits Note (NR)** $a Creation/production credits note (NR)				For film only
513	**Type of Report and Period Covered Note (R)**				

	$a Type of report (NR) $b Period covered (NR)				
515	**Numbering Peculiarities Note (R)** $a Numberin eculiarities note (NR)			Serials	
516	**Type of Computer File or Data Note (R)** $a Type of computer file or data note (NR)				For Computer File
520	**Summary, Etc. (R)** $a Summary, etc. note (NR) $b Expansion of summary note (NR) $c Materials specified (NR)				
525	**Supplement Note (R)** $a Supplement note (NR)				
530	**Additional Physical Form Available Note (R)** $a Additional physical form available note (NR) $b Availability source (NR) $c A vailabili conditions (NR)				
534	**Original Version Note (R)**				

	$p Introductory phrase (NR) $a Main entry of original (NR) $t Title statement of original (NR) $b Edition statement of original(NR) $c Publication, distr., etc. of original (NR) $e Physical description, etc. of original (NR) $x ISBN (R)				
536	**Funding Information Note (R)** $a Text of note (NR)				
538	**System Details Note (R)** $a System details note (NR)				
546	**Language Note (R)** $a Language note (NR)				
550	**Issuing Body Note (R)** $a Issuing body note (NR)				
586	**Awards Note (R)** $a Awards note (NR)				
590	**Local Notes (R)** $a Local Notes (R)				
600	**Subject Added Entry -Personal Name (NR)**				

	$a Personal name (NR) $b Numeration (NR) $c Titles and other words associated with a name (R) $d Dates associated with a name (NR) $f Date of a work (NR) $l Language of a work (NR) $n number of part/section of a work (R) $p Name of part/section of a work (R) $q Fuller form of name (NR) $t Title of a work (NR) $x General subdivision (R) $y Chronological subdivision (R) $z Geographic subdivision (R)				
610	**Subject Added Entry -Corporate Name (R)** $a Corporate name or jurisdiction name as entry element (NR) $b Subordinate unit (R) $c Location of meeting (NR) $d Date of meeting or treaty signing (R) $f Date of a work (NR)				

	$l Language of a work (NR) $n number of part/section/meeting (R) $p Name of part/section of a work (R) $q Fuller form of name (NR) $t Title of a work (NR) $x General subdivision (R) $y Chronological subdivision (R) $z Geographic subdivision (R)				
611	**Subject Added Entry -Meeting Name (R)** $a Meeting name or jurisdiction name as entry element (NR) $c Location of meeting (NR) $d Date of meeting (NR) $e Subordinate unit (R) $f Date of a work (NR) $l Language of a work (NR) $n Medium of art/section/meeting (R) $p Name of part/section of a work (R) $q Name of meeting following jurisdiction name entry element(NR) $t Title of a work (NR)				

	$x General subdivision (R) $y Chronological subdivision (R) $z Geographic subdivision (R)				
630	**Subject Added Entry -Uniform Title (R)** $a Uniform title (NR) $d Date of treaty signing (R) $f Date of a work (NR) $k Form subheading (R) $l Language of a work (NR) $m Medium of performance for music (R) $n number of part/section of work (R) $o Arranged statement for music (NR) $p Name of part/section of a work (R) $t Title of a work (NR) $x General subdivision (R) $y Chronological subdivision (R) $z Geographic subdivision (R)				
650	**Subject Added Entry -Topical Term (R)** $a Topical term or geographic name as entry element (NR) $b Topical term following geographic				

	name as entry element (NR) $x General subdivision (R) $y Chronological subdivision (R) $z Geographic subdivision (R)				
65'	**Subject Added Entry- Geographical Name (R)** $a Geographic name (NR) $v Form subdivision (R) $x General subdivision (R) $y Chronological subdivision (R) $z Geogaphic subdivision (R)				
653	**Index Term -Uncontrolled (R)** $a Uncontrolled term (R)				
700	**Added Entry -Personal Name (R)** $a Personal name (NR) $b Numeration (NR) $c Titles & other words associated with a name (R) $d Dates associated with name (NR) $e Relator term (R) $f Date of work (NR)				

	$k Form subheading (R) $l Language of a work (NR) $n Number of part/section of a work (R) $p Name of part/section of a work (R) $q Fuller form of name (NR) $t Title of a work (NR)				
710	**Added Entry -Corporate Name (R)** $a Corporate name or jurisdiction name as entry element (NR) $b Subordinate unit (NR) I$c Location of meeting (NR) $d Date of meeting or treaty signing (NR) $f Date of work (NR) $k Form subheading (R) $l Language of a work (NR) $n Number of part/section/meeting (R) $p Name of part/section of a work (R) $t Title of a work (R)				
711	**Added Entry -Meeting Name (R)** $a Meeting name or jurisdiction name as entry element (NR)				

	$c Location of meeting (NR) $d Date of meeting (NR) $e Subordinate unit (R) $f Date of a work (NR) $h Medium (NR) $k Form subheading (R) $l Language of a work (NR) $n Number of part/section/meeting (R) $ Name of art/section of a work (R) $q Name of meeting following jurisdiction name entry element (NR) $t Title of a work (NR)				
730	**Added Entry -Uniform Title (R)** $a Uniform title (NR) $d Date of treaty signing (R) $f Date of work (NR) $k Form subheading (R) $l Language of a work (NR) $m Medium of performance for music (R) $n Number of part/section of work (R) $o Arranged statement for music (NR)				

	$p Name of part/section of a work (R) $s Version (NR) $t Title of a work (NR)				
740	**Added Entry -Uncontrolled Related/ Analytical title (R)** $a Uncontrolled related/analytical title (NR) $h Medium (NR) $n Number of part/section of a work (R) $p Name of part/section of a work (R)				
777	**Issued With Entry (R)** $a Main entry heading (NR) $b Edition (NR) $c Qualifying information (NR) $d Place, publisher, and date of publication (NR) $g Relationship information (R) $x ISSN (R)				
780	**Preceding Entry (R)** $a Main entry heading (NR) $b Edition (NR) $c Qualifying information (NR) $d Place, publisher, and date of				

	publication (NR) $g Relationship information (R) $u Standard Technical Report Number (NR) $x ISSN (NR)				
785	**Succeeding Entry (R)** $a Main entry heading (NR) $b Edition (NR) $c Qualifying information (NR) $d Place, publisher, and date of publication (NR) $g Relationship information (R) $x ISSN (NR)				
800	**Series Added Entry -Personal Name (R)** $a Personal name (NR) $b Numeration (NR) $c Titles and other words associated with a name (R) $d Dates associated with a name (NR) $f Date of a work (NR) $l Language of a work (NR) $n Number of part/section of a work (R) $p Name of part/section of a work (R)				

	$q Fuller form of name (NR) $t Title of a work (NR)				
810	**Series Added Entry -Corporate Name (R)** $a Corporate name or jurisdiction name as entry element (NR) $b Subordinate unit (R) $c Location of meeting (NR) $d Date of meeting or treaty signing (R) $f Date of a work (NR) $l Language of a work (NR) $n Number of part/section/meeting (R) $p Name of part/section of a work (R) $t Title of a work (NR)				
811	**Series Added Entry -Meeting** **Name (R)** $a Meeting name or jurisdiction name as entry element (NR) $c Location of meeting (NR) $d Date of meeting (NR) $e Subordinate unit (R) $f Date of a work (NR)				

	$l Language of a work (NR) $n Number of part/section/meeting (R) $p Name of part/section of a work (R) $q Name of meeting following jurisdiction name entry element (NR) $t Title of a work (NR)				
830	**Series Added Entry- Uniform Title (R)** $a Uniform title (NR) $b Date of treaty signing (R) $f Date of a work (NR) $g Miscellaneous information (NR) $h Medium (NR) $k Form subheading (R) $l Language of a work (NR) $n Number of part/section of a work (R) $p Name of part/section of a work (R) $t Title of a work (NR)				
850	**Holding Institution (R)** $a Holding institution (R)				
852	**Location (R)**				

	$a Location (NR) $b Sublocation or collectaion (R) $c Shelving location (R) $h Classification part (NR) $i Item part (R) $j Shelving control number (NR) $n Country code (NR) $p Piece Designation (NR) $t Copy number (R)				
856	**Electronic Location and Access (R)** $a Host name (R) $b Access number (R) $c Compression information (R) $d Path (R) $f Electronic name (R) $g Uniform Resource Name (R) $h Processor of request (NR) $i Instruction (R) $j Bits er second (NR) $k Passward (NR) $l Logon (NR)				

	$m Contact for access assistance (R) $n Name of location of host (NR) $o Operating system (NR) $p Port (NR) $q Electronic format type (NR) $r Settings (NR) $s File size (R) $t Terminal emulation (R) $u Uniform Resource Locator (NR) $v Hours access method available (R) $w Record control number (R) $x Nonpublic note (R) $z Public note (R) $2 Access method (NR)				
886	**Foreign MARC Information Field (R)** $a Tag of the foreign MARC field (NR) $b Content of the foreign MARC field (NR) $2 Source of data (NR) $a-z Foreign MARC subfield (R) $0-9 Foreign MARC subfield (R)				

Note: Indicators for fields must be defined as per the value given in MARC21 concise format. Mandatory and Optional of fields also need to be defined as per given in MARC21 concise format.

MARC21 Field List for Name and Subject Authority Database

Tag No.	Name of the Field	Person Name	Corporate Name	Meeting Name
001	Control Number (NR)			
003	Control Number Identifier (NR)			
005	Date and Time of Latest Transaction (NR)			
008	Fixed-Length Data Elements -GI (NR)			
035	System control number (R) $a System control number (NR)			
040	Cataloguing Source (NR) $a Original cataloguing agency (NR) $b Language of cataloguing (NR) $c Transcribing agency (NR) $d Modifying agency (R) $f Subject heading/thesaurus conventions (NR)			
042	Authentication Code (NR) $a Authentication code (R)			
045	Time Period of Heading (NR) $a Time period code (R) $b Formatted 9999 B.C. through A.D.	This field is for Subject Authority		

	time period (R) $c Formatted pre-9999 B.C. time period (R)			
073	Subdivision Usage (NR) $a Subdivision usage (R) $b Source (NR) $6 Linkage (NR)	This field is for Subject Authority		
100	Heading -Personal Name (NR) $a Personal name (NR) $q Fuller form of name (NR) $b Numeration (NR) $c Titles and other words associated with a name (R) $d Dates associated with a name (NR) $t Title of work (NR) $f Date of a work (NR) $k Form subheading (R) $l Language of a work (NR) $n Number of part/section ofa work (R) $p Name of part/section of a work (R)	Person name		
110	Heading -Corporate Name (NR) $a Corporate name or jurisdiction name as entry		Corporate body	

	element (NR) $b Subdivision unit (R) $c Location of meeting (NR) $d Date of meeting or treaty signing (R) $k Form subheading (R) $n Number of part/section/meeting (R) $t Title of a work (NR) $f Date of a work (NR) $l Language of a work (NR) $p Name of part/section of a work (R).			
111	Heading -Meeting Name (NR) $a Meeting name or jurisdiction name as entry element (NR) $q Name of meeting following jurisdiction name entry element (NR) $d Date of meeting (NR) $c Location of meeting (NR) $e Subordinate unit (R) $n Number of part/section/meeting (R) $t Title of a work (NR) $f Date of a work (NR)			Meeting name

	$k Form subheading (R) $1 Language of a work (NR) $ Name of art/section of a work (R)			
150	Heading -Topical Term (NR) $a Topical term or geographic name as entry element (NR) . $b Topical term following geographic name as entry element (NR) $x General subdivision (R) $y Chronological subdivision (R) $z Geogaphic subdivision (R)	This field is for subject authority		
151	Geographic Name (NR) $a Geographic name (NR) $x General subdivision (R) $y Chronological subdivision (R) $z Geogaphic subdivision (R)	This field is for subject authority		
180	Heading -General Subdivision (NR) $x General subdivision (R) $y Chronological subdivision (R) $z Geographic subdivision (R)	This field is for subject authority		
181	Heading -Geographic Subdivision (NR)	This field is for subject authority		

	$z Geographic subdivision (R) $x General subdivision (R) $y Chronolo ical subdivision (R)			
182	Heading-Chronological Subdivision (NR) $y Chronological subdivision (NR) $x General subdivision (R) $z Geographic subdivision (R)	This field is for subject authority		
260	Complex See Reference -Subject (R) $a Heading referred to (R) $b Explanatory text (R)	This field is for subject authority		
360	Complex See Also Reference -Subject (R) $a Heading referred to (R) $b Explanatory text (R)	This field is for subject authority		
400	See From Tracing -Personal Name (R) $a Personal name (NR) $q Fuller form of name (NR) $b Numeration (NR) $c Titles and other words associated with a name (R) $d Dates associated with a name (NR) $t Title of a work (NR)	Person Name		

	$f Date of a work (NR) $1 Language of a work (NR) $n Number of part/section of a work (R) $ Name of art/section of a work R) $x General subdivision (R) $y Chronological subdivision (R) $z Geographic subdivision (R)			
410	See From Tracing -Corporate Name (R) $a Corporate name or jurisdiction name as entry elment (NR) $b Subdivision unit (R) $c Location of meeting (NR) $d Date of meeting or treaty signing (R) $n Number of part/section/meeting (R) $t Title of a work (NR) $f Date of a work (NR) $1 Language of a work (NR) $p Name of part/section of a work (R) $x General subdivision (R) $y Chronological subdivision (R) $z Geograhic subdivision (R)		Corporate body	

411	See From Tracing -Meeting Name (R) $a Meeting name or jurisdiction name as entry element (NR) $q Name of meeting following jurisdiction name entry element (NR) $d Date of meeting (NR) $c Location of meeting (NR) $e Subordinate unit (R) $n Number of part/section/meeting (R) $t Title of a work (NR) $f Date of a work (NR) $l Language of a work (NR) $p Name of part/section of a work (R) $x General subdivision (R) $y Chronological subdivision (R) $z Geographic subdivision (R)			Meeting name
450	See From Tracing -Topical Term (R) $a Topical term or geographic name as entry element (NR) $b Topical term following geographic name as entry element (NR)	This is for subject authority		

	$x General subdivision (R) $y Chronological subdivision (R) $z Geographic subdivision (R)	
451	See From Tracing -Geographic Name (R) $a Geographic name (NR) $x General subdivision (R) $y Chronological subdivision (R) $z Geographic subdivision (R)	This is for subject authority
480	See From Tracing -General Subdivision (R) $x General subdivision (R) $y Chronological subdivision (R) $z Geographic subdivision (R)	This is for subject authority
481	See From Tracing -Geographic Subdivision (R) $z Geographic subdivision (R) $x General subdivision (R) $y Chronological subdivision (R) $i Reference instruction phrase (NR) $w Control subfield (NR) $5 Institution to which field applies (NR) $6 Linkage (NR)	This is for subject authority

482	Heading -Chronological Subdivision (NR) $y Chronological subdivision (NR) $x General subdivision (R) $z Geographic subdivision (R)	This field is for subject authority
550	See Also From Tracing -Topical Term (NR) $a Topical term or geographic name as entry element (NR) $b Topical term following geographic name as entry element (NR) $x General subdivision (R) $y Chronological subdivision (R) $z Geographic subdivision (R)	This field is for subject authority
551	See also From Tracing -Geographic Name (R) $a Geographic name (NR) $x General subdivision (R) $y Chronological subdivision (R) $z Geographic subdivision (R)	This field is for subject authority
580	See Also From Tracing-General Subdivision (R) $x General subdivision (R) $y Chronological subdivision (R) $z Geographic subdivision (R)	This field is for subject authority

581	See Also From Tracing -Geographic Subdivision (R) $z Geographic subdivision (R) $x General subdivision (R) $ Chronological subdivision (R)	This field is for subject authority
582	See Also From Tracing -Chronological Subdivision (R) $y Chronological subdivision (NR) $x General subdivision (R) $z Geographic subdivision (R)	This field is for subject authority
640	Series Dates of Publication and/or Volume Designation (R) $a Dates of publication and/or volume designation (NR) $z Source of information (NR)	This field is for subject authority
641	Series Numbering Peculiarities (R) $a Numbering peculiarities note (NR) $z Source of information (NR)	This field is for subject authority
642	Series Numbering Example (R) $a Series numbering example (NR) $d Volumes/dates to which series	This field is for series authority

	numbering example applies (NR)			
643	Series Place and Publisher/Issuing Body (R) $a Place (R) $b Publisher/issuing body (R) $d Volumes/dates to which place and Publisher/issuing body apply (NR)	This field is for series authority		
644	Series Analysis Practice (R) $a Series analysis practice (NR) $b Exceptions to analysis practice (NR) $d Volumes/dates to which analysis practice (NR)	This field is for series authority		
645	Series Tracing Practice (R) $a Series Tracing practice (NR) $d Volumes/dates to which tracing practice applies (NR)	This field is for series authority		
646	Series Classification Practice (R) $a Series classification practice (NR) $b Volumes/ dates to which classification practice applies (NR)	This field is for series authority		
670	Source data Found (R) $a Source citation (NR) $b Information found (R)	Person name	Corporate body	Meeting name

675	Source Data Not Found (NR) $a Source citation (R)	Person name	Corporate body	Meeting name
680	Public General Note (R) $a Heading or subdivision term (R) $i Explanatory text	This field is for subject authority		
681	Subject example Tracing Note (R) $a Heading or subdivision term (R) $i Explanatory text	This field is for subject authority		
688	Application History Note (R) $a Application history note (NR) $5 Institution to which field applies (R)	This field is for subject authority		

Note: Indicators for fields must be defined as per the value given in MARC21 concise format. Mandatory and Optional fields also need to be defined as per given in MARC21 concise format. Fixed fields need to be taken from as given as in MARC21 format.

INFLIBNET Proposal for Manuscript Database

Field Names As Per AACR2	Tag Number as per the MARC21
Title and Statement of Responsibility Area	
1. Title Proper	245$a
2. Parallel Titles	245$b, 246
3. Other Title information	246
4. Statements of responsibility	245$c
5. Itmes without a collective title	245
Edition Area	
1. Edition Statement	250$a
2. Statements of responsibility relating to the edition	250$b
Publication and Date Area	
1. Place of Publication	260$a
2. Name of Publisher	260$b
3. Date of the Manuscript	260$c
Physical Description Area	
1. Extent of item	300$a
2. Other Physical Details	300$b
3. Dimensions	300$c
Note Area	
1. Nature, Scope, or form	500
2. Language	546
3. Source of title proper	500
4. Donor, source, etc. and previous owner(s)	561

5. Place of writing	535
6. Published versions	534
7. Access and literary rights	506
8. Reference to published descriptions	510
9. Summary	520
10. Contents	505
11. Ancient, medieval, and Renaissance manuscripts (Style of writing, Illustrative matter, Collation, Other physical details, Opening words)	556

Proposed Fields for Manuscript Database

001 Record- Id (for Union Database)

003 Record Id of University

005 Date and Time of Latest Transaction

006 Fixed-Length Data Elements -Additional Material Characters (R)

008 Fixed-Length Data Elements -General Information (NR)

040 Cataloguing Source

080 UDC Number

082 DDC Number

084 Other Class Number

1XX Main Entries -General Information

100 Main Entry -Personal Name (NR)

130 Main Entry -Uniform Title (NR)

20X-24X Title and Title -Related Fields-General Information

240 Uniform Title (NR)

245 Title Statement (NR)

246 Varying Form of Title (R)

25X-28X Edition, Imprint, Etc. Fields -General Information

250 Edition Statement (NR)

260 Publication, Distribution, etc. (Imprint) (NR)

3XX Physical Description, Etc. Fields -General Information

300 Physical Information

340 Physical Medium

5XX Notes- General Information

500 General Note

501 With Note

504 Bibliography Note

505 Fomlatted Control Note

520 Summary, Etc.

544 Location of other Archival Materials Note

546 Language Note

561 Ownership and Custodial History

6XX Subject Access Fields -General Information

600 Subject Added Entry -Personal Name (R)

630 Subject Added Entry -Unifoml Title (R)

650 Subject Added Entry -Topical Term (R)

651 Subject Added Entry -Geographical Name (R)

653 Index Term -Uncontrolled (R)

70X -75X Added Entries -General Information

700 Added Entry -Personal Name (R)

730 Added Entry -Uniform Title (R)

740 Added Entry -Uncontrolled Related / Analytical Title (R)

841 -88X Holdings, Alternate Graphics, Etc. -General Information

845 Terms Governing Use and Reproduction (R)

850 Holding Institution (R)

852 Location (R)

856 Electronic Location and Access

9XX Local Use Fields

900 Date of Merging to Union Database

$a Date of Merging

905 Cataloguers Name

$a Name of cataloguer

910 Reviewers Name

$a Name of Reviewers

6

Recent Trends In Library Cataloguing

FUTURE OF LIBRARIES

Before considering the new concepts in cataloguing which are likely to govern bibliographic control in the future it is important to look at the future of libraries. There are a number of developments in place at the moment which will force libraries and professional librarians to face a crisis in credibility unless they are prepared to take advantage of these new developments and at the same time accept that they may alter the shape of the library they know and the profession that they practice. Three factors are likely to bring this change about. The first two are inter linked; the increase in electronic publishing and the digitising of conventional library materials. Electronic publishing and digitizing add up to a situation where the library and in particular the academic library will find that most of its heavy demand can be satisfied in electronic form. From the library's point of view this would be a major step forward: the need for additional space would disappear and demaand could be satisfied much more quickly by downloading the full text in electronic form from databases. These databases, however, need not necessarily be held by the library or accessed through the library. Any user with a PC or access to a PC will be able to bypass the library from office or home and obtain the items that are required from data warehouses which might be anywhere. This mean that the library catalogue will cease to be an independent unit providing an entry to a particular local collection. It will form part of a world-wide network catalogue and the library will become a switching and control centre for those seeking the information.

Alongside these developments and forming an integral part of them is the Internet and the second revolution in information that it is going to create. It is probably true to say that the first information revolution took place half a millennium ago with the invention of printing. This dramatically speeded up the way in which information was disseminated. However, it took mankind over five centur..s to capitalize on the ability to transfer information and to devise methods of information retrieval. This is perhaps a misnomer as we never retrieve information, only the containers of information. The Internet will have an impact as great as the invention of printing but will differ from it because the effects will not take half a millennium before they are felt-the second information revolution is taking place almost while we watch. In the area of bibliographic control it has opened a number of doors. It is now possible to access nearly every important catalogue through the Internet and many of them belong to clumps or clusters which can be accessed as a group because they are linked by the Z39.50 protocol.

What is not clear is how libraries and cataloguers in particular will adopt to the new information environment that the Internet is bringing in with almost dramatic speed. Librarianship as a profession has been very successful in adapting to and exploiting automation. However, it is difficult for most librarians to abandon a system of bibliographic control that has been so successful and to adopt an entirely new set of concepts that will take full advantage of a new and foreign environment. The recent International Conference on the Principles and Future Development of AACR held in Toronto seems more concerned with improvements needed within the present framework and did not look in any great depth at new concepts in cataloguing which are needed to take full advantage of the new technical developments appearing with almost frightening speed.

NEW CONCEPTS

For over a century the writing and thinking on bibliographic control has been dominated by collocation. This is not surprising since the assembly of related items is the basis of the cataloguing function. Much of the strong feeling that still seems to exist for the main entry is founded on the conviction that it is the basis for good collocation. Innovative new OPACs like BOPAC2 which has been developed at the University of Bradford have demonstrated that this is simply not true. For example, the user, by making full use of the select options that BOPAC2 provides, is able to collocate in a number of different ways: by edition, by date, by format, by publisher as well as by title or author. Because the options that are available to the user have been increased, it is now possible to use search terms which are broad or even fractured. For example a search using Bleak House can be narrowed down quickly to Dickens as an author, videos as a format or OUP as a publisher. This means that the user will be able to work within broad retrievals and collocate using a wide selection of options to narrow down the original query.

A Research Project was funded by the British Library and completed in February 1998. Its object was to exploit the results of a previous research project which developed an entirely new kind of OPAC. This provided a facility for organising a retrieval in a number of different ways. Using this as a prototype BOPAC2 was set up on the Internet and used the Z39.50 protocol to enable it to act as a front end to libraries in Britain, Ireland and America. When the Project started Java as a programming language was just beginning to be used on the Internet and it seemed the right tool to use in order to achieve the Project objectives. This proved to be the right decision because by the end of the Project Java applets were being used successfully and extensively on the Internet on a world wide basis. Because it was set up on the Internet it was possible for anyone who was interested to evaluate the Project while it was in progress and contribute to its development. By the end of the Project the site had been visited over two thousand times and a number of constructive suggestions for improvements had been made. Although the Project has now ended attempts are being made to obtain development funding. In the meantime BOPAC2 has remained on the Internet and has had an additional fifteen hundred visits.

CHANGING THE FOUNDATIONS

Because there is a fundamental difference between what cataloguing was and is and what it can be in the future there is a need for a reassessment of the foundations on which it is based. The difference is a conceptual one which is already to be found in information retrieval where two basic types of searching have become established. These are pre-coordinate and post-coordinate. In the first the searching terms are allocated at the indexing stage while in the second the search terms are chosen by the user and are not restricted to terms which have already been allocated. Cataloguing, on the other hand, has always been a pre-coordinate operation and is based on what the cataloguer does at the input stage. The user then works within the framework created by the cataloguer. This means the cataloguer lays down the way in which a retrieval is displayed through ISBD, the way in which it can be searched through the access points and links that are provided, the way in which some of its elements can be collocated and some cannot and through authority control the preferred forms in which access points are provided. This is what AACR2 and the MARC Format are all about. Within the technical limits that were until fairly recently the only ones available it was probably the best that could be done. To the user it is a partial straight jacket but nothing like the straight jacket imposed by the card catalogue. It means that the user is restricted to certain ways of searching because they are the only ones provided by the cataloguer at the input stage. BOPAC2 has shown that there is another way from the present process where the cataloguer pre-coordinates and in doing so sets the parameters within which the searcher carries out his search. With post-coordination the cataloguer would have a different function. This would be to set up a system which would provide a range of options for the searcher to choose from. For the benefits of post-coordination to be maximised the cataloguing process must ensure that all the necessary links are in place.

Many cataloguers will be unhappy because they will feel that their creative professionalism is being taken away from them but this is not true. It is much more productive and creative to provide an open ended structure through which the users can navigate and arrive at their chosen destinations easily than to provide a rigid structure which often provides a blinkered search path. It is significant that the Toronto Conference seemed to loose sight of the user in their deliberations. Perhaps the most important concept that cataloguers must accept is that the searching process must be user driven.

The steady work that the library profession has put into improving bibliographic control has enabled library users to make better use of the resources of their libraries. If this is not to be lost then the concepts that have formed the basis for cataloguing need to change. The aim should be to expand the present options and to provide more and better linking systems. The changes that are called for are dramatic and it will not be easy to convince many in the profession that they are necessary and are a viable alternative.

OPACs

The introduction of OPACs in our professional lives to largely responsible for a renewed, widespread interest in library research. At the center of this interest is a willinganess to conduct a fresh, unbiased appraisal of our traditional collection access policies and practices, and to re-examine the means by which we have therefore provided catalogue-based collection access to our library users. OPAC research is urging us to re-examine our traditional assumptions and is providing us with the stepped advantage points upon which we may more eagerly glance over the near horizons of inproved information service opportunities.

There are at least three roles open to librarians in today's dynamic community of OPAC research and development:

(a) you can engage in research, part-time at least- research teams always need extra help, and local OPAC use studies or evaluation are frequently needed;

(b) you can keep well informed and, in your role as educator, help to disseminate knowledge gained through research; and

(c) you can directly impact the path of commercial system design and developement through your key levarage point as a system evaluator, system selector and, ultimately, system purchaser through the formal system specification and procurement process.

Online catalgues: a case for the user, that is, the need for user-oriented OPAC research and development, is presented by

Hancock-Beaulieu with special insight gained from years of professional experience combined with findings from a recent well-conducted study of actual information seeking behaviour of users within the library. Hancock-Beaulieu reviews earlier, pre-online catalogue research studies and casts serious doubt on the efficacy of the research methods employed and the reliability of the findings of many of the studies. The warning is clear: we must always be on guard against allowing old perspectives and outdated professional biases to influence the selection of research issues to be addressed or, worse; the interpretation of study findings. Because the online catalogue is so malleable, extendable and perfectible, a fresh perspective is required if the new design opportunities are to be moulded to the advantage of library users.

Hancock-Beaulieu calls for studies of so-called catalogue use that will le conducted in the wider context of user information-seeking behaviour throughout the library. OPAC design should be guided by what we can learn about user behaviour and searching strategies employed in shelf, browsing as well as at the traditional catalogue. If the OPAC is to evolve into a better collection access tool, able to satisfy a variety of search behaviours and search objectives, then improved online browsing facilities must be incorporated to support interactive discovery and user-system negotiation of better expressions of information needs.

Another discussion further explores the concept of negotiation as an essential ingredient of effective interaction between the user and the OPAC system at the communications interface. Present-day OPACs are fundamentally flawed, for two reasons:

a) the systems' language found in the command structures and the bibliographic records is incompatible with the language brought to the systems by their users, and

b) the typical OPAC interaction process requires the matching or crude translation of user vocabulary to system vocabulary.

Studies confirm that this matching process fails more often than not. It is believed that the conventional search term, system vocabulary matching approach employed in most OPACs are not suited to a variety of searching needs and different retrieval objectives. It is suggested to separate query processing design requirements, for the situation where the user's information need is well defined from browsing operations, where the need is not precisely understood or defined.

A desire to achieve a better understanding of online browsing requirements and OPAC browsing support features is shared by all the contributors. Tague defines negotiation as a two-way process of communication, whereby the user and the stem exploit interface design mechanisms to gain an understanding of the other's langua e usage and processing capabilities. A retrieval experiment is reported with an adaptive interface which responds to the user's level of knowledge about the system, and which gradually teaches the user its language conventions as well as how it formulates and processes the user's initial queries.

Tague's studies of user-system interaction in bibliographic searching led her to urge improvements of OPACs in two areas: increased variety in the language of bibliographic description and subject indexing; including an expanded 'entry' vocabulary linked to terms in the systems vocabulary; and the development of adaptive, responsive interfaces able interactively to teach and explain the content and workings of the OPAC system being used.

Markey gives us a well-structured overview of the Dewey Decimal Classification (DDC) online retrieval research project carried out at the Online Computer Library Centre (OCLC) Office of Research. The DDC Schedules and the Relative Index vocabulary were incorporated in a test OPAC to enhance online subject searching, browsing and displays. In Makey's account of this research, she reviews the project's background and objectives, and concisely summarises the study's findings. The Dewey-enhanced OPAC was compared with a more conventional OPAC to assess subject searching performance, ease of use and user satisfaction with the systems.

Markey cleverly closes the gap between theory and practice by giving us detailed functional descriptions of four types of enhanced subject searching capabilities for OPACs through the use of DDC. She convincingly explains that these yet-to-be implemented, performance-enhancing searching capabilities have been derived from the analyses and interpretation of data collected in the online retrieval tests.

Walker reports on perhaps the longest running series of OPAC experiments, the Okapi online catalogue research studies conducted at the Polytechnic of Central London (PCL) since 1982. These are funded mainly by the British Library Research and Development Department. Several reports of the experiments have been published, but the important Okapi research programme is still too little known in North America and Europe.

Walker surveys the history of the projects from 1982 until 1987, and discusses the results of the more recent design experiments and Okapi user studies. The Okapi research programme which utilizes an evolving demonstration, test OPAC, represents more of a research environment, that is, a 'field laboratory', than a mere designer's experimental OPAC. Okapi is permanently placed in one of the PCL libraries with that library's collection represented in the Okapi OPAC database. The library also offers a commercially supplied OPAC for access to its collection.

New versions of the Okapi retrieval and display software have been installed and field tested from time to time very rich study opportunities have thereby been created not only for Walker's research teams, but also for students from UK library schools. The research team's design goals include building an OPAC, that requires no training to use, yet which employs powerful, more effective retrieval capabilities than are found in conventional retrieval systems. Some of the advanced 'post-Boolean' retrieval techniques investigated in information retrieval (IR) system research experiments are being tested in the Okapi OPAC.

Since 1986, Okapi researchers have focused primarily on the problems associated with online catalogue subject searching. A recent version of Okapi addressed the faulty term matching operations of conventional OPACs. The automatic or semi-automatic processes tested in this version of Okapi were: automatic search term stemming routines, automatic cross-referencing using a synonym table, and semi-automatic search term spelling correction.

Each of these tested positive to some extent in improving OPAC search performance. A current objective of the Okapi researchers/ designers is to improve OPAC responsiveness to search needs which change or develop during a search in progress by semi-automatically exploiting user evaluations of intermediate search results. The 'extended OPAC' has become a popular topic in library conference programmes. Discussions of extensions to the OPAC assume a starting-point, a 'basic' OPAC, that may not actually exist anywhere. However, the extensions discussed most often are either functional extensions or data extensions.

Data extensions include fuller, augmented catalogue records for monographs and additional types of records such as those found in online indexes to and abstracts of the periodical literature. Extending OPAC functional access to include access to the indexed periodical literature joins the two basic kinds of OPAC extension.

Mischo and Moore describe their funded 'demonstration' project to build and test an intelligent, interactive, instructional search interface to the online periodical literature within an existing OPAC environment (the LCS/ WLN OPAC at the University of Illinois). Mischo designed and built a software interface that could be integrated into the local OPAC at its IBM PC user terminals. The major aim of the project was to address major subject searching difficulties identified in earlier OPAC user studies.

The Illinois IBM PC-based software interface tested enhanced, assisted subject access to the periodical literature through the OPAC terminals. Using interactive communication and instruction, the new interface assists untrained users with the selection of search terms, the development of search strategies and the formulation of Boolean queries.

As online catalogue use and evaluation research mature, it must continue to build on a sound theoretical base and employ rigorous empirical procedures among its various study methods and tools. Lynch explains how the automatic collection of OPAC system performance and usage data through monitoring and logging can fruitfully guide the ongoing evolution of an installed online catalogue. As a major developer and evaluator of the MELVYL OPAC at the

University of California throughout the 1980s, Lynch describes the problems inherent in the automatic collection and analysis of data and the pay-offs it offers for an improved user interface. Logged data, although difficult and costly to gather and analyse to good purpose, provides essential information to system designers charged with improving OPAC system performance.

Logged data reflecting actual OPAC user behaviour on the system can be used to balance or complement personal experience and anecdotal evidence. This 'transaction' data can be used, to 'validate' fine-tuning efforts or proposals' for fundamental changes in search and display features or capabilities. The emerging consensus among librarians and researchers about what makes OPACs special is that they are self-serviced interactive online IR systems, not merely computerized card catalogues. This realisation opens the door to insights and knowledge gained through interdisciplinary studies of similar interactive computer systems. Many of the usage problems and design issues associated with various interactive systems are common to all, and these issues are being addressed in a new field known as human-computer interaction (HCI) research. Mitev, a former member of the Okapi research team, focuses the attention on OPAC usability and ease of interaction issues. She explains why and how theoretical advances in HCI apply to the design of improved OPACs. She also discusses the concepts and specific findings in HCI research that are useful for improving our understanding of users' needs and problems as they interact with online computer catalogues.

Mitev urges library researchers and designers to expand their interests beyond the improvement of bibliographic and authority control and access to catalogue records, and also to address OPAC usability and related human factors issues.'Hypertext' and 'hypermedia' have just become hyperhot topics throughout the popular world of microcomputing. Recently introduced software products like Apple's HyperCard are much discussed among microcomputer enthusiasts. Yet, back in 1981-82, a hypermedium library catalogue, HYPERCAT, was ' launched, at least conceptually, at Sweden's LIBLAB. Faced with the daunting task of explaining an entirely new, non-linear, electronic, multidimensional catalogue form via a conventional printed narrative, Hjerppe attempts to describe and illustrate what such an OPAC might look like and how it would function. We are challenged to escape from all conceptions of earlier forms and media of the library catalogue, and to visualise a new catalogue which exists at the cutting edge of computer technology and at the frontiers of conventional comprehension. Yet Hjerppe's vision is well grounded in the best of traditional catalogue theory regarding the proper role and function(s) of the library catalogue. HYPERCAT is all about networks of linkages throughout the catalogue, linkages between related terms and related items in special-purpose subcollections and discovery - pathways and trails tailored to personal information needs.

A library catalogue in a hypermedium can be understood as an extension of cross-referencing and the collocative function of the traditional, print-bound catalogue. In simple terms, it permits us to shift from effective online known-item finding to enhanced pluralistic collection-contents access and discovery, HYPERCAT gives us a glimpse of the personal, responsive adaptive, multi-use OPAC we may encounter around the next corner or two.

Today's second-generation online catalogues represent a marriage of the library catalogue and conventional online information retrieval (IR) systems familiar to librarians who search online abstracting and indexing databases via DIALOG, BRS, DATASTAR, MEDLINE, etc. Improved card catalogue like 'main entry' searching and browsing by heading capabilities have been joined with the conventional IR keyword and Boolean searching approaches. Much of the power and flexibility familiar to online database search specialists which enables the post-coordinating of search concepts and terminology has been brought to the OPAC searcher.

Many online catalogues support the ability to restrict searches to specified record fields, to perform character- marking and/or right-hand truncation, and to limit the results by date, language, place of publication, etc. Also, bibliographic records may be viewed and printed in a number of different display formats. Second-generation online catalogues should be viewed as online bibliographic IR systems. But when compared with conventional keyword/ Boolean commercial database search and retrieval systems, these key differences should be kept in mind:

— the online public access catalogue must be usable directly by untrained and inexperienced users where online assistance is usually provided to help with the mechanics of searching.

— records in the catalogue database lack abstracts, the subject indexing is sparse and the vocabulary is often not representative of current terminology; and

— the catalogue database, in covering a library's collection, includes information on a wide variety of disciplines and subject areas.

Designers of second-generation online catalogues have addressed these differences in two ways:

(a) by providing card catalogue-like pre-coordinated phrase searching and browsing options along with keyword/ Boolean capabilities and

(b) by providing more and more online user assistance in the form of menus, help displays, suggestive prompts and informative error messages.

Post-coordinated keyword searching on subject-rich fields titles, corporate names, series entries, notes and subject headings, supported in most of today's OPACs can be used to alleviate the twin problems associated with the sparse subject indexing of most library materials and the users' unfamiliarity with the controlled subject indexing vocabularies.

Two fundamentally different search approaches can be found in second-generation OPACs. It is commonly recognised that keyword, Boolean searching (Post- coordinating) is different from pre-coordinated phrase searching, but the difference in addressing now cuts deeper across the OPAC interface territory. It is the difference between exact match querying and browsing. These different search approaches are best understood by considering differences that may exist in:

(a) users' searching objectives,

(b) system query specification and input requirements, and

(c) system output displayed and subsequent interaction with the searcher.

There are two kinds of query searching: phrase matching and keyword matching. A query consists of a term or terms (e.g., a character, number, word or words, or a phrase) and the specification, sometimes called the query 'formulation', which defined:

I. QUERYING

A. Phrase Matching

(Text strings or controlled vocabulary)

B. Keyword Matching

(Discrete words, with Boolean or proximity formulations)

**Query search requirements: Search aim/criteria known and can be expressed with relative precision and completeness

II. BROWSING

A. Pre-sequenced, linear, inflexible

(typically, lists of index terms, headings, descriptors or brief titles)

B. Non-linear, multidirectional, flexible

('navigation', 'chain', 'bridge', 'relational', 'serendipitous' browsing)

**Browse search requirements: search aim/criteria not specific, not known, and/or cannot be expressed in appropriate query/ indexing language

---

Two online catalogue search/access options

how the component term(s) of the query are to be interpreted or related for matching purposes (e.g., word truncation, Boolean combinations, word adjacency). The matching function of an OPAC is the mechanism through which the retrieval software makes a comparison between index terms which represent documents and query terms to effect retrieval. The matching criteria are specified through the query by the user or applied automatically by the system. Query searching of either kind (often called just 'searching', to distinguish it from an OPAC's browse mode) utilizes an exact matching function on the part of the system, regardless of the manner in which the matching criteria are specified.

In this all or nothing approach, documents (bibliographic records in OPACs) will be retrieved in response to a search only if an exact match of the query is found. The query may consist of a pre-coordinated phrase (with or without truncation) or a post-coordinated Boolean expression of keywords. In either case the query search matching requirements are precise and rigid.

The burden on the searcher is to enter terms that will match the entry terms in the database and to specify appropriate proximity or term relationship logic. Bates criticises this predominant approach to subject searching for requiring a 'perfect pinpoint match on the one best term'. No match means no retrieval, as viewers of our silent OPAC screens witness too often.

The search may fail (i.e., not identify relevant documents that are in the collection) unless the searcher knows or guesses the exact way the term (word or phrase) appears in the subject index. In keyword, Boolean queries, the system's matching mechanism makes a binary (yes/no) split of the database between bibliographic records that conform exactly to the requirements of the query and all the rest. Only the former are retrieved as 'hits'. Partial or 'closest' matching operations are generally not supported in second-generation OPACs and conventional retrieval systems.

Query searching is an appropriate, useful search option when the aim of the search is specific, when the searcher knows precisely what he wants, and when this request can be expressed in the language of the database. Even in subject searching for books or articles on a topic, the searcher may know his topic exactly and may be able to ; express it in the language of the system (e.g., the assigned subject headings or descriptors).

Typically, the system displays ordered lists of terms, descriptors, or brief bibliographic records for scanning by the searcher. Lists of index terms are usually presented in alphabetical order. The arrangement of brief citation records may be according to date, and some systems support short record browsing in shelf-list order. Usually the only 'navigation' option for browsers is to go back and or forward through the list in a constrained, linear manner. Cross-references, if included, represent a way of jumping out of the sequence and over to related areas of the database. Hypertext operations, which permit navigation throughout the database in many different directions and the dynamic definition of 'related areas and interests', have not been implemented in second-generation OPACs.

Conventional browsing assumes a vocabulary aim on the part of the searcher. It assists in identifying the correct form of a term and related terms. Other forms of browsing, rare in today's OP ACs, support related record/document discovery through non-linear explorations of the database. Browse searching is the most useful and preferred approach when the search aim is not specific, for example, discipline or topic, type of publication, level of treatment, perspective, etc. the desired results are not precisely known in advance, or the correct terms for representing the user's query are not known at the outset. One or more of these circumstances may be present in most subject searching activities. Researchers are coming to believe that some combination of the above circumstances is the most common situation database searchers present to the IR system.

More often than not, searchers want to use an OPAC or IR system because they recognise a gap or anomaly in their state of knowledge. Even if they have some sense of what information they need to resolve the anomaly, they cannot precisely describe in a search query what they do not yet precisely know or do not know at all. It is reasonable to assume that there may be a mismatch between an information need that cannot be specified and the fundamental requirement of conventional IR systems for an exact logical expression.

Some designers of online catalogues have recognised the difference in these search requirements and have provided some rudimentary browsing facilities, such as scanning index terms in the same alphabetical neighbourhood. This feature is not intrinsically tied to either phrase matching or keyword matching search facilities. Phrase matching often incorporates index term browsing automatically in the search dialogue, whether or not an initial match occurs, but there are exceptions to this. Most keyword match OPACs now offer the searcher an option to browse alphabetical term and descriptor indexes.

Most of today's OPACs support both phrase matching and keyword-matching query searching. However, these are hybrid systems that do not integrate or link these separate approaches in any useful way during a search. It is usually up to the searcher to choose, through commands or menu selection, one query type or the other. If the system assumes a particular search operation, the user is not informed which specific operation is being carried out on the search terms. Phrase searching, of course, generally assumes a word adjacency, same word order, matching specification.

Keyword searching on two or more words requires the specification of a Boolean operator either by the searcher or by the system. Most OPACs supply the Boolean AND as a default operator between words. When a search term like 'economic indicators and business cycles' is entered into an OPAC, if not explicitly instructed by the user the system automatically will decide precisely how to interpret the statement for matching purposes. The primary decisions to be made to include the indexes to be searched and the logic to be applied to specify the word relationships. Each type of query search has its advantages, but each may produce very different results even when the 'same search statement' is being processed. This can be a source of confusion for the untrained user, who may not understand the relative value of each approach. Such a user may not even know that both ways of searching are supported in a given OPAC, or how to invoke one or the other. Within a given catalogue database, one search choice on the same term can produce poor results, another choice can produce good results. Given these dual, unintegrated search approaches in many OPACs, it is a new responsibility of many librarians to understand their differences and to interpret these differences in a meaningful way for the users of these OPACs.

Subject searching in today's largely machine readable catalogue-based OPACs is supported by a variety of exact match query methods and browsing facilities. Exact match query searches are basically of two types: (a) phrase searching on pre-coordinated subject headings, and (b) keyword searches on cataloguing or indexing data in the bibliographic record (e.g., titles, notes, subject headings and their subdivisions). Keyword subject searches may be formulated as Boolean expressions to indicate the desired relationship between search terms, and some OPACs also permit explicit proximity designations in the formulation of the query.

The syntax and mechanics of entering subject searches have been simplified, and the task of precise search statement/query formulation has been delegated to the system software. Choice of subject query type is selected from a menu, or invoked by a pressed function key or simple typed command. Phrase searches are automatically processed as straightforward character string matches or word adjacency, same order matches. In most of the cases, the match must begin with the leftmost significant word or character of the indexed entry.

Keyword searches with more than one word are automatically processed as Boolean AND queries in most OPACs. Keyword searches may be targeted by the user or the system to one or more field indexes (e.g., title, notes. series statement, subject headings). Some flexibility is permitted in most keyword search OPACs. When searchers choose not to identify in their queries fields for subject keyword searching (or are not permitted by the system to do so), the trend is towards automatically searching both subject and title. ANDed keywords do not have to appear together in either the title field or the subject field to cause a match. Matching records would include those having one word in the title and another word in the subject heading.

Successful subject phrase searching in most OPACs still requires an exact match on at least the initial, main portion of the subject heading in the catalogue record. In the USA, this usually requires a perfect match on a LCSH. However, if a LCSH is entered as a search term and the heading has been modified or replaced in the local catalogue record, no match will occur.

In some OPACs, when no match occurs on the user's search term, the system displays headings in the alphabetical neighbourhood of the term. This may or may not help the searcher to find a heading which expresses his search interest. In today's OPACs, browsing is even less developed and is generally provided as an intermediate or secondary stage in the subject search process. Some keyword OPACs offer the searcher an unpublished option to browse alphabetical lists of index terms or headings. Phrase search OPACs typically display these lists after a search is constructed and entered, even when an exact match occurs.

A few OPACs are beginning to include cross-references and related terms in these browsing displays. This will make them more useful browsing tools for certain kinds of subject searching. More informative, flexible and intelligent browsing facilities can be provided in the online environment.

It is time for librarians and OPAC designers to recognise that subject browsing may be a primary search activity in the user's quest to discover materials on a topic, or to discover unknown items of potential interest. This kind of search activity requires more than term selection browsing facilities or even thesaurus-based automatic switching among related terms.

Related document browsing and discovery can be facilitated in OPACs through richer pre-coordination in the database of multiple subject/topic clues found in bibliographic records (e.g., linking title terms with subject headings with call numbers, etc.), and by providing more search navigation options between retrieved and unretrieved but linked records, that is, record-to-record 'jumping' at the discretion of the searcher.

Most of today's OPACs also fail to provide the more traditional subject search aids. For example, they do not suppurt browsing in displays of classification outlines or schedules. Neither do they permit related term look-ups in online subject thesauri or lists of subject headings.

Markey's research has shown the first of these to be useful in OPAC subject searching. Classification schedule terminology and systematic subject information can lead the searcher to relevant records not likely to be retrieved by the traditional phrase and keyword subject search methods. It is seldom recognised that even Cutter favoured this approach. Immediately following the famous passage where he lists the 'objects' of the library catalogue, Cutter proposes the means for achieving them. To enable the finding books on a subject, the catalogue needs the subject entry, cross references and a 'classified subject table'.

Online catalogue research studies have shown a number of common problems experienced by users of second-generation online catalogues. In general, the major problems include:

— too many failed searches (search attempts that are aborted, that result in no matches or that result in unmanageably large numbers of items retrieved);

— navigational confusion and frustration for the user during the search process ('Where am I?', 'What can I do now?', 'How can I start again?');

— unfamiliarity with subject indexing policy and vocabulary, leading too often to the failure to match search terms with the system's subject vocabulary;

— misunderstanding and confusion about the fundamentally different approaches to retrieval and search methods employed in todays online catalogues (e.g., pre-coordinate phrase searching and browsing and post-coordinate keyword Boolean searching; and

— partially implemented search strategies and missed opportunities to retrieve relevant materials (e.g., searches in which large retrieval sets are not scanned or narrowed in size, and title keyword searches that are not followed by searches on the call numbers or subject headings of the found records).

Conventional IR systems place the burden on the user to reformulate and re-enter the queries until satisfactory results are obtained. This is typically the case with second-generation online catalogues as well. This approach assumes however, that the user knows what he wants and can describe it in the language of the computer database being searched. Even the best second-generation catalogues do little to help the user transform an information need to explicit expressions of the need acceptable by the system but these catalogues do not lead the user from 'found' information to related, linked information that has not yet been discovered.

It is unrealistic to expect our catalogue users to know in advance the structure and language of our library databases. It is equally unrealistic to expect online catalogue users to be proficient in the various search approaches and techniques before they engage an interactive system in the retrieval process.

LCSH : Introduction and Its Improvements for Use in Online Catalogues

LC's publication of its subject headings list did not really begin in 1898. That was instead the year in which the Library of Congress converted from an author-plus a classed-catalogue to a dictionary catalogue, which incorporated author, title, and subject entries into a single file. For its first subject headings, LC used the American Library Association's List of Subject Headings for Use in Dictionary Catalogues (1st ed., 1895; 2nd ed., 1898), to which the LC cataloguers added new headings as they were needed. Meanwhile, with the ALA community clamoring for greater standardization as well as more cooperative cataloging, there arose a ready and appreciative market for the LC catalogue Card Distribution Service, which began in 1902. To the larger and "outside" library world, then, that was when subject headings formulated and assigned by LC began to be noticed and utilized. The first actual printing of Subject Headings Used in the Dictionary Catalogues of the Library of Congress (later to be titled Library of Congress Subject Headings) began in the summer of 1909, was issued in parts, and was completed in March 1914. In 1906 the Library of Congress published a preliminary list of subject subdivisions for place names and of subjects that could be subdivided by place. With all of these different dates to mark a beginning, perhaps it is the most sensible thing to choose 1898, assuming this to have been the year that the very first modification to the ALA List was made for LC use, and hence, the evolution of the Library of Congress Subject headings was begun.

There are frequent references to the guidelines for subject access delineated by Charles Ammi Cutter and this is remarkable because his Rules for a Dictionary Catalogue was originally published in 1876. A textbook on cataloging published in 1963 attested that "nothing has been written since that is any clearer than Mr. Cutter's explanation of this aspect of cataloguing. Certainly, we are indebted to Cutter for the concepts of direct entry, the use of natural language, and the syndetic structure meant to compensate for the "scattering" of related topics in the dictionary catalogue. And yet, the influence of Cutter on the LCSH was not acknowledged by the Library of Congress until 1972, when that acknowledgment was made unofficially by the Chief of the LC Subject Cataloguing Division. However, during the early development of the LCSH, J. C. M. Hanson at the Library of Congress adopted a more pragmatic approach than what Cutter had intended, resulting in some inconsistencies in the forms of subjed headings and the choice of cross-references. Inverted headings, meant to bring some subjects together in logical groupings, were established in the early LCSH lists to a much greater extent than had been recommended by Cutter.

It has also been noted that, whereas Cutter's Rules eventually led to much greater elaboration of rules-and examples-in the area of descriptive cataloguing, in subject cataloguing the efforts resulted in lists rather than codes. Paul Dunkin believed that our excessive focus on the lists and their growth actualy hindered the further development of the basic philosophy of the rules for subject headings. Perhaps this explains why throughout the century the library community made numerous requests for explanations of the fundamental rules or theory behind LC's subject heading lists.

The Library of Congress developed the LCSH for use in its own catalogues. The list was also considered appropriate for the very largest public libraries, some colleges and many university libraries. Smaller libraries continued to use the ALA List, last published in a 3rd edition (1911), and later, the Sears List of Subject Headings, which first appeared in 1923. LCSH was criticized for its aforementioned inverted headings, as well as its subdivided headings, which seemed to be a carryover from the days of the alphabetico-classed catalogue. Also, in the 1920's and 1930's the LC list lacked some of the syndetic structure found in ALA or in

Sears. It was not until 4th LCSH (1943) that "refer from" references were included, in addition to the "see" and "see also" cross-references, but printed in a separate volume; the 5th LCSH (1948) incorporated the "refer from" references in the main list. Nevertheless, by the 1930's more and more libraries found themselves doing a retrospective conversion of subject headings. They abandoned their homegrown lists, the outdated (1911) ALA List, or Sears, and converted to the LCSH for several compelling reasons: as their library collections grew, the desire for more precise subject headings increased; it was no longer economically feasible to continually revise subject headings appearing on LC catalogue cards; and, the LCSH was the only general list that made a consistent practice of keeping up to date by creating new subject headings for new topics. LC had been publishing supplements from time to time, but many outside cataloguers reported using the card distribution service as an informal notification about the newest subject headings.

Simultaneous to the increased adoption of LCSH in the 1930's, the library community began to demand a textbook on understanding and applying the LCSH. As a compromise, in the early 1940's "notes on L.C. methods and authorities used to establish certain types of headings, geographic headings, names of Indian and African tribes and languages, were obtained and published in column of Library Journal, largely through the efforts of the ALA Committee on Subject Headings and the "friendly cooperation of the Library of Congress. Finally in 1946 a treatise on subject headings by Julia Pettee, librarian of the Union Theological Seminary in New York, was published; later in same year the Library of Congress indicated that it was also working on a manual which could not be published until 1951. Written by the Chief of the LC Subject Cataloging Division, David J. Haykin, it was a 140-page book that basically reiterated most of Cutter's principles and tried to explain or rationalize some of the seeming inconsistencies in LCSH. Neither of these books, however, provided a true manual of practice for using and applying the LCSH. Another controversy that flared up in the literature of the 1940's was a debate over whether or not published subject bibliographies were superior to catalogue subject headings as a means of access to subject information.

At mid-century there was a growing dissatisfaction with LCSH; libraries were feeling the pressures of the increased publication and acquisition activities of this postwar period. There was a need to improve subject access but also to make subject cataloguing less costly, goals which are often in conflict with each other. Critics complained that "the basic rules and techniques for the construction of subject catalogues and the development of subject heading lists have undergone virtually no change in the last 75 years, and that such practices did not reflect any clear understanding of function or purpose. One trend that gained popularity in the 1950's and 1960's was a move to the divided catalogue. Considering the complexity of catalogue filing rules, along with the ever-lengthening, more precise subject headings, the rise of the "subject catalogue" (separated from the author/title catalogue) undoubtedly did benefit the library staff, but some librarians worried that it often diminished access-especially access of the serendipitous sort-for 'the catalogue user. Pettee observed the irony that libraries had gone "full circle"-from author and classed catalogues to dictionary catalogues and then back to divided catalogues. As another result of the Cold War period's rapid expansion of knowledge and information, many cataloguers felt that the Library of Congress was too slow in adopting new subjects or revising antiquated terminology. Nevertheless, LC did demonstrate a greater sense of responsibility in educating the library community during this time, principaly by including in its Cataloguing Service Bulletin explanations and guidelines on the use of certain types of subject headings or subdivisions, as well as notices of major revisions. The reporting concerning LCSH printed in Cataloguing Service Bulletin has continued and increased from the 1950's to the present day. In 1957 the 6th edition of LCSH was published; its innovation was the increase from two to three columns of subject headings per page, a format which would remain constant through to 1999.

Another development of the latter half of the 20th century was the experimentation with automation as a means for resolving the problems of subject access; this resulted in several efforts to create or discover a viable alternative to the LCSH. In the 1950's there was much discussion of "uniterms"which later were called "descriptors", designed for coordinate indexing via machine manipulation. A proliferation of keyword indexes (KWIC, KWOC, etc.) was witnessed in the 1960's-1970's, succeeded in later years by the keyword/Boolean search techniques utilized in most online public catalogues (OPACs). Thesauri became popular, particularly in special libraries, during the same period. And, in the 1970's-1980's a powerful string index language, PRECIS, was used by the British Library which even studied briefly by the Library of Congress as an augmentation to LCSH. These new techniques, experiments or functinalities proved to be useful, to a point. But ultimately it was generally concluded that none of these means for subject access could fully match the effectiveness of a precoordinated, controlled vocabulary such as the LCSH system. In the 1980's and 1990's the emphasis shifted to enhancing, rather than eliminating, the LCSH access, e.g., through mapping to other vocabularies or linking to classification numbers.

Social changes also had an impact, resulting in complaints in the 1960's-1970's about bias in the LCSH. Gradually, and often after much study and input from the ALA Subject Analysis Committee or other special-focus groups, the Library of Congress did revise many of the offensive terms or subtly-discriminatory wordings of headings related to racial, ethnic, religious, or gender groups. More technical changes occurred in the 1970's: the LC practice of using free-floating subdivisions was named in 1974 and later was expanded to new types or categories of headings; the 8th LCSH (1975) grew to two volumes and adopted its modern title, Library of Congress Subject Headings; in 1976 LC discontinued its practice of dual methods for geographic subdividing ("direct" and "indirect" instructions); and the LCSH began to print some headings that had previously been omitted i.e., legendary and fictitious characters, works of art, chemicals, ancient cities, structures, buildings, parks and reserves, and others. Also in 1976, the Library of Congress offered the list in a microfiche version for the first time. This made it affordable for libraries desiring to have multiple copies; the microfiche was portable, and very convenient for libraries that had converted to or were planning for computer-output microform catalogues.

Practitioners and professors writing in the literature began to propose the creation of a subject cataloguing "code" to do for subject analysis and practice what the Anglo-America". Cataloguing Rules 2nd ed. (AACR2) did for descriptive cataloguing. Although technically of a general code, the expressed need was partially fulfilled by the Library of Congress in 1984 through the publication of its Subject Cataloguing Manual: Subject Headings (SCM:SH). It was necessary, it may be argued, to publish such a manual in order to promulgate the rules for assigning the numerous and complicated free-floating subdivisions to be used under various categories or pattern headings. But the manual provided much more information, including LC policies and procedures, scope notes, and detailed guidance on applying subject headings for particular disciplines or forms of material. For the first time, "outside" cataloguers were able to read the same memoranda, or instruction sheets, available to LC cataloguers, and thus acquire the opportunity to become more consistent and improve the quality of the LCSH strings that they assigned to original-cataloguing records for the bibliographic utilities. From this point forward, the LCSH ceased being simply a list, and became the LCSH system; a cataloguer could no longer select or verify a subject heading using the LCSH alone, but instead must use the list in conjunction with the Subject Cataloguing Manual: Subject Headings. The SCM:SH has been issued in a looseleaf format, to allow for the ease of updating. Updating of the LCSH also became more timely during this period. Subscriptions to the "Weekly Lists" of new and changed subject headings and references were first offered in 1984.

In 1985 the Library of Congress began to regularize its practices regarding the provision of cross-references for new subject headings, and hoped to conduct a review and revision of the syndetic structure under older headings, as time allowed, to bring them into conformity with the new criteria. The criteria called for making links between subject headings only under certain circumstances, e.g., when the concepts or objects represented by the terms had a whole/part or genus/species relationship, among other rigorous conditions. At this time, the LCSH converted its notation devices to those most often used in thesaurus construction, i.e., BT for "broader term," NT for "narrower term," and so forth. The late 1980's also saw the introduction of two new formats for LCSH: one was the CDMARC Subjects for use on personal computers with CD ROM drives; the other was the Subject Alithorities in MARC format issued on magnetic tape which later also available via FTP transfer. The latter product enabled bibliographic utilities such as OCLC and RLIN to load the LCSH authorities in their databases and make searching of them available to their member libraries. While these improvements in the sharing of guidelines and dissemination of additions and changes were occurring, the LCSH continued to grow, expanding to three volumes beginning with the 11th ed. (1988). It was also in that year that new editions of the printed LCSH began to be published on an annual basis.

The 1990's ushered in a new era of cooperation, seeming to suggest that the Library of Congress no longer took a proprietary view of the LCSH, but rather, was finally acknowledging its responsibility to all users of the LCSH system. In May 1991, LC hosted an invitational Subject Subdivisions Conference, which resulted in many changes to LCSH, still ongoing and regularly summarized in Cataloguing Service Bulletin. Perhaps even more significant has been the development, under the auspices of the Program for Cooperative Cataloguing of the Subject Authority Cooperative Program (SACO). The SACO process allows specially-trained "outside" cataloguers to propose new subject headings based on their libraries' new acquisitions or their users' needs, rather than those exclusively of the Library of Congress. Clearly, the Library of Congress has accepted its leadership role, while encouraging the wider cataloging community to contribute to the list. That list, by the way, grew to four volumes by 1992, and reached five volumes beginning with the 21st ed. (1998).

There are many other issues and important moments in The LCSH Century. The collection begins with three essays that focus on the history or theoretical aspects of LCSH practice. Elaine Svenonius presents an analysis of the LCSH system as a language, describing some of its semantics and syntax as well as the pragmatics of specificity, and the effect of these on precision and recall. Hoerman and Furniss, investigated many of the same principles in light of recent guidelines developed and approved by the International Federation of Library Associations and Institutions (IFLA). Not only, a good deal of similarity between the IFLA Principles and those of the LCSH is discovered, but also indicated two major defects: the principles are often in conflict with each other; and, the principles are derived from tradition and practice rather than being based on users'-searching behaviours and needs. The essay contributed by Hope Olson is a successor to earlier books and articles which blew the whistle on the apparent or subtle biases inherent in the terminology found in LCSH; she uses the theories of a postcolonial critic as a framework to argue that LC could choose to eschew the exclusion or marginalization of certain peoples or cultures and instead become a change agent aspiring to the enrichment of the lives of all library users.

Pauline Cochrane first covered LCSH online environment in two works published in 1981 and 1986, and now offers an "update" on the progress made and the issues that still remain in improving the LCSH for use in OPACs. A topic which has seldom been addressed in the literature is examined by Gregory Wool. Because librarians have relinquished their control over the traditional catalogue's filing rules by merely accepting the limitations imposed by programmers and designers of OPACs, the result has been an accidental (or, unintended) deregulation of standard arrangements of subject headings in the indexes. Wool illustrates in particular how the Library of Congress Filing Rules, which arranges entries differently according to the punctuation that is present (e.g., commas for inverted headings, parentheses for qualified headings, etc.), takes advantage of the highly developed syntax and semantic features of the LCSH and result in logical groups that can benefit the searcher. These structured but perceivably helpful collocations are lost, however, in most online catalogues that simply arrange LCSH strings in a word-by-word fashion, causing Wool to wonder if LC and the library community as a whole have virtually abandoned their faith in a precoordinated controlled vocabulary. On a more positive note,

Stephen Hearn reports on the potential for online validation and updating of LCSH strings; he examines three approaches being studied, and discusses improvements to the LCSH authorities, including the establishment of authority records for all types of free-floating subject subdivisions.

Thomas Mann explains how he uses and teaches others to use the LCSH, for the most effective and thorough results in subject searching. His techniques-illustrated by cogent examples-combine explorations of adjacencies, cross-references and precoordination in the LCSH "red books" with redirections and browsing within the subject catalogue itself. He also addresses the differences between keyword and LCSH searches, pointing out several advantages to the controlled vocabulary approach.

For the public library perspective, we could hardly choose a better representative than the Cleveland Public Library, whose catalogue was among the five library catalogues examined in order to compile the first edition (1895) of the ALA List later used as the foundation for developing the Library of Congress Subject Headings. Louisa Kreider looks at a sample of subject searches executed at the urban library, and finds that LCSH terms and phrases match fairly well on the vocabulary used by the users. She also discusses the library's participation in SACO through which they have proposed new subject headings that have indeed been established in LCSH, the application of subject headings to works of fiction, and certain accommodations made locally for differences between the LCSH and the standard LC Annotated Card program headings (i.e., subject headings for juvenile literature). Hemmasi and Young present a comprehensive history of the development of music-related headings in LCSH. They include discussions on the LC Music Division's long-held preference for a classed catalogue, problems such as a bias in favour of Western "art" (or, classical) music. and the potential for the ongoing Music Thesaurus Project to assist in future improvements to LCSH. Perhaps most instructive to other "special interest" groups is the authors' account of the proactive role taken by the Music Library Association, in furthering the additions and revisions to LC subject beadings for music.

Although designed for library catalogues, the LCSH have also been used over the years in published or online bibliographies, abstracts, and periodical indexes too. Miller and Kuhr describe the vocabularies used in periodical indexing at the H. W. Wilson Company, with examples of various adaptations to LCSH that have been necessary. Their analysis highlights the fact that, whereas the LCSH is an excellent tool as a general system, for highly specialized indexes such as those geared to children, or lawyers, the LC terminologies are often either too specific or not detailed enough. David Miller treats the issue of LCSH's handling of access for different formats of materials, an area of concern for libraries with extensive audiovisual collections, or even, for those desiring better access to the genres/forms found in collections of literature. Recent developments such as the implementation of a new MARC code for subject "form" subdivisions have made this a hot topic of the 1990's. It is contended that, despite the LCSH inclusion of such terms, the form of a work is distinct from its subject; it is therefore questionable whether or not a subject heading list is really the proper venue for documenting practice.

Chronology of Official LCSH-Related Publications

1906	Preliminary List of Subject Subdivisions Under Names of Countries or States and of Subject Headings with Country Subdivisions.
1909-14	Subject Headings Used In the Dictionary Catalogues of the Library of Congress.
1910	Preliminary List of Subject Subdivisions: (a) Under Names of Countries or States (b) Under Cities; (c) Under General Subjects.
1913	Preliminary List of Literature Subject Headings.
1915	Preliminary List of Literature Subject Headings. 2nd issue.
1916	Preliminary List of Subject Subdivisions. (2nd ed.]
	Preliminary Lists of Subject Headings with Local Subdivision: (A) Headings with Indirect Subdivision; (8) Headings with Direct Subdivision; and (C) Preliminary List of Local Divisions (States, Provinces, etc.) to Which Subdivision Is Always Direct.

1917	Preliminary List of Literature Subject Headings, with a Tentative List for Shakespeare Collections. 3rd issue.
	Preliminary Lists of Subject Headings with Local Subdivision. 2nd ed.
1919	Subject Headings Used in the Dictionary Catalogues of the Library of Congress. 2nd ed.
	European War: Preliminary List of Subject Headings.
1920	Literature Subject Headings with List for Shakespeare Collections and Language Subject Headings. 4th ed.
	Subject Subdivisions: (A) Under Names of Countries, Stales, etc.; (8) Under Names of Cities; (C) Under General Subjects. 5th ed.
	Subject Headings with Local Subdivision. 3rd ed.
1924	Subject Subdivisions. 6th ed. (reprinted 1928.1936)
1925	Subject Headings with Local Subdivision. 4th ed.
1926	Literature Subject Headings with List for Shakespeare Collections and Language Subject Headings. 5th ed.
1928	Subject Headings Used in the Dictionary Catalogues of the Library of Congress. 3rd ed.
1935	Subject Headings with Local Subdivision. 5th ed.
1943	Subject Headings Used in the Dictionary Catalogues of the Library of Congress. 4th ed.
1945	Cataloging Service Bulletin. (Ongoing publication; issued quarterly; includes, among other topics on LC cataloging and classification, information on new subject headings, revised subject headings, and changes in practice or procedures.)
1948	Subject Headings Used in the Dictionary Catalogues of the Library of Congress. 5th ed.
1950	Period Subdivisions Under Names of Places Used in the Dictionary Catalogues of the library of Congress.
1951	Subject Headings: A Practical Guide/by David Judson Haykin.

1952	Music Subject Headings Used on Printed Catalogue Cards of the Library of Congress.
1957	Subject Headings Used in the Dictionary Catalogues of the Library of Congress. 6th ed.
1966	Subject Heaiings Used in the Dictionary Catalogues of the Library of Congress. 7th ed.
1969	Subject Headings for Children's literature.
1975	Library of Congress Subject Headings. 8th ed. (2 v.)
	An Introduction to Library of Congress Subject Headings. (Reprinted from the 8th LCSH, principally for users of the microfiche ed.)
	LC Period Subdivisions Under Names of Places. 2nd ed.
	Subject Headings for Children's Literature. 2nd ed.
1975-	Library of Congress Subject Headings [microform]. 8th ed. (22 microfiches). Publication in microfiche has continued from Jan. 1 Mar. 1976-, with slight title variations, issued quarterly.
1978	Working List of Subject Headings for Children's Literature.
1980 1981	Library of Congress Subject Headings. 9th ed. (2v.) Library of Congress Subject Headings: A Guide to Subdivision Practice.
1982	Working List of Subject Headings for Children's Literature.
1984	Subject Cataloguing Manual: Subject Headings. Prelim. ed.
1984-	L.C. Subject Headings Weekly lists. (published 1984-1994 in monthly cumulations; continued 1995-by an online file accessible via the LC website, updated weekly)
1985	Subject Cataloguing Manual: Subject Headings. Rev. ed. (loose-leaf)
1986-	Subject Authorities [database] (Ongoing publication of LCSH authority records in MARC format; issued weekly; available as 9-track magnetic tape, on IBM tape cal1ridge, or via Internet FTP; 1996- also include

	Subject Headings for Children's Literature)
1987	LC Period Subdivisions Under Names of Places, 3rd ed, 1988 Library of Congress Subject Headings, 11th ed, (3 v,)
	Subject Cataloguing Manual: Subject Headings, 3rd ed, (2 v,. loose-leaf)
1988-99	CDMARC Subjects [computer laser optical disk] (Replaced quaterly; consisted of machine-readable LCSH on compact disk; ceased with final issue of 1996)
1989	Library of Congress Subject Headings, 12th ed, (3 v,)
	Free-floating Subdivisions: An Alphabetical Index.
1990	Library of Congress Subject Headings, 13th ed, (3v.)
	LC Period Subdivisions Under Names of Places, 4th ed,
	Free-floating Subdivisions: An Alphabetical Index, 2nd ed,
	Library of Congress Subject Headings: Principles of Structure and Policies for Application/by Lois Mai Chan,
1991	Library of Congress Subject Headings, 14th ed, (3v.) Subject Cataloguing Manual: Subject Headings, 4th ed, (2v., loose-leaf)
	Free-Floating Subdivisions: An Alphabetical Index, 3rd ed,
	Revised Library of Congress Subject Headings: Cross-References from Former to Current Subject Headings, 1st ed,
1992	Library of Congress Subject Headings, 15th ed, (4 v,)
	Free-Floating Subdivisions: An Alphabetical Index, 4th ed,
	The Future of Subdivisions In the Library of Congress Subject Headings System: Report from the Subject Subdivisions Conference/ed, by Martha O'Hara Conway,
1993	Library of Congress Subject Headings, 16th ed, (4v,)
	Free-Floating Subdivisions: An Alphabetical Index, 5th ed,

	Subject Headings for Children's LIterature [Microform]. (Ongoing publication, issued quarterly as part of the LCSH-microfiche)
1994	Library of congress Subject Headings. 17th ed. (4v.)
	LC Period Subdivisions Under Names of Places. 5th ed.
	Free-floating Subdivisions: An Alphabeticallrmex. 6th ed,
1994-	Cataloguers Desktop [Computer Laser Optical Disk] (Ongoing publication, replaced quarterly; includes the full Subject Cataloging Manual: Subject Headings)',
1995	Library of Congress Subject Headings. 18th at. (4 v.)
	Free-Floating Subdivisions: An Alphabetical kmex. 7th ed.
1996	Library of Congress Subject Headings, 19th m (4 v.)
	Subject Cataloguing Manual: Subject Headings. 5th ed. (4 v., loose-leaf)
	Free-Floating Subdivisions: An Alphabetical Index. 8th ed,
1996	Classification Plus [Computer Laser Optical Disk] (Ongoing publication, replaced quarterly; includes the full Library of Congress Subject Headings)
1997	Library of Congress Subject Headings. 20th ell. (4 v.)
	Free-Floating Subdivisions: An Alphabetical Index: 9th ed.
1998	Library of Congress Subject Headings. 21st m (5 v.)
	Free-Floating Subdivisions: An Alphabetical Indax. 10th ed.
1999	Library of Congress Subject Headings. 22nd es. (5 v.)
	Free-Floating Subdivisions: An Alphabetical Index. 11th ed.

LCSH: some Illustrations

D. J. Haykin recognised that the specific entry principle is applied in a limited fashion in Library of Congress practice, but added no further explanation beyond claiming that the non-specific entry policy is based on the experience of assisting readers. One suspects that the accumulation of a large amount of material on a generically entered subject often leads to a change to specific entry. Such a policy would be closely in line with Cutter's use of subdivisions to break up large numbers of entries under the same heading.

It is suggested that the effectiveness of a system of connective references depends upon the extent to which it is a system; that is to say upon the extent to which it is based upon a map of subjects symbolising their mutual relationships. A scheme of classification is just such a map, and we find that the Library of Congress list does appear to stem from such a classificatory background.

There seem to be two distinct and separate layers of relational references in the list. The first layer comprises a more or less complete net- work of downward directed hierarchical references and horizontally directed co-ordinate references, apparently based upon a classification scheme which often reveals the lineaments of the Decimal Classification. Superimposed upon this is a second layer of references, the content of which is unpredictable and apparently unrelated to any under-lying principle. It would appear, according to Library of Congress reasoning, that a connective reference- system based on classification alone does not suffice for a dictionary catalogue.

Miss Pettee, perhaps the most articulate expositor of the American type of dictionary catalogue, reveals a curiously ambivalent attitude to the whole question of the relationship between classification and subject cataloguing. On the one hand she affirms that the classificatory "horse" pulls the logical load of the alphabetical subject references in a dictionary catalogue, on the other she refers to the power of the dictionary catalogue to express relationships in several dimensions at once as its supreme advantage over the classified catalogue. She is right in stressing the multi-dimensional nature of subject relationships, but wrong, it may be thought, in supposing that the freedom of the alphabetical subject catalogue to set up multi-dimensional connective references is necessarily an advantage. Knowledge that such a miscellany of undefined relational dimensions exists is of no help to the subject cataloguer, whose whole task is to select a few of the possible lines of relationship to be embodied in 'see also' references. What the subject cataloguer requires above all are some principles defining and limiting those relationships which are to be expressed in references. Such questions are in current dictionary catalogue theory and practice put on one side in favour of casual selection in Miss Pettee's multi-dimensional continuum.

The multi-dimensional theory is evidently represented in Library of Congress practice by the superimposed or secondary layer of references mentioned above. A single example from the list will illustrate the two layers. At the heading 'Drawing', the following connective references are given:

Drawing

See also * Anatomy, Artistic
Architectural drawing
Blackboard drawing
Brush drawing
Caricature
Charcoal drawing
Crayon drawing
*Design, Decorative
Drawing books Drawings
Figure drawing
Geometrical drawing
*Graphic methods
*Human figure in art
*Illustration of books
Landscape drawing
Map drawing
Mechanical drawing
Military sketching
Painting
Pastel drawing
Pen drawing

Pencil drawing
*Perspective
*Projection, Art
*Proportion, Art
*Shades and Shadows
Topographical drawing

and Art
Design, Decorative
Illustration of books
Manual training
Perspective

See also * Drawing

The items here asterisked are neither subordinate nor co-ordinate references. They are in fact the superimposed layer corresponding to the multi-dimensional linkages mentioned by Miss Pettee. It is worthwhile pausing to try and define the relationships of some of the asterisked headings to the concept 'Drawing'.

The idea to which they all have a common affiliation is that of Art. Drawing is a particular kind of Art which involves the placing of materials such as charcoal, crayon, etc. on a surface. Artistic Anatomy, Human Figure in Art, and Shades and Shadows are related to Art in a different manner. They are examples of what may be depicted in Art (not only in Drawing). Yet another kind of relationship with Art is suggested by the quartet Design, Decorative; Perspective; Projection, Art; Proportion, Art. Here we have neither a kind of Art nor what is depicted in Art, but some principles belonging to artistic activity and technique. Finally we have Illustration of Books which is an example of a particular kind of Art being applied to an extraneous object. Here, then, we have four relational 'dimensions' radiating from Art and tentatively designated as Kind, Subject depicted, Principle of Activity, and Application. These are what Ranganathan would call separate 'facets' of the subject Art.

Now each of these topics is related to others in the other facets of Art indirectly through the common concept (Art) from which they spring. Any system of 'See also' references which tried directly to connect all these subjects would collapse under its own sheer volume. The Library of Congress list links together merely an indeterminate selection. Fortunately it is not necessary to represent indirect relationships by direct reference links.

Direct linkage between topics in different facets occurs when a compound subject such as Perspective in Drawing, or the Human Figure in Book Illustration is formed. But by its very nature a compound subject poses no problem of subject relationship which requires 'see also' references. It merely needs a set of references from each of those parts of the heading not used as entry word in the subject heading. Thus the heading 'Perspective, Drawing' and the supporting references from 'Drawing, Perspective' provide everything that is required to signal the relationship between Drawing and Perspective. 'See also' references are needed only to show relationships between those subjects which cannot (because they are in thc same faect or in hierarchical relationship) form compound subjects. Why has this simplification of the pattern of 'see also' references evaded the compilers of the Library of Congress list? The reply to this question is to be found in thc fact that except for a few special categories avoids compound subject headings as much as possible. This policy in turn stems back to Cutter's refusal of specific entry for non 'established' subjects. Semantically compound subjects are certainly, by and large, less 'established' than, simple ones, and the general effect in Library of Congress practice is that a compound is often entered under one or more simple generic headings. Thus 'Perspective, Drawing' cannot apparently be admitted as an 'established' subject and books on this subject may expect to receive two generic entries under 'Perspective, Art' and 'Drawing' respcctively. But double entry makes no contribution to signposting the relationship between Perspective and Drawing, hence it is necessary to make cross-references between the two headings. Undoubtedly many of the superimposed references compensate for the absence of compound subject headings.

A further consequence of the generic entry of 'unestablished' topics is that it is possible to have 'see' references from an unused specific term to a used generic one. Apparently there is a half-way condition of 'establishment' which warrants a reference but not an entry in the list. Thus we have 'Kneejerks see Reflexes', 'Public Libraries see Libraries', 'Dungeons see Prisons'. The opposite situation can also occur. 'See' references are made from certain generic terms which for unexplained reasons are not used as subject headings. Examples are 'Exports see Commerce' and 'Exports see Tariff'

Not all terms listed as subject headings are included explicitly in the reference network. Names of concrete objects and materials are frequently not signalled by references from the generic headings which logically contain them. To a certain extent access to material on such subjects is made possible by the use of general references in the form:

Materials. For special materials see under their names.

Such general references offer the possibility of vast economics both in respect of the actual size of the catalogue as well as in the tracings which need to bc maintained. They fail, however, to provide for the collective enquiry which demands access to all the library's resourccs within a particular subject field. Probably their use in the Library of Congress list is confmed to cases where intelligent anticipation suggests that collective enquiries are not likely to be made. As an aid to enquirers whose approach to a specific subject commences by resort to a generic term, the general reference is satisfactory provided that its use is limited to subjects of concrete character. To invite an enquirer to seek headings on 'the various aspects, kinds and applications' of say Biology would certainly fall short of reasonable subjcct catalogue service. Rather remotely allied to the general reference in Library of Congress is the scope note. This defines the range of meaning of a particular heading, and includes general directions for the finding of subjects which might conceivably be sought under the heading concerned but are in fact entered elsewhere.

Two further ways in which the reference-system of the Library of Congress list departs from the pattern outlined in Chapter III may be mentioned here. The reference pathway leading down from the generic to the specific does not always modulate. A direction may be given not only to the next subordinate term in the hierarchy, but also to a further subordillate term, one or more further stages down in the hierarchy. Thus we have both 'Economics see also Finance, Public', and 'Economics see also Taxation'. This practice is authorised by Cutter, but once again it is difficult to detect any rationale underlying its employment in some cases but not in others. It is not unknown for intermediate subordinate terms to be omitted altogether from the chain of referencs'. Thus there is no reference linking Carving with Ice carving. The second peculiarity in Library of Congress practice is that 'see also' references between collateral subjects are sometimes unaccountably made in one direction only. Thus, we have 'Rime see also Rhythm', but not 'Rhythm see also Rime'.

Perhaps the chief lesson to be drawn from the referencing system in the Library of Congress list is that it is not enough for the purposes of the alphabetical subject catalogue to lay down the rule that collateral or co-ordinate subjects are to be linked by references. It is necessary to define with more precision just what collateral subjects are, otherwise the collateral relationship may be invoked to justify indiscriminate reference linkages. Examples of such false collateral references have been mentioned already in connection with the discussion on the heading 'Drawing' and its associated references. There are many others. Hygiene and Air are not a collateral pair, nor are Publicity and Journalism, nor Book Industries and Trades and Publishing and Publishers, nor Aesthetics and Classicism. The only possible closer definition of collateral relationship appears to lie within the concept of faceted classification. Tentatively we may say that the lateral relationship is restricted to terms which lie within the same facet of a given generic subject. The relationship between such a pair as Aesthetics and Classicism is almost always to be expressed by a compound subject heading (such as Classicism, Aesthetics).

Compound subject headings are admitted in the list provided that they can be regarded as 'established'. Following Cutter, the Library of Congress usually enters phrases as they stand, inversion being an exceptional procedure. According to Haykin, every effort is made to avoid subheadings because they amount to 'indirect entry' which is supposedly incompatible with the specific entry principle. Some subjects are designated in ordinary language by a combination of words. We can, indeed we must, use such a combination as a subject heading in the alphabetical subject catalogue, and provided that the idea signified in the subject heading corresponds to that covered by the document in hand, we have specific subject entry. Such compound headings as 'Personnel Management' (phrase form) and 'Personnel, Management' (subheading form) are equally direct and specific for a document on personnel management. Most subject headings with subheadings are really inverted phrases with the connecting preposition omitted. No doubt the dual reluctance of the Library of Congress to use either the inverted phrase form or the subheaded form springs from a common source. With regard to Haykin's appeal to directness it is difficult to see in what sense 'Air, Hygiene' is less direct than the two generic headings-'Air' and 'Hygiene' which would presumably replace the single compound heading in Library of Congress practice. The exact contrary would seem to be true. One objection to subheadings voiced both by Haykin and Margaret Mann suggests that their use is appropriate only to the alphabetico-classed catalogue. This is erroneous. The alphabetico-classed catalogue does provide indirect entry via a generic term, according to the scheme of subdivision and main classes adopted, irrespective of whether the subheading term standing alone could in fact represent the subject. This is an entirely different matter from the use of subheadings in cases where there is no single word or phrase which denotes the subject. It is hardly an exaggeration to say that the reluctance to use subheadings is the greatest contributory factor to the deficiencies of the Library of Congress Catalogue as a reference tool.

In an effort to avoid the reproach of either non-specific entry or the use of subheadings, the Library of Congress sometimes uses phrase headings which from no point of view can be regarded as established. We find, for instance, 'Medicine, Magic, Mystic and Spagiric'. Another form of phrase without currency outside the list and its derivatives is the conjunctive form employed as a means of distinguishing homonyms. 'Files and Rasps' is an example of a phrase heading of this type. The second term' Rasps' is a substitute for a qualifying subheading such as 'Tools' which is required to differentiate the files from the office equipment bearing the same name.

In the recent editions of its list, the Library of Congress has found itself obliged to relax, to some extent, its veto on subject sub-headings. Haykin says that the purpose of these subheadings is "not to limit the subject but to provide for its arrangement". This is a mere play upon words; in the alphabetical subject catalogue the degree of subject specification and the mechanics of arrangement are simply two aspects of a single operation. One decides upon a particular heading and by the same token determines the position of the entry in the catalogue. Where such subject subheadings appear in the list, there is sometimes confusion because the same entry word is also part of one or more phrase headings. Thus we have

Aeroplane racing

but

Aeroplanes —Piloting

This weakness also appears in the Australian subject heading list of Sherrie and Jones, which has

Animal ecology

but

Animals — Behaviour

and

Aeroplane engines

but

Aeroplanes — Design

It is probably necessary to include both phrases and subject sub-sheadings in dictionary catalogues, but there is a field of choice in deciding whether to use phrases whenever possible or subheadings whenever possible. The Library of Congress and those under its influence have chosen the former method for entangled reasons, which include intractable though indefinite reservations about the specific entry principle and what can only be emotional a version from the superficial appearance of the alphabetico-classed catalogue.

The Library of Congress list also permits the use of form, chronological, and locality subheadings. The form subheadings. which include subjects such as societies and law, which classification schemes have for some time placed among common subdivisions, can be applied to any heading in the list. The time and place subheadings can only be used as headings where permission for their use is given. Haykin explains the procedure followed when literature occurs giving local treatment to a topic precluded in the list from taking a locality subheading. For example 'Gnatcatchers' is a term for which locality subheadings are not authorised. A book on 'Gnatcatchers of California' is given double entry as follows:

(1) Gnatcatchers

(2) Birds — California.

The rule here appears to be that a second entry is made under the nearest generic term at which locality subheadings are allowed. It is hard to see what advantage is to be found in double non-specific entry over a single specific entry

Gnatcatchers — California with inversion reference

California — Gnatcatchers. See Gnatcatchers California

No doubt in evading specific subject entry in this fashion the Library of Congress Catalogue achieves a superficial appearance of simplicity. Under the generic heading or headings books covering the whole generic subject field are interspersed in random order with books on various sections of the field which possess no "established" subject name. Such lack of specification impedes the enquirer, whether he is seeking generic or specific subject material.

A few further details of Library of Congress subject cataloguing practice are given which will serve to pin-point some minor practical problems not hitherto discussed.

The subheadings for historical periods in Library of Congress practice normally consist of verbal headings followed by dates: the latter are, however, the arranging symbols. The subheadings represent ad hoc historical eras worked out for particular subjects. Presumably historical specification in any field awaits the accumulation of a large amount of material under the heading. Historical episodes are normally entered under the place.

The form of geographical heading or subheading has exercised a great deal of the attention of Library of Congress cataloguers. In the first place there is the distinction to be made between ethnic adjectives and the names of places as such. The ethnic adjectives are used to name national schools in many of the fine arts, literature and philosophy. Usually they appear as the second word of an inverted phrase heading, e.g. 'Painting, English'. But in topics connected with language and literature the ethnic adjective is the first word, the phrase in this case not being inverted. The Sherrie and Jones list usefully treats some religious and period adjectives in exactly the same way as ethnic adjectives. Two further problems arise in connection with geographical headings proper. The first is concerned with the possible conflict between geographical names and the names of states. Library of Congress regularly prefers geographical names to political names on the ground of permanency. Against this must be placed the fact that political names are almost always better known, that they are usually more precise in meaning than geographical ones, and some denote areas which have no purely geographical name. The second problem is concerned with whether a locality subheading denoting an area within a country should be given directly or subordinated under country, giving such an entry as

Agriculture —France —Coutances

Directions for direct or indirect subordination are given in the list under each heading for which geographical subdivision is permitted. It is not possible to discern any controlling principle. The indirect method of subordination is contrary to specific entry and the result is a true alphabetico-classed entry. The motive for this practice is undoubtedly to link, say. Agriculture in France' with 'Agriculture in Coutances'. The alternative mechanism would of course be a 'see also' reference.

Agriculture —France, see also Agriculture —Coutances.

Any system of subheadings poses this problem, which is not peculiar to Library of Congress methods. Rigorous linkage of subheadings under the same heading by means of 'see also' references would be prohibitive for most catalogues and indexes. Perhaps here the general reference, reminding the enquirer in effect that the alphabetical subject catalogue does not physically group related topics, may come into its own. Thus the direction

> Agriculture — France. See also names of parts of France amongst these subheadings under Agriculture

would appear to meet all reasonable needs provided that the number of subheadings under the particular heading is not too great for scanning by the enquirer.

A situation which seems to challenge the whole principle of alphabetical arrangement arises when subheadings representing forms, periods, places and subjects appear together under a particular heading. Few dictionary catalogues are so firmly wedded to thorough going alphabetical arrangement that they would arrange all subheadings in a single sub-sequence. Conventional practice attempts grouping of kinds of subheadings and arrives at some such arrangement as the following:

HEADING
References from Heading
Subheadings
— Forms
— Periods
— places
— Subjects

Library of Congress, in its annual subject catalogues, adopts a simpler scheme, namely:

HEADING
References from Heading
Subheadings
— Forms, Periods (introduced by the term 'History') and Subjects in one sequence
— places

Heading as first word of an inversion

With this final passing glance at a particular sector of the alphabetical catalogue structure, at which the alphabetical principle appears to be insufficient, it is concluded that this form of catalogue considered mainly from the point of view of heading language. Reference has been made from time to time to the relevance of classification for all forms of subject catalogues; its importance as the foundation of attempts to signal subject relationship has béen underlined.

LCSH Online :

In 1986 the book, Improving LCSH for Use in Online Catalogs,' Exercises for Self-Help with a Selection of Background Readings was published. In the early 1980s library automation developments were changing the basic design of our traditional card catalogues and there was a need to reconsider the subject access information as it was put into MARC format for bibliographic and authority records. The results of catalogue use studies and research into subject access problems were not being headed. This was the period before vendors' turnkey systems and OPAC (Online Public Access Catalogue) design was being done on college campuses (UC-Berkeley, Mankato State, Syracuse, Ohio State, Toronto, VTI-Blacksburg, Northwestern, etc). OPAC design efforts were not concentrating on subject access even though we learned from the 1982 Council on Library Resources national study of OPAC use that the majority of users were searching by subject and that they needed help.

At that time, almost twenty years ago, many of us "knew the new facts early" but no matter what we did to alert librarians and designers, OPAC system design evolved with few enhancements for the subject searcher. One reason for their reticence to embark on such improvements may have been the slowness with which LCSH was prepared to serve as a thesaurus in electronic format. The Subject Authority File at the Library of Congress was not really ready until 1986, almost a decade after the first OPAC design efforts. As these systems have been revamped over the years because of developments such as graphical user interfaces, the Internet, and computer games, we are beginning to see the design of OPACs improve. Subject searching still needs improving.

A recent publication has taken up the call for further improvements and this effort is to be lauded because its recommendations are based on a thorough knowledge of the catalogue records that make up the database being searched and the findings of the most relevant use studies in the past twenty years.

Keyword searching is often touted as the best feature of OPACs, but any subject searcher knows that this mode of searching puts the burden on the user with little or no help provided to track down synonyms, homonyms, or related terms. Surely we can do better than that after twenty years of automated catalogues and indexes?

Another publication from almost twenty years ago and the Shubert update in 1992 provide a critical bibliography concerning the world's leading vocabulary control mechanism, namely LCSH (Library of Congress Subject Head ings, hereinafter refemd to as LCSH/SAF because this list, in the MARC Authority record format, presents the most complete version of LCSH records). Through the years almost 300 separate articles and research reports have addressed the general structure and features of LCSH/SAF, with critical comments and suggestions for improvements. In Improving LCSH some of those suggestions were developed into a coordinated series of steps which could be taken to make improvements in subject access mechanisms in an OPAC. If the staff of the Library of Congress did not have the time or inclination to make those improvements, others could (Sanford Berman's efforts at the Hennepin County Public Library and later in NoveList have served as independent models of LCSH/SAF). The chapters in improving LCSH covered such improvements as more notes, more entry vocabulary, more complete trackiag of logical and associative relationships between terms, a better way to handle period, place, form and topical subdivisions, and links between subject headings and class numbers.

Recent changes at the Library of Congress will have an impact on the presentation of subject headings from bibliographic records.

In September, 1999, the new Integrated Library System has been launched at the Library of Congress. Separate products such as Classification Plus will probably be incorporated into that system and other OPAC systems will do likewise. Relationships between classification schedules and subject heading lists, between bibliographic records and authority files, between parts of the MARC bibliographic reord and other files will all be important aspects of OPAC design and related processes such as cataloging, searching, and retrieval.

In Improving LCSH, several reprinted selections on this aspect of a subject authority list was covered. The index refers the reader to: cataloguer's note, general reference note, history note, refer from note, scope note, and see also reference note. These are the notes that appear in subject authority records, some of which are displayed for OPAC searchers. Alan M. Greenberg's review prompted Lois Chan to include information about the construction of such notes in later editions of her book on LCSH because of their importance, and the Subject Cataloguing Manual: Subject Headings (SCM:SH) has a section (H400) to document policies followed at the Library of Congress.

The 22nd LCSH (1999) indicates that about of 2% of the headings now have scope notes. Scope notes for the subdivision records (18X in MARC format for subject authority records) can now be found in the Subject Authority File. These notes were previously only available in a separate publication. They can now be accessed by anyone using LCSH/SAF.

Scope notes are now in two MARC/SAF fields, 680 and 667, the former a "public" general note and the latter a "nonpublic general note." Until February 1999 there were no 667 notes in LCSHISAF, but now they appear in geographic subject heading records, for example, to record "Heading not valid for use as geographic subdivision."

Exercise One in Improving LCSH included eight subject headings with scope notes with revisions suggested to improve the note for catalogue searchers who were not cataloguers. Four had been revised, two deleted, and two remained identical. That is progress! In Exercise 2, where three headings (New thought,

Sandwich construction, and Open and closed shelves) needed dictionary definitions as scope notes, there were no scope notes in the 22nd LCSH (1999). Apparently a third suggestion caused no overall review of the need for scope notes at such places as headings beginning with the word "State. .., Municipal. ..., or Local....". Notes still appear only erratically at such places in LCSH/SAF. For example, why should Local finance have a scope note but not Local budgets, Local laws but not Local option etc.?

Since so few headings have scope notes (in the 680 field of the MARC/ Subject authority record), the review was not continued any further. Instead "note-type" information in LCSH/SAF, in fields 670, 675, and 952 was checked. As a subject cataloguer at the Library of Congress (or elsewhere) prepares a subject authority record for a new term, justification for that term and any cross references especially entry vocabulary appears in field 670. It shows sources checked and if the LCSH heading is not identical to that used each source, the variation is noted. If a source is checked and there is no entry found, that is recorded in the 675 field. Local information is given in field 952.

Let's examine the LCSH/SAF records given as examples in Lois Chan's book on LCSH to see how valuable these fields might be for OPAC users who are doing multifile or crossfile searching. Figures 1-7 illustrate seven of these records from Chan. There is a wealth of information for multifile or crossfile earching if and when OPACs are redesigned to accommodate such a feature. For example:

Look at the LCSH/SAF record for the Tailhook Scandal, 1991-1993 (Figure 1). Out of the four sources checked three did not agree with the approved LCSH heading, and the variations are shown. Three of the sources are online bibliographic databases.

FIGURE 1. LCSH/SAF Record for Tailhook Scandal

010 sh 93007668

040 DLC DLC

150 Tailhook Scandal, 1991-1993

550 Sexual harassment of women-United States *broader term*

670 Work cat.: 93-138159: Women in the military: the Tailhook affair and the problem of sexual harassment, 1992.

670 Wash. Post index, 1992 (Tailhook Association ...sexual harassment scandal)

670 NYT index, Jan.-Mar. 1993.

670 MAGS (Tailhook scandal scars Naval aviation)

670 LC data base, 10/5/93 (Tailhook Association)

FIGURE 2. LCSH/SAF Record for Golden Parachutes

010 sh94002701

040 DLC DLC

150 Golden parachutes (Executive compensation)

680 Here are entered works on severance benefits paid to executives in the event of a corporate takeover.

450 Golden umbrellas (Executive compensation) used for 550 Executives-Salaries, etc. broader term

550 Severance pay *broader term*

670 Consolidation and merger of corporations related term

670 UMI business vocab.

670 LIV.

670 Scott, D.L. Wall Street words, 1988: (Golden parachutes, also known as Golden umbrellas)

FIGURE 3. LCSH/SAF Record for Lost Architecture

010 sh93000146

040 DLC DLC DLC NJR

053 NA209 (General)

150 Lost architecture

680 Here are entered works on buildings, structures, etc., that were accidentally or purposefully destroyed or demolished.

450 Architectural heritage, Lost *used for*

450 Buildings, Lost *used for*

450 Lost architectural heritage *used for*

450 Lost buildings *used for*

550 Architecture *broader term*

670 Work cat.: 92-43452: Jones, C. Lost Baltimore, c1993.

670 92-73620: DeAngelo, D. The law offices of Shook ...Kansas City as seen through its lost architecture, c1992.

670 LC database, Dec. 15, 1992 (lost architecture; lost architectural heritage)

670 Art. human. cit. index (lost architecture)

675 Bibl. guide art arch.: Hennepin; LIV; IAC; Readers' guide; NYT index; Random House; Art index

FIGURE 4. LCSH/SAF Record for Crop Circles

010 sh 93000098

040 DLC DLC

150 Crop circles

450 Circle formations in crops *used for*

450 Circles, Corn *used for*

450 Circles, Crop *used for*

450 Corn circles *used for*

450 Crop circle formations *used for*

450 Crop field circles *used for*

450 Cropfield circles *used for*

450 Formations, Crop circle *used for*

550 Curiosities and wonders *broader term*

670 Hennepin (Crop circles x Crop field circles; Crop field circles)

670 LC data base, 1/8/93 (crop circles)

670 Ox. dict. new words (crop circle: a (usually circular) area of standing crops which has been inexplicably flattened, apparently by a swirling, vortex-like movement (sometimes also called corn circles))

670 Crop circle enigma, 1990: pp. 10, 12 (Circle formations in crops, corn circles)

335

675 IAC

Look at Figure 2, where the heading was glossed (qualified in parentheses) in such a way that the related and broader terms are sensible relationships and the 670 fields contribute to our understanding.

Look at Figure 4, the record for Crop circles. Eight "used for" references are included in LCSH/SAF and justified by what was found in the Hennepin County Public Library catalogue and elsewhere.

FIGURE 5. LCSH/SAF Record for Health Care Reform

010 sh 93007525

040 DLC DLC

150 Health care reform

450 Health reform *used for*

450 Health system reform *used for*

450 Medical care reform *used for*

450 Reform of health care delivery *used for*

450 Reform of medical care delivery *used for*

550 Medical policy *broader term*

550 Insurance, Health *related term*

670 Work cat.: 93-35883: Domestic Policy Council (U.S.). Health security, cl993 (health care reform)

670 MESH 1994 (Health care reform)

670 Washington Post (health care reform, health reform)

670 IAC (health care reform)

FIGURE 6. LCSH/SAF Record for Time Pressure

010 sh93005764

040 DLC DLC

150 Time pressure

450 Pressure, Time *used for*

450 Temporal stress *used for*

450 Time stress *used for*

550 Stress (Psychology) *broader term*

670 Work cat.: 93-11985: Time pressure and stress in human judgment" and decision making, c1993 [Time stress, time constraints, time urgency)

670 LC data base, 7/26/93 [Time pressure)

670 Keyes, R. Timelock, 1991 [Time pressure)

670 Faulkner, H. W. (Spatio-temporal stress)

675 Hennepin; Thes. psych. index terms

FIGURE 7. LCSH/SAF Record for World Music

010 sh 93002569

040 Mn MHCL DLC

150 World music

680 Here are entered popular musical works combinig traditional rhythms from around the world with clements of jazz and rock.

450 World beat music *used for*

550 Popular music *broader term*

670 Work cat.: Spencer, P. World beat, 1992 : a listener's guide to contemporary world music on CD, 1992 (World music)

670 BDNE (World Beat)

670 Hennepin (World beat music)

670 Ox dict. new world (World music)

670 M. Ziomek visited Tower Records, 5/18/93 (World music)

Look at Figure 5, the record for Health care reform. If this information were used in multifile searching, catalogue users would have direct links, with correct headings for searching, in three popular databases, Medline (where MeSH is used), the Washington Post, and IAC.

Look at Figure 6 where the field 675 tells that the heading, Time pressure, is not found in the Thesaurus of Psychological Index terms.

Such information could prompt the searcher to do a keyword search in the abstract and title fields of *Psychinfo*. The same is true in Figure 3 where the 675 field of the record for Lost architecture, shows that eight databases do not use this term as a descriptor.

In Figure 7, the authorized heading chosen, World music, must have been a toss-up in the mind of the subject cataloguer. The sources checked show that various terms (World music, World beat music, and World Beat) are used. The helpful scope note in 680 provides the searcher with more useful information.

As more and more books will be in electronic form and accessible from OPACs through hyperlinks in the 856 field of the MARC bibliographic record, the information about book citations in the 670 and 675 fields of LCSH/SAF will become more important (See the "work cat." notes in the 670 field of records in Figures 1, 3, 5, 6, and 7. See also the notes about reference works in Figures 2, 4, and 7.)

These fields truly contain notes for the 21st century library catalogue. Thompson-Yee, at the Library of Congress, reported that as on September 30, 1998 there were 87,424 of the 244,747 LCSH/SAF records that have a 670 field, with a mean of 2.07 occurrences, and this is only for headings established or revised after 1986. There was no breakdown given by heading tag, but figures 1-7 show how full the records are for such topics as public affairs issues, technology, news events, and even humanities headings.

A follow-up study of this feature of LCSH/SAF is recommended so that we can judge how truly valuable this information will be as OPACs are transformed into gateways to electronic library collections and help us locate other resources on the Internet. No doubt the availability of electronic thesauri will transform the way we use metadata to access full text in the OPACs of the future.

A subfield in the 6XX fields of the MARC bibliographic records now shows the source of the subject heading if it is not from LCSH/SAF. This prompts to suggest a related study of the OCLC/OLUC file to determine how many different thesauri are used and to find out how many of these thesauri are in electronic form. As we begin to experiment with relationships between LCSH and other thesauri, between MARC bibliographic records in OPACs and all relevant thesauri, we may find some other features which can enhance OPAC use.

Cross-Reference Stnlcture in LCSH/SAF

Phyllis Allen Richmond's seminal 1959 paper started most of us thinking about the hierarchic structure within LCSH. Before then all we knew was that there were relationships between headings in the printed LCSH such as an unapproved heading cross-reference to an approved heading (the old A see B reference with an x notation at the B heading); cross-references between two approved headings (the old B see also C reference, sometimes combined with C see also B (shown as a *sa* or *xx* tracing, or both at B and C, depending on the nature of the relationship). At the time there were no principles or theory for establishing these relationships except for some discussion by David Haykin these references were more or less made by subject cataloguers at the Library of Congress as needed. There were no computers around to manipulate and trace the entire hierarchical structure of any subject heading list if such a structure could be discerned. This is why Richmond's "manual analysis" was so very revealing. Other research followed and in only a year or so some lexicographers started using categorization and classification schemes to help to determine hierarchic relationships in their lists. The term "thesaurus" came into vogue about 1960 in the information science field and constructing such a list of controlled vocabulary terms was defined as the practice of relating approved headings or descriptors in a list to each other in either a BT-NT (Broader-Narrower Term) hierarchic relationship or a RT-RT (Related term) relationship by association. The x and see relationship were coded *used for* and *use* and talked about as entry vocabulary or synonym equivalents. Retrieval tests at Cranfield, England and elsewhere tested the value of these relationships during the search process. By the time of the Elsinore Conference in September 1964 the value of a classification scheme for the formation of a thesaurus was recognized and the relationship of subject headings and class numbers was considered as integral parts of an information retrieval system.

As thesauri were constructed for abstracting and indexing services and for special libraries in scientific and technical fields, national and international standards were developed for the construction of such vocabulary control mechanisms. The ERIC Thesaurus and MeSH (Medical Subject Headings from the National Library of Medicine) are two notable examples which have been used in library science education classes for more than thirty years. We could never use LCSH as an example because study after study showed how incomplete the structure was. The Library of Congress has repeatedly explained that only headings needed for cataloging were in the list and there was no attempt at an underlying structure of relationships. But by 1948, in the Introduction to the 5th edition of LCSH, there was a telling statement:

A growing awareness of the need of a statement of principles and rules of practice in subject cataloguing has tended to correct deviations from logic and consistency, and has led to the gradual improvement of the headings in the Library's catalogues. (Subject Cataloging Manual: Subject Headings (SCM:SH) policies H373, 370, 375 document those principles and practices today).

The Library of Congress, for many editions of the printed LCSH, reported that the logical arrangement of concepts in their classification scheme was a complementary structure to what seemed missing in LCSH. Unfortunately they have been lax in relating these two vocabulary control mechanisms for almost one hundred years. Only thirty-six percent of the headings in the 22nd LCSH (1999) show a corresponding LCC class number.

With a syndetic structure that did not show proper hierarchic relationships there is no wonder that there was a flurry in the professional literature when the Library of Congress decided to adopt the standard thesaurus encoding for term relationships in LCSH/SAF during the 1980s and 1990s. There was no overall review of the structure of LCSH/SAF until the mid-1990s. Such a review is a monumental task, given that the number of topical headings is well over 180,000 and the linkage of all these headings to a classified outline has never been done. Now that both LCSH/SAF and LCC exist in electronic form, we may see more effort to get this done. For comparison purposes, consider that the total review and updating of the ERIC Thesaurus, in the late 1970s, took more than twenty man-years. It was called the Vocabulary Improvement Project. A similar plan for LCSH/SAF will involve much more time and resources but the information technology developments such as thesaurus editing software and hypertextual thesaurus browsers that now exist should make the review more efficient.

The review of LCSH/SAF cannot be done fast enough if we are to provide OPAC designers with the wherewithal to show the logical structure and other relationships between headings in hypertextual thesaurus browsers and in improved intermediate displays of search results in OPACs. Figure 8 shows Eric Johnson's IODyne system operating within Cancerlit using MeSH as the controlled vocabulary.

Several features in this system serve as a useful model for what should be a part of every OPAC someday, because these features will prove quite useful to catalog searchers. Many of these features go beyond those recommended in Yee and Layne. For example, IODyne:

1. dynamically unifies keyword searching with controlled vocabulary searching. The searcher can open a search window and see a keyword- in-context display as the search term is entered. The searcher can decide whether this KWIC list will be for thesaurus terms and/or the concept space.
2. displays in the thesaurus window all levels of the hierarchy related to the search term. In Figure 8 this looks much like the outline of a classification schedule or the MeSH tree structure-which indeed it is without the numbers. For compactness in the first thesaurus display IODyne opens only those parts of the hierarchy needed to place the search term in context (the opened parts of the hierarchy are shown by downward pointing radio buttons). The searcher is free to "punch" other buttons and open up more of the display (or close it), or switch to another hierarchy if the search term has more than one BT. (This latter feature is not shown in Figure 8 because the term only appears in one part of the MeSH tree structure.)
3. the free text searching option opens the Concept Space

window where the co-occurrence analysis of the search term is shown with other terms or phrases in the title or abstract. Included in this anaylysis, but not shown in Figure 8 are authors' names and descriptors (subject index terms such as MeSH headings) that frequently co-occur with the search term in the file where the search is being made (in this case, CancerLit). The concept space information is shown in rank order. The most frequently occurring thesaurus terms could be shown in the concept space window if the scroll bar were used.

4. When any terms in these vocabulary displays are found useful by the searcher they can be moved into the search window or thesaurus window and from the search window back into the thesaurus or concept space windows by a drag and drop procedure.
5. IODyne provides the user with an efficient and effective search environment to search in several repositories (or OPACs) at the same time, displaying all the available electronic thesauri associated with those files, and shows "concept spaces" if the bibliographic files have been processed for a concept space analysis.

Coupled with the useful information to be found in the 670/675 field of records in LCSH/SAF we could begin to see how future developments of an OPAC or a system like IODyne could provide aids to the searcher which would result in a very functional multifile and crossfile searching capability.

There is an enormous potential for LCSH/SAF in this new world of graphical user interface, hyperlinks and object oriented programming. What is needed is preparation to move structure and logical relationships away from the rigidity and incompleteness of the MARC Authority Format and to free up the fixed field string of topical headings with subdivisions which are found in bibliographic records. To this day a continuing source of aggravation is the way LCSH/SAF records are displayed in some other bibliographic utilities or OPACs. All LCSH/SAF displays, in all OPACs and bibliographic utilities, must be improved. Too often the following minimu processing is not done when LCSH/SAF is included in various bibliographic systems.

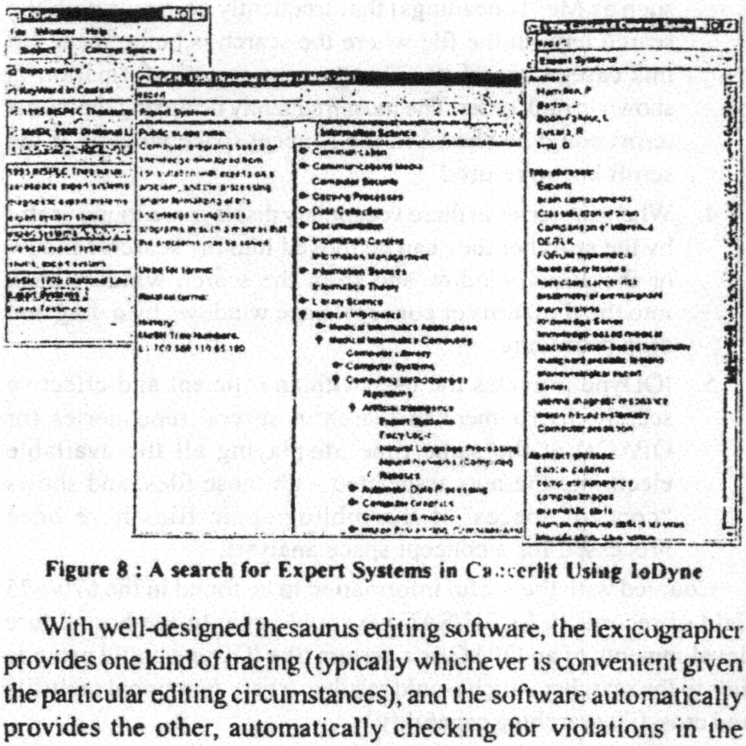

Figure 8 : A search for Expert Systems in Cancerlit Using IoDyne

With well-designed thesaurus editing software, the lexicographer provides one kind of tracing (typically whichever is convenient given the particular editing circumstances), and the software automatically provides the other, automatically checking for violations in the structure of the hierarchies affected by the change. Each term in a thesaurus can have multiple NTs as well as multiple BTs.

Referring back to Figure 8 shows what would be possible if retrieval system designers understood more about the value and content of thesaurus records, including all levels of the BT-NT relationships in the thesaurus. (Downward pointing "radio buttons" in the middle of the display show how MEDICAL INFORMATICS in the INFORMATION SCIENCE hierarchy has been "opened" to show where EXPERT SYSTEMS fits under MEDICAL INFORMATICS COMPUTING/COMPUTING METHODS/ ARTIFICIAL INTELLIGENCE.)

When hierarchies in LCSH/SAF are more complete and when

we have a standard for complete display of subject authority records, we will have made substantial improvements in our subject access mechanisms. The ERIC Vocabulary Improvement Project pointed the way but it was not followed.

LCSH-based subject searching in OPACs

Markey's research has shown that online searchers are not very successful in matching their subject terms with the catalogue's controlled subject vocabulary. The assigned subject headings in the catalogues she investigated were derived form the LCSH list, this being the subject vocabulary used in most library catalogues in North America. In one study of subject searching on a university OPAC, a total of 859 search statements entered in 188 subject searches were analysed; 45 per cent of these search statements resulted in no retrievals. Markey reports, 'We were concerned about, and subsequently sought an explanation for, the surprisingly large percentage of subject searches resulting in no or very few retrievals.' In comparing the subject statements with LCSH, only 29 per cent of searchers' terms matched or closely matched LCSH. Yet only 7 per cent of these LCSH searches resulted in no matches. This is not surprising since OPAC subject headings are extracted from actual bibliographic records in the collection. More often than not, searchers used whatever terms popped into their minds; this produced no retrievals for 65 per cent of the time. These depressing findings have been corroborated in studies of other university OPACs.

Another finding in Markey's SULIRS study raises questions about the effectiveness of LCSH subject searches for retrieving only the most relevant documents for a query: 29 per cent of the LCSH searches retrieved 100 or more citations. When this occurred, searchers either aborted their searching or looked individually at all the results. Very few searchers entered valid LCSH cross-references. A good guess is that they usually entered and matched LCSH terms broader than their topic of interest. Markey concludes that the study, 'drives home the need for online vocabulary assistance. Alphabetically arranged or rotated lists of subject headings only scratch the surface.'

Based on a variety of OPAC subject searching research studies, Markey lists the major problems subject searchers face, with little or no assistance from OPACs:

— mathing their terms with those indexed in the catalogue.

— identifying terms that are broader or narrower than their topic of interest,

— improving search results when little or nothing is retrieved,

— reducing search results when too much is retrieved,

— grasping LCSH indexing policies and idiosyncracies.

To summarise, second-generation online catalogues are deficient tools for subject searching because they:

— do not sufficiently assist with the translation of entered query terms into the vocabulary used in the catalogue,

— do not provide online thesaurus aids useful for subject focusing and topic treatment discrimination,

— do not automatically assist the user with alternative formulations of the search statement or execute alternative search methods when the initial approach fails,

— do not lead the searcher from successful free-text search terms (e.g., title words) to the corresponding subject headings or class numbers assigned to a broader range of related materials,

— do not provide sufficient information in the retrieved bibliographic records (such as tables of contents, abstracts and book reviews) to enable the user to judge the usefulness of the documents,

— do not rank the citations in large retrieval sets in decreasing order of probable relevance or 'closeness' to the user's search criteria,

— do not facilitate open-ended, exploratory browsing through following pre-established trails and linkages between records in the database, in order to retrieve materials related to those already found.

In the early 1980s many librarians and OPAC researchers urged vendors and system designers to upgrade their OPACs to keyword, Boolean retrieval systems. Many thought that the provision of Boolean search formulation and retrieval methods in OPACs would provide more search flexibility and subject access points than first generation OPACs arid, by offering term/query post-coordinated searching, would give subject searchers an effective alternative exact matches on unknown LCSHs. Some librarians welcomed keyword/Boolean OPACs as the panacea for the problems of subject searching in early OPACs.

This enthusiastic anticipation of the arrival of Boolean OPACs in libraries is easy to explain as first-generation OPACs were not very good retrieval systems. Many of them are still in place alongside the new interactive CD-ROM reference retrieval systems and search terminals used to access the commercial online database search services. Boolean retrieval is the predominant mode of access in the world of commercial online reference searching, and has over the years acquired an immense prestige in the librarians' world. The commercial database search services have steadily grown in the number and size of their databases, and the number of libraries and librarians using one or more of them has increased greatly in the 1980s.

Reflecting on the popularity of Boolean retrieval, Porter and Galpin remark, 'This is unfortunate, since it has a number of inherent weaknesses.' What is behind this prevalent anti-Boolean opinion which seems to pervade the IR research community? In a nutshell it is this: much research and experience with Boolean retrieval systems (including OPACs) indicates clearly and repeatedly that Boolean search formulation syntax and retrieval techniques are not very effective in search performance and not very usable or efficient search methods for end-users.

The accumulating evidence dearly-supports this summary critique of Boolean retrieval by Porter and Galpin: The number of documents retrieved is usually too large or too small, and a certain amount of juggling with terms is necessary to get a retrieved set of manageable size. Users frequently cannot compose Boolean expressions, and require an expert to do it for them. The retrieved set of documents is usually not ranked in any way, so it is necessary to inspect the entire list in the search for relevance. Much advanced (post-Boolean) IR research and theoretical analysis has been directed to improving the search performance and retrieval effectiveness of IR systems in controlled, experimental environments. While the research has focused on system perfonnance factors, actual human searchers have been excluded from most IR experiments.

IR researchers and theorists generally have been critics of Boolean logic-based IR systems, and have experimented with a variety of alternative approaches that either attempt to ameliorate the shortcomings of classic Boolean methods (e.g., 'extended Boolean' processing and 'fuzzy-set' retrieval) or offer radically different, non Boolean retrieval operations (e.g., query and document term vector processing and statistical, probabilistic retrieval methods).

A consensus seems to exist among IR theorists and investigators regading the shortcomings of IR systems that rely solely on Boolean logic query expression and processing. Salton presents the following list of the reasons why conventional Boolean retrieval methodology is not well adapted to the IR task:

1. The fonnulation of good Boolean queries is an art rather than a science; most untrained users are unable to generate effective query statements without assistance from trained searchers.
2. The standard Boolean retrieval methodology does not provide any direct control over the size of the output; some query statements may provide no output at all whereas other statements provide an unmanageably large number of retrieved items.
3. The Boolean methodology does not provide a ranking of the retrieved items in any order of presumed usefulness, thus all retrieved items are presumed to be equally good, or equally poor, for the user.
4. The Boolean system does not provide for the assignment of weights to the terms attached to documents or queries; thus each assigned term is assumed to be as important as

each other assigned term, the only distinction actually made is between terms that are assigned (with an implied weight equal to 1) and terms that are not assigned.

5. The standard retrieval methodology may produce results which appear to be counter-intuitive:
   (a) in response to an or-query (A or B or ...or Z) a record or document with only one query term is assumed to be as important as a document containing all query terms;
   (b) in response to an and-query (A and B and. ..and Z) a document containing all but one of the query terms is considered as useless as a document with no query term at all.

Recent online catalogue design efforts have centred on making post-coordinate, Boolean logic, library retrieval systems easier to learn and easier to use than the commercial models used by trained intermediaries: However, too little attention has been given to the performance limitations of Boolean OPACs, and no university developed or commercially available OPAC uses any of the advanced post-Boolean retrieval methods which have been tested with some success in the retrieval laboratories by the probabilistic and fuzzy-set retrieval theorists. The shortcomings of second-generation OPACs and Boolean retrieval systems are now well known. There is no doubt that a vigorous dialogue between IR researchers and online catalogue designers could lead to improvements in online catalogues and other IR systems intended primarily for use by the 'everyman' end-user rather than by trained search specialists. Much is to be gained by a sharing of their separate insights and theoretical or design advances.

Careful reflection on the growing body of findings produced by online catalogue and IR system research leads inescapably to a fundamentally revised perspective on users' subject searching needs and OPAC design to respond to those needs. The fact that users bring different types of subject search needs and different subject search requirements to OPACs cannot be ignored any longer. A single search interface and a single retrieval model (e.g.. Boolean) are not adequate for the variety of searchers and search needs that exists. 'Moving up' to conventional Boolean retrieval enhanced with a friendly interface has not bought OPAC users much retrieval effectiveness.

There is a large category of search needs and behaviour for which the Boolean exact match query model is simply wrong. The online interface and retrieval requirements of OPAC and IR system end users differ considerably from those of trained search intermediaries.

In building the search intermediary into the interface of 'expert' retrieval systems we may be following the wrong model. The behaviour of trained search specialists is product/ output oriented. Their aim usually is to produce a high-quality list of citations or other references for the end-user. The 'quality' of the output product is measured by such limited variables as recall, precision and search efficiency minimising the costs to the user of the retrieval process. The search topic or need is usually well understood (a 'known subject') and well expressed in advance of the search, and the search is typically processed in a highly structured, subject-specific domain. The search situation is fundamentally different in the case of scholars and many others who use online catalogues for their own purposes. These searchers, a growing heterogeneous population have a variety of information-seeking needs and behaviours. Furthermore, the document collections available to them for online searching are multidisciplinary in coverage and, at present, are poorly structured and indexed. Evidence indicates that the process of searching and discovery is more central to end-user searching objectives and satisfaction than the delivery of any pre-defined product.

Most end-users are not going after a specific 'known item', nor do they have a well-defined output product in mind at the outset of their interaction with the online system. Typically, they wish to discover materials on a topic of interest, and they seldom have or wish to present a precise expression of that interest. Both the expression of the topical interest and the interest itself may change dynamically during the search and browsing activity. Unlike the linear, highly structured, logical search strategy approach pursued by the efficient search intermediary (human or machine), much end-user searching can best be described as exploratory, circuitous and, fully interactive.

The search process is likely to be largely a trial-and-error process, having no particular pre-determined end or outcome. In trial-and-error exploratory searching, both the experience of the search process and its initial results can lead the user to new or altered information needs and may lead to additional materials or information of value. Effective search and retrieval methods must also be provided for the OPAC subject browser, and for searchers who cannot, or do not wish to, precisely describe their information need or problem in advance of the activation of the retrieval process.

Librarians have long understood the differences between 'known-item' searches and 'subject' searches in the catalogue. Now, we need to equally appreciate different kinds of subject searches and searching requirements; Alternative design models and retrieval methods which support these separate needs and modes of searching behaviour should be integrated into improved subject OPACs. Users should be given a choice of (a) how they want to access the subject catalogue, (b) how they wish to use it (to match searching styles or requirements), and (c) how much automatic and/or semiautomatic assistance they want from the system.

AUTHORITY CONTROL

The present authority control mechanism is expensive to set up, expensive to maintain and expensive to use. Nevertheless, it is firmly based, it is widely used and it is the foundation stone of sound cataloguing. This is true for today but it is not true for tomorrow when the Internet is in widespread use and computing power is as readily available as electricity. The suggestion to disband authority control or use it in another way is not lightly made and it is only made because there is an alternative. The alternative is to use authority control to provide the link rather than the preferred heading. The cataloguer must not dictate the preferred heading. To the user the preferred beading is the heading that he searches by and when he searches he wants the headings that he has thought about to be linked to the heading that he has not thought about. This means that the place for authority control is not at the cataloguing stage but at the searching stage. It is a post-coordinate and not a pre-coordinate operation. Or put in another way authority control files will be used by the user at the searching stage and not by the cataloguer at the cataloguing stage. Again this is revolutionary and stands present practice on its head. It makes the search for a preferred and standardised heading unnecessary and the present Authority Control Files will become linking files. The cost savings of this are enormous. Up to now it has not been possible to post-coordinate the searching process but the situation has changed with the advent of Z39.50 and systems like BOPAC2. It is now possible to download a retrieval which can be broad and unrefined and then let the user and systems like BOPAC2 to carry out the search using linking mechanisms and different methods of display.

OTHER LINKING METHODS

Authority control, or whatever its new name, will not be the only linking mechanism. Uniform title will be another, but not collective uniform title. At present the uniform title is used infrequently and only works when it is used consistently for complex headings like the Bible. Because it is used erratically and infrequently it causes more harm than good. In future it must be applied universally and according to agreed principles. All works will have a common ancestor and this should be used as the uniform title. With a simple example there is probably no difficulty. A uniform title like Dickens Bleak House is not difficult. The user would expect to be able to select different forms such as collected works, selections, videos, etc. or different displays such as short, full, Marc or citation. Some of these are already available and most are available in BOPAC2. There are, however, more complex situations which will call for the use of the same sort of nesting system found in computer programs. One example of this would be the Handbuch der Physik where each volume covers a specific area which in its turn may be split into parts. This will call for a uniform title for Handbuch der Physik and an additional nested one for the parts of it covering a specific subject. Another would be the publications of the Open University which are rarely correctly or consistently catalogued.

Another linking system and a very powerful one would be a link between bibliographic relationships. In many ways this exists already but not by intent but by accident. For example the collective uniform title does this spasmodically but not consistently. What is needed is an obligatory link between one relationship and another. Some would argue that this is what the main-entry does. But this is only true some-times and in some cases. It should always be done and a new tagging structure is needed to ensure that this is done at the pre-coordinate stage. A link from one relationship to another would be very powerful. It would be something like a collective uniform title where some relationships are concerned, in others it would not. Catalogues of the future would have a much larger range of selection options, all of which would be based on relationships. This would mean that the user would have an option to collocate by selections, collective works and many others.

ISBD

The International Standard Bibliographic Description (ISBD) is associated with the descriptive function of the cataloguing process. Because it attempts to pre-coordinate the form in which the bibliographic record is presented to the user it relies heavily on ISBD, a standard which uses principles which have little relevance in a computing environment. It lists all the elements which are required to describe and identify all types of material which are likely to appear in library collections. It then assigns an order to the elements of description and specifies a system of punctuation to differentiate the various parts of the bibliographic record. In all stages of its development the ISBD has been more concerned with the printed versions of the national bibliography and the exchange of bibliographic records. This is a necessary and important concern but it is not more important than the result that the catalogue user sees. The use of punctuation to prescribe the order in which the elements of a bibliographic record are described and demarcated is not only confusing to the user but it is unnecessary in a computer environment. Because it tries to pre-coordinate the form of the display that the user sees there is little room for manoeuvre at the. post-coordinate stage. Of course each element of the description has to be tagged but having done this it should be possible for the user to choose from a number of different displays, one of which will be a citation display. If no type of display is requested there will be a default display. Those who advocate the retention of ISBD must be clear what function it performs in a modern automated catalogue and in what way it assists the user. Judging by the many uncritical comments on ISBD at the Toronto Conference nobody thought it necessary to justify its use. This seems to be a strange oversight in view of the disbelief in its function expressed by many users, particularly those with computer backgrounds.

THE INTERNET

The Internet is, many things to many people from children to those seeking information of a dubious nature. However, it has grown in the way it has because of its commercial potential both for sales and for advertising. In spite of this, its long term potential will be for information. Information which is provided quickly and reliably will eventualy have a dramatic effect on the decision making functions of society. The control of information on the Internet relies on a variety of search engines both general and covering specific subject areas. It can be very effective but more often than not it misfires because it produces irrelevant or too much information. The challenge is to filter out this irrelevant information. The search engines are already trying to solve this problem with more sophisticated methods of searching and techniques like the advanced search facility or the refining option of Alta Vista and the folder system of Northern Lights. The challenge for professional librarianship is to see if the control techniques that have been used successfully in library catalogues have a place in helping to control the additional information that is on the Internet.

At this point it is important to be clear about what is meant by 'information' and information retrieval' in its purest form. The latter term is usually used for what is in fact the retrieval of information containers and not the information itself. The oldest form of obtaining information and probably still the most efficient is to ask the expert. Information obtained in other ways is of three kinds. First is quick information or information that can be obtained from a reference source. This can range from the time of a train to basic information on a particular drug. A lot of this is quickly and freely available on the Internet. The second type is background information-the sort of information contained in books on a particular subject or the required background material that students need to get from their reading lists. Finally there is hard information that has to be mined for in the containers of information brought up by a subject retrieval search in a library catalogue or an abstracting service. Some hard information is available free on the Internet but most is only available through sites to which a paid subscription is necessary in order to gain access. This is inevitable as information is increasingly going to be something that will have to be paid for. At first sight this is a disadvantage but it also has advantages because all this information will have some sort of entry point which will either be a bibliographic record or a meta tag performing the same function. The Internet's search engines and the bibliographic control methods used by librarians need to be coordinated if the information potential of the Internet is to be exploited to the full.

SEARCH ENGINES

It is probably safe to say that the first search engine was the library catalogue. However, what is known to users of the Internet as the search engine has none of the discipline and formal structure of the library catalogue. Search engines have grown almost as fast as the Internet itself both in their coverage and in their specialisation. They vary from being dramatically successful to being a total failure. It is difficult to see why they are so successful sometimes and so totally ineffective at others. Nevertheless, library users with experience with search engines will expect to find the sort of facilities that they provide in their library catalogues. This is particularly true of the full text search facility provided by the search engines. The only comparable equivalent in library catalogues is the FIND facility in BOPAC2, which is able to provide a full text searching function of the bibliographical record or its MARC format. It can provide a valuable additional tool to the use of traditional library catalogue searching methods. Whatever their faults search engines are so firmly established and widely used that they cannot be ignored. In general, librarians tend to write off the Internet and the search engine as inefficient and of limited use in information retrieval. This overlooks its potential and the speed with which new developments are taking place.

In the long run it will not be either the search engine or the library catalogue but a coming together of the two. The strength of the search engine is that it indexes the full text of an item while the library catalogue provides a descriptive picture of the item that is being recorded. The search engine is computer generated while the library catalogue relies on human decision making and is based on rigorous and well established standards. When information is freely available on the Internet then the techniques of bibliographic control will probably have little to offer the search engine. However, as the importance and commercial value of information on the Internet becomes apparent then the access to more and more sites will have to be paid for. In this situation something like the bibliographic control which provides access to library collections will be needed to give a preliminary access to these sites and this will have to be enough for the user to assess whether the information on offer is worth paying for.

CATALOGUE 2000

At a time when technology is changing so fast it is dangerous to try to forecast what the library catalogue will be like in the new millennium but it is essential to at least try to foresee trends. It is probable that if the user is looking for a particular work for which the reference is known then the traditional methods will still be used. The difference is that Z39.50 widens the area which is searched and developments like BOPAC2 will find the required item more quickly and will use minimal information or even severely fractured information to do so. If necessary it will do this from large retrievals which have been obtained by using broad search terms. What will change and change dramatically is the user's expectations from a subject enquiry. It will no longer be acceptable for a query to produce a list of containers of information. The requirement will be for the information itself and for it to be tailored to the user's needs. This may be provided by the written word but it is more likely to be a mixture of media forms. It will be achieved by the same process that is used in BOPAC2 where the aim is to download a retrieval and then give the user a number of options which will help to arrive at the optimal answer to the request. Where the digitized version of the required work is available then an option to search the whole text will be required.

This will not be achieved easily. BOPAC2 works as well as it does because it uses material which has been subject to standards which may be imperfect in some ways but which by and large are universally used and which provide a format and framework which can be built on. This enables BOPAC2 to offer a range of options for the user to choose from. If the same sort of control which works well in a library environment is to be used to control the information on the Internet then new standards will have to be developed which will operate successfully in the volatile new atmosphere.

The Internet does not provide the same sort of structure for non library databases as the library catalogue does for library databases. However, developments which are being proposed for revisions of the Z39.50 protocol mean that it will be able to do the same thing for other material on the Internet as it does for bibliographic records. This means that the cluster record can 'contain' a mixture of bibliographic or meta data records and full documents. Thus it is possible to model the move, from meta data or bibliographic record to the full document, as simply another step along the path of increasing detail. The likely link between the two is the meta tag which in many ways is like a bibliographic record. Although meta tags are used they are only used in a minority of cases and unlike the bibliographic record they do not seem to follow any standard. An attempt by the library information lobby to introduce some systematic standard with the Dublin Core meta tag seemed to be a promising development. However, it is unlikely to be readily accepted by the search engine lobby. The question of meta tag standards is very important and if control of information is going to be achieved then standards which are accepted by all Internet users are essential. Although there is a super abundance of information on how to use search engines and which ones to use there is a dearth of information on how they work and in particular how they work so well sometimes and how they result in total failure at others.

To a very much greater extent than at present information is going to become a commercial product and will have to be paid for. This will lead to more sites to which access is restricted and if use of these sites is to become more profitable their contents will need a process like bibliographic control to maximise their use. It is in this area that librarianship has a contribution to make. But it will not be done by advocating standards that were effective in a pre automation era. Many librarians seek only to improve and perfect existing systems and to make changes only within the existing framework. This must be the wrong approach at a time when the Internet is developing so fast, library schools are closing down and university libraries and university computing departments are merging throughout the world. There is a time for change and it is now.

CATALOGUING NETWORKS

One of the major objectives of forming cataloguing networks is to perform the cataloguing operations centrally by one library/ organization while other participating members can use the catalogue. They are also called bibliographic utilities for they provided bibliographic utility services such as catalogues of materials to the members. Library of Congress, in Washington, D.C. (USA), since 1901, has made printed card available containing cataloguing data, classification numbers (Library of Congress as well as Dewey Decimal Classification number) and subject headings. Mechanization was introduced as early as in 1970s to meet the growing demands for this service among libraries, Currently cards are printed from Marc records on demand and the Library of Congress (LC) also operates an 'alert service'. A participating library establishes a profile consisting of the subejct areas that are of interest. Then, when LC enters a bibliographic record that matches this profile into its MRAC databse, a catalogue card is automatically produced and is sent to the library.

The United Kingdom was half a century behind the United States in providing a centralized service similar to that of LC. Though the British National Bibliography (BNB) started in 1950, a printed card service, called BNB cards, began in 1956. These BNB cards could be obtained by libraries for porducing their own catalogue records. A MARC districution service began in UK in 1969 and a large number of UK libraries and other institutions use BLMARC records for local cataloguing and housekeeping operations.

The United Stated led world in setting up cataloguing networks and bibliographic utilities such as OCLC (Online Computer Library Center), RLIN (Reșearch Libraries Information Network) and WLN (Western Library Network). Among these OCLC is the pioneer and is the most highly used bibliographic utility service.

OCLC is a nonporfit computer service and research organization whose network and servies link more than 27,000 libraries in 64 contries and territories. OCLC services help libraries to locate, acquire, catalogue, access, and lend the library materials. OCLC, he world's largest library information network, offers the following services that help libraries further access to information and reduce information costs:

* WorldCat, the OCLC Online Union catalog is the world's largest and most comprehensive bibliographich database. Libraries use the WorldCat database and OCLC's computerized telecommunication network to porcess materials and share information. WorldCat offers libraries and their users resources that not single library could provide:
    * 38 million records in eight bibliographic formats representing 400 languages with holdings information;
    * Growth by approximately 2 million bibliographic records each year; and
    * Easy searching from First Search, EPIC, and other services
* The OCLC system. Extensive online cataloguing, interlibrary loan, union list, and selection services.
* OCLC First Search service, Online reference service that provides flexible searching and subject access to over 70 databases for end users.
* OCLC First Search Electroing Collection Online service: Provides remote access to large collections of journals through the Web. Now also available through the First Search Web interface.
* OCLC Access Services: Telecommunications and stand alone systems that facilitate online and offline cataloging, resource sharing, reference, and selection services.

Now a question comes how can library benefit from a

networked favility. Let us take the example of the services offered by the largest cataloguing network or bibliographic qutility services in the world, viz., OCLC. OCLC offers a range of cataloguing services that help to increase productivity and reduce cost. From batch services to CD-ROM, you can transfer records quickly, efficiently, and cost-effictively to your card catalogue or local system. The OCLC Cataloguing service is the largest and busiest online cataloguing system in the world. It handles over one billion transactions a year and supports a range of services that help libraries increase porductivity and reduce costs. And with OCLC Cataloguing, only one library needs to originally catalogue an item. OCLC offers a range of cataloguing options to meet the library's need. You can:

* have bibliographic records automatically delivered at the time your vendors ship books using the OCLC PromptCat service;
* catalogue online, where the hit rate is more than 95 percent for English materials;
* input your own original records;
* export records from OCLC and edit them on your local system;
* tapeload your cataloguing that is done outside OCLC's cataloguing systems;
* have OCLC convert your older cataloguing to machine-readable form;
* move records to an offline environment to edit and export and then batch your edits and holdings back with OCLC;
* cataloguing Micro Enhancer software;
* have OCLC staff catalogue current materials, foreign language materials, or backlogs;
* seamlessly link selectors, acquisitions department, book vendors, and your local system to an online, ready for filling; and
* order custom-printed cataloguing cards according to your specification. Cards arrive at your library- ready for filing.

Cataloguing with WorldCat gives you an incomparable knowledge resource. You can :

* use high quality records to improve search results;
* catalogue all materials;
* reduce staff time for copy cataloguing with OCLC PromptCat service; and
* custom order machine-readable tapes or catalogue cards.

The OCLC Catalogue service is an interactive online system that provides access to WorldCat (the OCLc Online Union Catalogue) and facilitates shared cataloguing. OCLC cataloguing increases porductivity and reduce cataloguing costs. Participating libraries retrieve and use bibliographic records contributed by other libraries and enter records for items not already catalogued. OCLC Cataloguing provides:

* global record sharing through worldCat;
* keyword and browsable searching;
* full secreen record editing and cut, copy, and paste capabilities;
* a high hit rate-find over 95 percent of the English records you need; and
* access to name and subject authority records.

Electronic export capabilities to local systems in North America join OCLC. Through their OCLC- affiliated Regional Networks, Libraries outside North America receive OCLC services through OCLC Asia Pacific Services, OCLC Europe, OCLC Latin America and the Caribbean, or via international.

One of the major porblem facing liraries in many countries, including those in India, related to what is known as retrospective coversion or Retrocon in short. This relates to a basic questions as to how libraires can convert their existing manual catalogues to machine-readable cataloges. Thus, simply speaking, retrocon is a process that is used in libraries to convert existing manual catalogues to machine-readable catalogues. There are several options available and each one has its own martis and demerits. The simplest way is to manually convert (i.e., keying-in), each and every catalogue record which is impossible for a large library collection where several hundred thousand cataluge entries are a vai'able in card forms, because this will be very time-consuming and expensive process. One alternative way could be to decide a cut-off year for the retrocon poocess. Indeed, whichever method is used, each library has a cut-off date, beyond which catalogue records are ot available in machine-readable forms; users looking for materials beyond certain date have to consult card catalogues. The cut-off year is decided by the library concerned on the basis of a study that determines beyond which year library materials are scarcely used.

Another option to retrocon is to scan the card catalogues (provided they are available in printed/neatly typed form) and then to use a custom-built program to convert the scannned files to machine-readable catalogues. This method has now found useful in certain situations, and several companies have taken this approach to do retroconversion job for libraries on a contract basis. If the cards are ot neatly printed or typed, then the quality of the scanned image and the corresponding ASCII file will be poor, resulting in number of errors in the catlogue entries. Hence, a significant amount of editorial time will be needed to snsoure the quality of the machine readable catalogue.

Yet another, and the most commonly followed method, is to use the services of bibliographic utilities like OCLC. As already mentioned earlier one can avail the WorldCat service form OCLC for downloading catalogue data of all the materials held in a library. This process is much easy and does not need any local expertise. However, there are two major problems. First, this may prove to be expensive, particularly for libraries in India, because the price to be paid for such service is calculated in the US Dollar and thus may be quite a big amount in local currency. The second problem may be that local materials and non-English language materials may not be available in OCLC's database.

Each of the above options has its own merits and demerits. One option, that has been chosen by many, is to set up a centralized cataloguing agency, mostly at the national library level, that produces catalogue entries for all types of materials and makes available to other libraries in the country in machine-readable form. This approach helps off-set the huge cost and other resource requirements of retroconversion.

Dewey Decimal Classifications and Online Cataloguing

A brief introduction to the Dewey Decimal Classification and the Library of Congress classification is provided here which examines whether, and in what ways, the DDC and LCC can be used to retrieve subject information through online catalogues. Almost all MARC records contain LCC notations and LC subject headings may also contain DDC notations. These subject labels, along with the keywords contained in the title, contents note, and other parts of the MARC record, can be used for retrieving the record through the subject or subjects it represents.

DESIRABLE FEATURES OF ONLINE CLASSED RETRIEVAL SYSTEMS

The quality of online subject retrieval via a classification scheme depends on the computer hardware and software capabilities, and on the structure and notation of the classification scheme. Among the latter's essential qualities for this purpose are a logical structure; a definite, standard and communicable way of handling material that relates to more than one field as such as city planning or the influence of religion on art, and a notation that is expressive and therefore permits truncation and hierarchical searching relatively easily.

The following is a list of some of the features that an online classed retrieval system should contain. The list goes far beyond the current abilities of such systems, but it reflects the opinions of several experts in the field and of the authors.

1. Access to individual entries by a known class or call number. Many systems already permit this, but typically only as a follow-up to bibliographic retrieval through alphabetical subject terms, in order to obtain circulation status or other item-level information.
2. Full-schedule browsing; that is, display of the classification schedule. Either a display of as many contiguous class numbers, with their captions, as tilc screen will hold including instructions and cross- references contained in the schedules, or a display of a range of notations, such as

DDC's 337 (International economics) and its immediate subdivisions or, if preferred, all levels of its subdivisions is desirable. Along with this feature, backward and forward scrolling should be permitted. Scrolling permits moving from a notation to the next notation and, through further scrolling, to broader or narrower notations, as if the user were looking at a classification schedule. The phrasing of the instructions and cross-references that are in most typical classification schedules would need to differ for retrieval use and for input use.

This, like most other suggested features, demands that the schedules exist in machine-readable form. The DDC schedules do; the LCC schedules not yet, with some very limited exceptions. Experts in the field generally agree that it will be a major undertaking, fraught with difficulties, to put the LCC schedules online.

3. Shelflist browsing; that is, display of as many contiguous brief entries in shelflist order as the screen will hold. One line per entry may suffice, but again the user should be able to scroll forward and backward to permit pinpointing a search. Instructions and cross-references should be included in this display as well. This amounts to an enhanced shelf-browsing feature.
4. Since points 2 and 3 are intended to permit pinpointing a search not only for retrieval but also for input (that is, for assigning call numbers), it is important that the display of entries in call number order (point 3) be available in two formats: (a) consolidated order, in which all items in a collection are shown in call number order regardless of where the individual item is located; and (b) shelflist order, in which the entries are shown in the shelf order of individual departments or branches.
5. Hierarchical display of class numbers with their captions is needed. The system should display a requested class notation as part of a hierarchical structure showing different levels of arrays, the notations as well as their captions. This is important in case nothing appropriate, or too little material,

is available in a specific class number sought, and because many people tend to begin searches under tenns that are broader than what is actually wanted.

6. With the hierarchical display should come menu ability, that is the ability to select from a hierarchical display one option and, when that option is displayed, to see how it is broken down, or how it can be broadened, and to keep on selecting options until the search has been refined or broadened sufficiently. The system thus would permit a combination of command functions (such as in point 1) and menu functions.
7. The notation should permit left, internal, and right truncation in order to permit broadening a search. This would usually consist of broadening a search within a discipline. If the notation does not pennit truncation, as is true in some instances with DDC and in most instances with LCC, other devices must be employed at considerable effort to achieve the same result.
8. The ability to switch from one class or call number to another, to permit following up on the instructions and cross-references in the schedules. This should permit pinpointing a search, including sometimes moving to another discipline.
9. Access to the schedules by the captions in the schedules and by terms in the index. Various devices have been suggested to overcome this obstacle to precise recall.
10. Access to the schedules by equivalent subject headings or descriptors. Since a concrete topic can often be distributed among various disciplines, this will often involve a reference from one subject heading or descriptor to several class numbers.
11. Since a keyword approach has been shown to be helpful, captions, index terms (point 9), subject headings, and descriptors (point 10) should be accessible by keyword as well as by their complete terminology.
12. Boolean search capability of many kinds is essential. For example: between keywords in the description, such as the title, and a class number; between class number and subject

headings; between author's surname and subject heading. This capability helps to make retrieval more precise.

13. Experts also desire additional features (some of which already exist in individual cases), all designed to help users to refine their searches or to forgive misspellings or the use of too-broad or "wrong" subject terms. Since computers are likely to access ever-increasing catalogues of whole groups of libraries, rather than of just one library, information overload is a very likely problem of the near future. The result of a fairly precise subject search may still be two hundred entries, Attempts are being made to develop intelligent systems which will, for example, match these entries against the searcher's interest profile or against previous checkouts by people in the searcher's field of interest, or some other automatic technique that will present these two hundred entries in order of the searchers likely interest or expressed need.

This is primarily a wish list, and most existing OPACs can do none, or only very few, of these things. Moreover, this wish list is limited to features useful to notational retrieval. Other features that are useful for alphabetical retrieval can be added,

In the above list, points 2, 3, 5, 6, 7, and 9 are related to the classification scheme and its notation rather than to the computer programme or hardware. The DDC and LCC will, therefore, be examined in the light of the following points:

Points 2-3: Relationship of concepts as expressed by contiguous class notations.

Points 5-6: Hierarchical structure of the scheme; expressiveness of the notation.

Point 7: Truncating ability of the notation.

Point 9: Suitability of caption and index terminology as access points.

Finally, the system must be hospitable to accepting new concepts logically, where the resulting structure still makes sense.

CHARACTERISTICS OF THE DDC

The Dewey Decimal Classification (DDC) was first published

by Melvil Dewey in 1876. It is now in its 22nd edition. It is basically a theoretical scheme, designed to contain room for all knowledge, without attention to the subject emphases of the holdings of anyone library. Although its use in North American libraries, especially academic libraries, diminished during the 1960s and 1970s, it is the most widely used library classification system in the world. It has been translated into thirty-four languages, from German to Gujarati.

The DDC uses a pure notation based on numbers, and is divided into ten main classes:

000-099	Generalities, including Knowledge, Library science, Bibliographies
100-199	Philosophy; Psychology
200-299	Religion
300-399	Social sciences, Statistics, Customs, Etiquette. Folklore
400-499	Language
500-599	Pure sciences
600-699	Technology, Manufacture
700- 799	The arts; Recreation and performing arts
800-899	Literature
900-999	History, Biography, Geography

Further subdivisions are again in groups of ten: e.g.,

300-309	Social sciences in general
310-319	Statistics
320-329	Political science
330-339	Economics
340-349	Law
350-359	Public administration
360-369	Social problems and services
370-379	Education
380-389	Commerce, Trade
390-399	Customs, Etiquette, Folklore

Still further subdivisions are also in groups of ten: As

370	Education

371	Generalities of education
372	Elementary education
373	Secondary education
374	Adult education
375	Curricula
376	Education of women
377	Schools and religion
378	Higher education
379	Education and the state

Numbers divided beyond three figures become decimal numbers; as for example

378	Higher education
378.1	Organisation and administration of institutions of higher education
378.11	Personnel administration
378.111	Academic personnel
378.14	College year
378.142	Summer school

Advantages for online catalogues

Like any classification scheme, the DDC has advantages and disadvantages when examined keeping automation in mind. Among th positive characteristics that make it a possible solution for, use in automated subject retrieval are:

— It obeys many logical principles of a well-designed classification scheme, for example that the whole of a subject should precede its parts.

— It has with some exceptions, an expressive notation in decimal form. These three facts (logic; expressive notation; decimal numbers) facilitate hierarchical search and permit truncation. The truncation technique is commonly found in keyword retrieval systems. When it is applied to notation. It makes the notation even more powerful retrieval tool with which the depth and breadth of a search subject can be quickly and easily amended.

Truncation— in this case, right truncation (that is, truncating the right side of a notations-applied to an expressive notation allows a search to be extended or broadened, with more material to be retrieved. A search that began with the notation for bowfins (597.41) could be extended by using the notation 597.4? so that the documents with class numbers 597.42, 597.44, 597.46, etc., could be retrieved, allowing items relating to the scientific study of not only bowfins but also other related species such as sturgeons. The search could be further expanded by using 597?, allowing all items relating to fish to be matched. While 59? would retrieve everything on zoology, and 5? would retrieve everything on the pure sciences, the quantity of material on such broad subjects suggests a need for some way of preventing such searches from being performed, probably by limiting the number of items that can be retrieved in response to a truncated-notation search.

— The DDC uses standard subdivisions, whereby to each subject, broad or specific (Social sciences, Education, Secondary education, Teaching French in secondary schools) can be added generally consistent symbols that indicate the format in which the subject is being treated or the geographic area with which it is concerned.

For example, — 0977583 added to a topical number always means "in Madison", -097758 always means "in South Central Wisconsin", -09775 always means "in Wisconsin",- 0977 always means "in North Central United States", -0973 always means "In the United States", and so forth. -06 added to a topical number always means "An organisation in that field", and -0207 always means "Humorous treatment of the topic". The use of consistent numbers with the same meaning throughout the schedules is a mnemonic or memory-aiding device.

500 Natural Sciences and mathematics

510 Mathematics

520 Astronomy

530	Physics
540	Chemistry
550	Earth sciences
550.21	Statistics of earth sciences
560	Paleontology, Paleozoology
570	Life sciences
580	Botanical sciences
590	Zoological sciences
591	Zoology, general aspects
591.021	Statistics of zoology
591.0941	Zoology of Great Britain
592	Invertebrates
593	Protozoa and other simple animals
594	Mollusca and molluscoidea
595	Other invertebrates
596	Vertebrata (Craniata, Vertebrates)
597	Cold-blooded vertebrates, Pisces (Fishes)
597.0021	Statistics of cold-blooded vertebrates
597.00941	Cold-blooded vertebrates in Great Britain
597.2	Agnatha (Cyclostomata)
597.2.02.1	Statistics of Agnatha
597.20941	Agnatha in Great Britain
597.3	Chondrichthyes (Cartilaginous fishes)
597.4	Chondrostei, Holostei, Sarcopterygii
597.41	Amiiformes (Bowfins, River dogfishes)
597.41021	Statistics of amiiformes
597.410941	Amiiformes in Great Britain
597.42	Polypterifomes (Fringe-finned ganoids)
597.44	Acipenserifomes (Cartilaginous ganoids)
597.46	Crossopterygii (Lobe-finned fishes)
597.47	Sensionotifomes (Gars)
597.48	Dipnoi (Lungfishes)

369

597.5	Teleostei (Fully-boned fishes)
597.51	Elopomorpha (Morays and true eels)
597.51021	Statistics of elopomorpha
597.510941	Elopomorpha in Great Britain

Selections from DDC class 500, with emphasis on class 597. Some topical numbers have standard divisions attached which indicate location or method of presentationof the topic.

In the online catalogue, standard subdivisions permit broadening a topical search while retaining the limitation "in country X", or 'in the form of'. This is desirable if the more limited notation does not provide sufficient material. The technique used is internal truncation. For example, the notation for bowfins in Britain is 597.410941, where the 0941 represents the British aspect. The user may want to broaden that topic without eliminating its British aspect. Middle truncation, as in 597?0941, will expand the topic to Fish regardless of species in Britain.

It would also be possible to use left truncation and enter ?0941 to retrieve information about books that deal with a large range of subjects relative to Britain. While this particular example may be unlikely, because an excessive quantity of material might be retrieved, left truncation could be of use to the person interested in some less well-known or smaller part of the world, such as Angelina County in Texas. It would be interesting and useful, for example, to be able to go into a national library and to retrieve all indexed information about one particular region regardless of the subject.

By using truncation in these ways, one broadens recall at the expense of decreasing precision; fewer of the items retrieved will be appropriate to the needs of the inquirer. However, the overall assessment of this technique is positive.

— The DDC uses mnemonics even in some of its topical numbers, particularly in Literature and Geography; Biography, and History. The DDC literature symbols are composed of the following elements:

	Discipline of literature	Language of writing	Literary genre	Period of creation	
Examples:	8	2	1	.7	: English poetry of the early 19th century: 821.7
	8	3	2	.6	: German drama of the classical period (1750-1830): 832.6
	8	91.44	3	7	Bengali fiction of : today : 891.4437

The numbers for the literary genre are consistent, while the numbers for the period of creation vary with the literature. Internal truncation thus permits queries like the following:

83134 for all types of German language literature of the Reformation period

Internal and right truncation permits, for example,

8?1? for all poetry in the collection, regardless of language or time period

The historical time periods of a country and of its subdivisions are the same. Internal truncation thus permits queries like

944?082 for the history of the various regions. towns, etc., of France during the Fourth Republic.

— The DDC is maintained by a well-funded, well-administered organisation and is, therefore, a live scheme that, within limits, keeps pace with progress, creating with each edition new class categories or adapting existing ones, as needed.
— The scheme's decimal notation permits the addition of new concepts as needed so the scheme is hospitable.
— There is considerable quality control in the revision and

updating of the scheme, based partly on advice and reactions from practicing librarians.

These three factors (willingness and ability to update in an effective manner) give searchers reasonable certainty that even relatively new topics can be searched in the spots where they can be logically expected, since provisions will have been made for them.

— The DDC symbols can-be found in many MARC records.

— The DDC is at least comparatively familiar to many librarians and information specialists and to a lesser degree, to the public. Its decimal notation makes it relatively easy to be directed to specific topics, and to remember favourite topics for future use.

These two factors (availability and familiarity) make it relatively inexpensive for an information facility to use the DDC, because the facility can copy existing numbers for many of its new acquisitions, and because the staff can direct the public orally to pertinent sections of the shelves or of the various classed records.

Disadvantages for online catalogues

In spite of its many excellent features, the DDC has disadvantages. It is old having been created over a century ago and then for a library that by today's standards would be regarded as very small. Originally designed for filing entries (document surrogates) in paper-based files, the DDC was developed primarily for use in shelf arrangement. not for use in a computer. A classification scheme, especially one that is to be used as a retrieval device in an online catalogue, should be consistent in structure and notation, although inconsistencies can sometimes be circumvented by sophisticated algorithms or retrieval programmes. While the DDC is in some respects a remarkably consistent scheme- far more so than the LCC— it also contains some inconsistencies that make the creation of menus, the display of arrays, and the use of truncation not only less than automatic, but often difficult to achieve. Also, while it has in several places a structure that resembles the more versatile and precisely structured faceted classification schemes, it is overwhelmingly enumerative, with the typical limitations of enumerative schemes.

DDC AND ONLINE CATALOGUE FEATURES

The following is an examination of the DDC in the light of the features previously listed as desirable in an online classed retrieval system.

Age, notational base, and logical structure

Since the DDC was created over one hundred years ago, its basic structure reflects the knowledge, attitudes, emphases, and political situation of that time. One example is the topic of Psychology which is still placed in the middle of Philosophy instead of with Medicine and health, to which it belongs according to current thought. The use of arrays and scrolling is not aided by this structure. Since the DDC was created before many of today's scientific and technical achievements were invented, and before many of today's social concepts,were developed, the scheme originally devoted proportionally far less space and detail to the social, pure, and applied sciences (300s, 500s, and 600s) than today's state of knowledge requires.

New fields can be, and are being, inserted, thanks to the DDC's hospitality. However, because of the limited notational base of ten, the resulting numbers are often quite long which is more of a problem for human beings than for computers. The notational base, however, also causes some new topics to be inserted in ways that cause problems in logical relationships and, therefore, online classed searching ability.

The DDC notation has a numerical base of ten. Therefore, if the notation were to be truly expressive, each topic could be divided into no more than ten subgroups. Unfortunately, nature does not work that way. Among the more obvious areas where the subject has broken the bounds of ten are:

Life sciences (570-599): conceptually, Botany (580-589) and Zoology (590-599) are subdivisions of Life sciences, but the notations do not read that way.

Manufactures (660-689): conceptually, this is one broad unit, subdivided into different types of manufacture, but the notations do not express, for example, that 685.22 (Leather goods manufacture) is a subdivision of 660.

While such situations cause problems when the actual numbers are used to produce arrays, the problems can be relatively easily solved through the use of menus.

The DDC is generally considered to be reasonably logical and effective for a general horary in its grouping of related concepts and in its separation of unrelated ones. However, while it breaks down each major topic reasonably, the relationships among the major topics themselves are often tenuous. This is true for any classification scheme. For example, while the concepts of Education and Commerce are broken down more or less reasonably, there is little obvious logical connection between the last notations in the 370-379 group and the first few notations in the 380-389 group: 379.982 (Government control of public education in Greenland) and 380.1 (Commerce) are hardly logically connected. Scrolling of class notations or of entries in call number order can, therefore, be limited to searches within anyone major topic, such as Education.

Like any enumerative scheme, the DDC suffers from the inability to assign a class number that truly reflects works relating to more than one field (such as "Effect of gasoline prices on automobile travel"). By tradition, if only one call number is assigned to such a work as a shelf location number, the work is classed under the topic affected, in the above case under 388.342 (Automobile travel). If the searcher looks, however, under 338.2328 (Prices in the oil and gas industry) for such a topic, or scrolls about it, the work will not be found in spite of the DDC's basically logical structure. This is not a flaw in the DDC, but in the policies with which it is applied. The solutions to this problem demand on the total configuration of an OPAC's retrieval posibilities. Possible solutions range from multiple clasification (assigning both class numbers, which would then be no longer shelf location numbers but retrieval numbers) to reliance on subject headings to reliance on kewords in the title or subject headings.

In an online system that permits broadening and narrowing a topical search by moving up and down the hirarchy, and that permits broadening a topical search through truncation, two of the most important features are consistently logical structure and a consistently expressive notation. This requires that topics at anyone level in the consistently logical hierarchy have a notation that has at last one more symbol at the end than the notation for topic at the immediately more general level, as shown below :

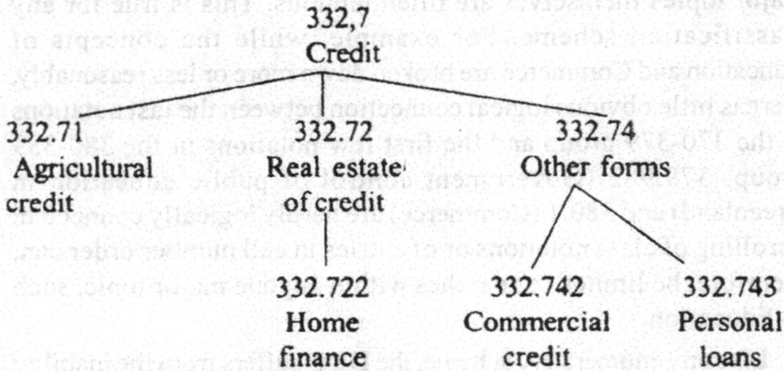

Example of an expressive notation that permits automatic move to the next broader array by truncating the last figure on the right

While the DDC does fairly well both with respect to logical structure and expressive notation, there are quite a few exceptions that make truncation and hierarchical display based solely on the notation less than automatic, and that affect hierarchical online searches negatively.

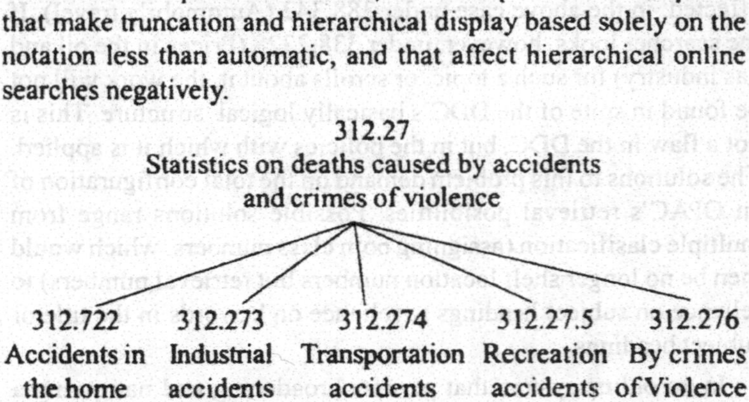

Breakdown of 312.27 in DDC's sixteenth edition.

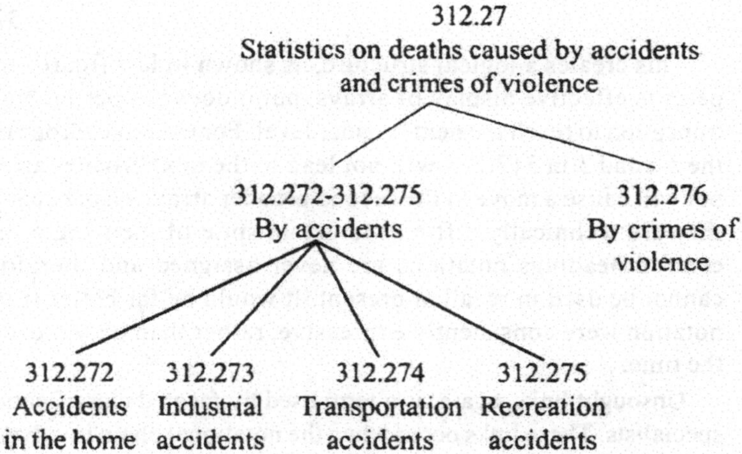

More logical breakdown of 312.27 in DDC's seventeenth edition.

In some places in the schedules, a step in the logical hierarchy was originally left out. It is difficult, especially in an online catalogue, to move in a search from a specific concept to the next broader one if that concept has no notation symbol. In the language of faceted classification specialists, this is the problem of the missing link.

In the sixteenth edition of the DDC, published in 1958, the concept "Statistics on deaths caused by accidents and crimes of violence" was broken down directly into five subcategories: one category for "Crimes of violence", and four for specific types of accidents.

There was no middle-level category for "Statistics on deaths caused by accidents". With the seventeenth DDC edition, published in 1965, the editors wished to introduce a more logical theoretical structure. To do this, they had to add a new hierarchical level for "Statistics on deaths caused by accidents", to balance "Statistics on deaths caused by crimes of violence". But they also did not want to disturb the meanings of the existing numbers, possibly to save libraries from having to reclassify works already in their collection. They invented the concept of "centred headings" with a range of numbers, and marked with the symbol in the margin (> in the twentieth edition).

This creates a logical structure, as shown in last figure, and permits effective display of arrays, but it does not permit right truncation to reach the next broader level. For example, dropping the second 3 in 312.273 will not lead to the next broader array, but will cause a move to the second broader array. Also, because they are technically difficult to use in spite of their logic, the centred headings notations are never assigned and therefore cannot be used in recall at present. It would be far better if the notation were consistently expressive, rather than only most of the time.

Unsought links, again, is a term used by faceted classification specialists. These links occur when the notational chain involves a link whose terms should be ignored in the compilation of an alphabetical index because the terms do not lead to a recognisable or useful concept. One example is notations with captions for which no single natural language term exists. Such notations are often created for the sake of a logical hierarchical structure, and , are therefore useful for displaying arrays, but the caption is not useful as a retrieval device.

BIBLIOGRAPHY

Allen, D.Y. 2001. Using the Dublin Core with CORC to Catalog Images of Maps. *Jl.* Of *Internet Cataloging.* 4(1/2): 163-77.

Ayres, F .H. 1999. Time for Change: A New Approach to Cataloguing Concepts. *Cataloging & Classification Qly.* 28(2): 3-16.

Bakewell, K.G.B. 1972. A Manual of Cataloguing Practice. Pergamon Press, Oxford.

Banerjee, K. 2001. Taking Advantage of Outsourcing Options: Using Punched Record set to Maximize Cataloging Effectiveness. *Cataloging & Classification Qly.* 32(1): 55-63.

Clack, H. 1990. Authority Control: Principles, Applications, and Instructions. American Library Association, Chicago.

Cochrane, P.A. 2000. Improving LCSH for Use in Online Catalogs Revisited; What Progress has been Made? What Issues stil Remain? *Cataloging & Classification Qly.* 29(1/2):73-89.

Cole, J. 1999. The Cataloging of Digitized Texts. *Cataloging & Classification Qly.* 28(3): 45-54.

Dhiman, A.K. 2003. Basics of Information Technology for Librarians and Information Scientists. 2 vols; Ess Ess Publications New Delhi.

Fleishcer, E and Goodman, H. 1980. Cataloguing Audio-Visual Materials: A Manual Based on the Anglo American Cataloguing Rules II. Neal- Schumann, New York.

Gorman, M. and Wrinkler, P.W.1988. Anglo American Cataloguing Rules. 2nd Edition. Canadian Library Association, Ottawa.

Gorman, M. and Wrinkler, P.W.1998. Anglo American Cataloguing Rules. 2nd Edition. 1998 Revision. Canadian Library Association, Ottawa.

Gorman, Michael. 1999. The Concise AACR2, 1998 Revision. The American Library Association, Chicago.

Gorman, M. 1999. Metadata or Cataloging? A False Choice. *Jl. Of Internet Cataloging* 2(1): 5-22.

Gopal, K. 2000. Library Online Cataloguing in Digital Way. Authorpress, New Delhi.

Hunter, E.J. and Bakewell, K.G.B. 1983. Cataloguing. 2nd Edition. Clive Bingley, London.

Jones, W. 2001. Dublin Core and Serials. *Jl.* Of *Internet Cataloging*. 4(1/2): 143-48.

Jonson, B.C. 2001. XML and MARC: Which is Right? *Cataloging & Classification Qly.* 32(1): 81-90.

Lam, Winh-The. 2000. Cataloging Internet Resources: Why, What, How? *Cataloging & Classification Qly.* 29(3): 49-61.

Larsgaard, M.L. 1999. Cataloging Cartographic Materials on CD-ROMs. *Cataloging & Classification Qly.* 27(3/4): 363-74.

Library of Congress Subject Headings, 21 st Edition, Volumes 1-5. Published by the Library of Congress, Cataloging Distribution Service, 1998.

Liheng, C. and Chan, W.S. 1998. Serials Cataloging Handbook: An Illustrative Guide to the Use of AACR2R and LC Rule Interpretations, 2nd Edition. American Library Association, Chicago.

MARC 21 Code List for Soul Software. 2001. INFLIBNET, Ahemdabad.

Maxwell, M.F. 1980. Handbook for AACR 2: Explaining and Illustrating Anglo American Cataloguing Rules. 2nd Edition. ALA, Chicago.

Maxwell, R.L. and Maxwell, M.F. 1997. Maxwell's Handbook foı AACR2R : Explaining and Illustrating the Anglo-American Cataloguing Rules and the 1993 Amendments. The American Library Association, Chiago.

Maxwell, M. F. 1989. Handbook for AACR2, 1988 Revision: Explaining and Illustrating the Anglo-American Cataloguing Rules. The American Library Association, Chicago.

McCroskey, M. 1994. Cataloging Nonbook Materials with AACR2R and MARC: A Guide for the School Library Media Specialist for the American Association of School Librarians, A division of the American Library Association, Chicago.

Needham, L. 2002. The Development of the Online Archive Catalogue at the University of Birmingham using CALM 2000. *Program: Electronic Library and Information Systems*. 36(1): 23-29.

Olson, N.B. 1982. Cataloging of Audiovisual Materials: A Manual Based on AACR 2. Minnesota Scholarly Press, Mankato.

Olson, N.B. 2001. Cataloging Remote Electronic Resources. *Cataloging & Classification Qly.* 31 (2): 101-37.

Riaz, M. 1989. A Manual of Practical Cataloguing. Atlantic Publishers & Distributors, New Delhi.

Russel, R. 2000. Making sense of Standards and Technologies for Serials Management. Library Association Publishing, London.

Saye, J. D. and Vellucci, S. L. 1989. Notes in the Catalog Record: Based on AACR2 and LC Rule Interelations. The American Library Association, Chicago.

Sehgal, R.L. 1993. Cataloguing Manual AACR-II. Ess Ess Publications, New Delhi.

Smits, J. 1999. Metadata: An Introduction. *Cataloguing & Classification Qly.* 27(3/4): 303- 19.

Stone, A. T. 2000. The LCSH Century: A Brief History of the Library of Congress Subject Headings and Introduction to the Centennial Essays. *Cataloging & Classification Qly.* 29(1/2):1-15.

Viswanathan, C.G. 1990. Cataloguing: Theory and Practice. Ess Ess Publications, New Delhi.

Ward, D. and VanderPol, D. 2000. Librarian, Catalog Thy Work! Getting Started Integrating Internet Resources into OPACs. *Jl. Of Internet Cataloging.* 3(4): 51-61.

Weigh, J. 1998. The Principles and Future of AACR: International Conference on the Principles and Future Development of AACR held in 1997 at Toronto, Ottawa (Canada). Canada Library Association, Ottawa.

Weighs, J. 2001. History of Audiovisual Cataloging. *Cataloging & Classification Qly. 31 (3.4): 159-88.*

Welch, G.D. and Williams, F. 1999.Catalguing Digital Cartographic Materials. *Cataloging & Classification Qly.* 27(3/4):343-62.

Witt, M. 1999. Cataloguing CD-ROMs using the ISBD (ER) Rules. Example of a French Public Library. *Cataloging & Classification Qly.* 28(1): 21-31.